THE BERLIN-DAHLEM GALLERY

THE BERLIN-DAHLEM GALLERY

THE
Berlin-Dahlem Gallery

GREAT PAINTINGS FROM THE FORMER
KAISER FRIEDRICH MUSEUM

With an Introduction and Commentary by

Edwin Redslob

Translated from the German by Sophie Wilkins

Berlin. Gemaldegalerie (West Berlin)

THE MACMILLAN COMPANY · NEW YORK

COLLIER-MACMILLAN LTD. · LONDON

This book was first published in West Germany in 1964 under the title
Gemäldegalerie Berlin-Dahlem, Ehemals Kaiser-Friedrich-Museum.
© Holle Verlag GmbH, Baden-Baden

Library of Congress Catalog Card Number: 67–19551
The Macmillan Company, New York
Collier-Macmillan Canada Ltd., Toronto, Ontario
Printed in West Germany
Bound in West Germany

Contents

INTRODUCTION

History of the Museum

I

The beginnings of the Berlin collections go back to Frederick William, the Great Elector of Brandenburg, who, with characteristic enterprise, sought to confer every sort of brilliance on the Prussian capital after the ravages of the Thirty Years' War (1618–1648). His collection was formed around a nucleus of paintings by Lucas Cranach that his family had acquired in the sixteenth century and that he subsequently inherited. As the husband of a Princess of Orange and in conformity with the taste of the period, he tended to prefer the art of the Netherlands—a predilection that led him to retain Willem van Honthorst as his court painter in Berlin for nearly two decades.

This emphasis on Dutch painting, still recognizable in the Berlin collections today, received additional impetus when the Great Elector's son, King Frederick I of Prussia, inherited a number of valuable pictures from the House of Orange—among them such prizes as Rembrandt's *Rape of Proserpine* (Pls. 124, 125) and *Joseph's Dream* (Pl. 127). His desire for magnificence led the first King of Prussia to set aside six rooms on the second floor of his palace, part of a grand suite decorated by Schlüter,[1] to house a major part of this inheritance.

But the first to acquire paintings systematically and make them available to connoisseurs and artists was Frederick I's grandson, Frederick the Great. As Crown Prince, he had followed the eighteenth-century bent for French art by purchasing major works by Watteau and his successors. As King, he consciously emulated Dresden, Kassel, and Brunswick by building up an art gallery in which the great Italian and Flemish painters also were represented. Special agents acted for him abroad, and he himself traveled to Amsterdam in 1755, in the guise of a flute virtuoso, to buy paintings for the gallery he was planning to build at Sans Souci, his residence in Potsdam near Berlin.

That same year, his architect Johann Gottfried Büring began construction on the picture gallery on the east side of the palace, to balance the orangery on its west flank. Following the Dutch style, the center of the long building was decorated with a small tower crowning the rotunda that makes an attractive break in the vaulted interior. The royal collector was haunted by the approach of war and its vicissitudes when he wrote to his sister Wilhelmine in Bayreuth: "I am having an art gallery built at Sans Souci, one more of my follies, if you like; but these are the things that make for progress in the world. If everyone always acted rationally, historians would have little to write about."

The gallery began to take shape in the picturesque Frederickian rococo style. In 1756, when the building was nearly completed, its paintings and statuary chosen, and more than a hundred frames carved specially with a view to giving unity to the ensemble, the Seven Years' War broke out.

Even while Prussia was fighting for survival, the King continued to busy himself with

[1] Andreas Schlüter (1664-1714), German architect and sculptor, noted exponent of the baroque style. – Tr.

thoughts of completing the building and planning its appointments. In the midst of battle, he wrote to his friend the Marquis d'Argens, philosopher of the Berlin Academy of Sciences, about his plans as a collector, "in order to occupy my mind for a while with thoughts of the gallery." And on another occasion, he wrote: "I do not know what disaster may be lying in wait for me at this very moment, yet I talk of pictures and galleries." But possibly this very preoccupation with art gave him the inner strength to prevail.

The war was barely over when, upon his return home in the spring of 1763, Frederick was able to enjoy the magnificent interior and appointments of his gallery. Strikingly set off by the colonnades supporting the cupola in the center, the paintings on the long left-hand wall were lighted by seventeen tall windows opposite. Museum technicians will be interested to know that this was not an outer wall, the dampness of which would have damaged the paintings, but that it was backed by a narrow passageway, while the cupola rested upon four pairs of columns inside the gallery. An anteroom at the far end of the gallery held smaller pictures, which were hung five rows deep.

Thus one of the first art museums ever built in Germany housed a rich collection in a harmonious blend of architecture, sculpture, and painting. True, many of the works, though bearing the names of great masters, were only copies, owing to the haste with which the King had brought the gallery into being. Still, the Dutch collection did boast six authentic major works by Rubens, including his *Perseus and Andromeda* and *St. Cecilia*. Rembrandt was represented by two large canvases, *Samson* and *Moses with the Tables of the Law*, as well as by the *Self-portrait with Velvet Beret*.

Some of the Italian masterpieces were also suspect. Correggio's *Jupiter and Io*, a painting for which Frederick had paid a huge price at a Paris auction in 1762, proved to be a copy, but three years later he did get Correggio's *Leda and the Swan* (Pls. 94, 95). Because most of Frederick's French paintings were left hanging in his various castles, French masters were almost entirely absent from the gallery; there was only a pair of paintings by Watteau, *The Italian Comedy* (Pls. 158, 159) and *The French Comedy*. As early as 1764, the curator of the gallery, Matthias Oesterreich, whom the King had summoned from Dresden in 1757, issued a catalogue, "Description of the Paintings in the Royal Gallery and Side-Chamber of Sans Souci," a revised edition of which appeared a few years later in both German and French. Today, of course, this catalogue—generously studded with names like Leonardo, Raphael, Andrea del Sarto, Titian, Veronese, as well as with attributions to Rubens and Van Dyck—is only a curiosity for the amusement of the connoisseur.

Nevertheless, the gallery, with its beauty of architecture and decoration, remains an important work of art. Even though the best of its paintings, about 25 out of 170, were transferred to Berlin in 1830, when the state museums were founded, other works were put in their place to maintain the effect of the whole. One hopes that the gallery of Sans Souci will continue to be preserved in this manner.

Surely what was built on the heights of Sans Souci can be called a museum, for here was a collection consecrated to art and scholarship and housed in a building especially designed for it. As early as June 1763—as we know from D'Alembert—the King was able to descend the forty steps from the terrace of his residence in order "to take a stroll in his gallery" and show its treasures to visitors. When Büsching, the Prussian Royal High Councillor of the Consistory and Director of the Gymnasium zum Grauen Kloster, traveled in 1775 from Berlin to his estate in Brandenburg, he stopped off in Potsdam. In a 332-page book published the same year, he wrote a detailed report of "the splendid edifice" and gave a "Schematic representation of the arrangement of the paintings in the Royal Gallery at Sans Souci." And when Goethe spent a few days in Berlin and Potsdam in 1778 with Duke Charles Augustus of Weimar while Frederick II was in the field with his army in Silesia, he took time to inspect both the gallery and the royal palace.

The gallery that King Frederick I had had installed in his Berlin palace, with the bulk of its paintings, was opened to the public in a limited way only in the last year of his grandson's reign, 1786, when it was decided to allow students at the Prussian Academy of Fine Arts to complete their studies by copying the masterpieces in the royal gallery four days a week during the summer months. Accordingly, by far the oldest of the Berlin museums that were opened to the public as state institutions in 1830 is the gallery of Sans Souci, founded by Frederick the Great in 1763–1764.

II

In the nineteenth century, the state replaced the prince as the custodian of culture, and museums took the place of the galleries of princes. From now on, art treasures would belong to the community, and art collections would be used to advance education and culture. The painter, who in the eighteenth century was also the connoisseur and guide in matters of art, gave way to the art historian—critic.

In Berlin, this transformation took its most tangible form. As early as 1815, the Prussian state had purchased in Paris a number of works from the Giustiniani collection, which had its beginnings in seventeenth-century Rome. Of the 157 paintings in the collection, 83 were purchased by the Prussian state, including some noteworthy examples of Italian art. Of this group, the present volume contains the *Portrait of a Young Man* by Lorenzo Lotto (Pl. 86) and Caravaggio's *Love Triumphant* (Pl. 101). The latter painting had been commissioned by the Marchese Visconto Giustiniani, at the home of whose heir in Rome Goethe himself had seen it.

In the early 1820's, a special commission under the chairmanship of Wilhelm von Humboldt[1] was charged not only with the selection but with the determination of the authenticity and value of paintings from the holdings of the royal palaces in Berlin and Potsdam for the projected state museum. In addition to the Rembrandts inherited from the House of Orange, the commission also selected the portrait of Saskia completed a year after her death. Altogether the commission chose some 260 paintings, but later it drew on the princely galleries to add to the state collections.

The selection attested to the connoisseurship of Baron von Rumohr.[2] He continued to concern himself with the expansion of the gallery on his travels in Italy, where the writing of *Italienische Forschungen* (1837–1841), a milestone in art history, had taken him. It was probably owing to him that the young Hamburg art historian Gustav Waagen[3] was entrusted with preparing the scholarly catalogue of the paintings. Since neither man fully appreciated the masters of the rococo, only a few examples from Frederick the Great's large and discriminating collection of French eighteenth-century painters came into the museum. For example, Watteau's last work, *Gersaint's Shop Sign* (Pls. 160–163), was not presented to the museum until much later by the Administration of Palaces and Gardens.

In line with nineteenth-century historical thought, from the first, the museum—especially where the picture gallery was concerned—concentrated on presenting the history of art as stages in an evolution. By a stroke of good fortune, it so happened that in Berlin in 1821, a great—one is tempted to say, a wild—collector, the English businessman Edward Solly, found himself obliged to sell his art treasures. Engaged as he was in the export trade, he had, with the help of many agents, gathered together rather haphazardly some three thousand paintings, several hundred of which were to go to the museum. The Solly collection made an ideal complement to the museum's already ample stock of paintings from the High Renaissance and the baroque, for his collection was exceptionally rich in earlier periods, the fourteenth and fifteenth centuries particularly. Works by Mantegna (Pls. 16, 18), Pollaiuolo's *Annunciation* (Pls. 22, 23), Sassetta's *Virgin and Child* (Pl. 20), some of the major works of Botticelli (Pls. 24–27), the *Portrait of a Young Lady* by Petrus Christus (Pl. 47), Holbein's *George Gisze* (Pl. 72), and Cranach's *Cardinal Albrecht of Brandenburg* (Pl. 62) were acquired for Berlin at that time.

Because of the economic depression following the Napoleonic wars, Frederick William III did not think that the state should be burdened with the cost of the collection; he therefore donated the large sum—for those times—of 200,000 talers from his private fortune.

A great many more works might have been chosen, but a large number of them did not pass the commission's test: it appeared that Solly had not confined himself to collecting; he had also acted as his own restorer, and in trying to remove a later varnish from various paintings, he had frequently managed to wash off some of the original colors.

Ten years of careful preparation were devoted to planning the museum. When the architect Karl Schinkel[4] accompanied Waagen on a trip to Italy, they stopped off at Weimar for Goethe's blessing. Later that same year Christian Rauch visited the poet in order to do a sculpture of him and reported that "Goethe expressed his wholehearted delight at the sketches for the great art museum that Schinkel intends to build in Berlin."

[1] Wilhelm von Humboldt (1767–1835), the great humanist, philologist, statesman, and reformer, was the brother of Alexander von Humboldt (1769–1859), the famous naturalist and explorer. – Tr.

[2] Baron Karl Friedrich von Rumohr (1785–1843), art historian. – Tr.

[3] Gustav Friedrich Waagen (1794–1868), author of a three-volume work on *Treasures of Art in Great Britain* (1854), among others. – Tr.

[4] Karl Friedrich Schinkel (1781–1841), German architect and painter in the classical tradition. – Tr.

Humboldt did not have an altogether easy time of it, having to overcome a good deal of resistance to the demands of the commission. Berlin wags delighted in making puns on the names of Waagen (*Wagen* = carriage) and Rumohr (*Rumor* = rumor), telling tales of rumor-laden carriages and driving rumors. There were special difficulties in erecting the building because of the marshy ground, which bolstered the arguments of those who had championed a site adjoining the Academy of Arts on Unter den Linden.

Thanks more to Humboldt's tenacity than to the efforts of the museum's General Director Count Brühl, the museum was ready to open on August 3, 1830, the King's birthday, and was called the Royal Museum. The King honored Humboldt's great achievement by conferring on him the highest order in the monarch's gift: Humboldt was made a Knight of the Black Eagle and, in reparation for an earlier wrong done him, was reappointed to the Council of State. Two years after the opening, he was justified in writing to his brother Alexander: "I believe I may say without vanity that without me the museum would still not be open."

With its imposing pillared hall rising above a lofty stairwell, Schinkel's edifice made a striking architectural terminus for the pleasure garden extending westward from the palace. Its front section had two stories, the lower of which was devoted to classical sculpture, while the upper story held the "truly royal gift" of the picture gallery, as it was described by the anonymous author of a book, *Berlin wie es ist (This Is Berlin)*, that appeared soon after the opening of the museum.

Its guiding principle was, as Humboldt put it, "the study of the human spirit through contemplation of the greatest masterpieces of all time." This principle had served him well when, two decades before, he had founded the University of Berlin in the spirit of German classicism, and it continued to do so as the art museum rounded out his lifework. The same was true of Schinkel, whose skill here was touched with genius, for he succeeded in giving a spiritual quality to a building that had to serve practical ends. This museum marked the beginning of a new kind of building. Up to now, sculpture and painting had been subordinate to the architecture in medieval churches and Renaissance and baroque palaces; even in the early art galleries built to house works of art, such as Frederick the Great's gallery at Sans Souci, architecture and decoration dominated the works of art. But now, with the Berlin museum—as it would be a few years later with the Pinakothek of Munich and the National Gallery of London—architectural form was subordinated to the demands of displaying a collection of works from widely different periods and countries. Schinkel solved this problem by giving architecture priority in the exterior, the vestibule, and the stairwell, then subordinating and adapting it to the contents of the rooms themselves.

Contemporary observers tell us how the Royal Museum was received by the public: the visitors, whether Berliners or from out of town, were not satisfied with one quick look. Struck by the beauty of the works of art as well as by the grandeur of the building itself, they took their time. Zelter,[1] for whose singing school Schinkel had put up a noble building, wrote to Goethe in 1830: "Since the opening of our new museum, I spend an hour there almost every day, working up an appetite for dinner in the best of company." Goethe replied: "How glad I would be to come to your priceless museum, there to verify my knowledge, confess my ignorance, enrich and broaden my ideas, but most of all to experience pure delight, without critics and without history books! It is fine to study a work of art, but one must enjoy it before judging it."

---

[1] Karl Friedrich Zelter (1758–1832), German composer—Goethe's favorite arranger for his own poems—and music director, whose correspondence with Goethe and Schiller was published in six volumes in 1833–1834.—Tr.

Goethe's words make a valid point. He realized that the direct encounter with the originals made possible by the museum could open new perspectives as the nonvisual, theoretical contemplation of art cannot.

The Old Museum, as the Royal Museum is now called, had exactly 1,189 paintings, divided among the various schools as follows: the Dutch came first, with 515; the Italians were a close second, with 497—among these, the High Renaissance was less well represented than earlier periods, of which there were a surprisingly large number of examples. There were only a few German paintings, and none by Dürer.

Since the taste of the period preferred the classical style to the graceful lightness of rococo, the commission had left the Watteaus and other eighteenth-century French masters, as we have said, in the various palaces, a lapse that was not corrected for some time. Waagen, as the guiding spirit, had nevertheless managed to provide an impressive survey of the evolution of European painting over half a millennium. The character and the value of the collection were thus securely established.

When Frederick William IV, who was a lover of art, came to the throne in 1840, a relatively large sum of money was made available to enlarge the gallery's holdings. Waagen was thus able to make important purchases in Italy, among them Titian's *Lavinia* and, later, Raphael's famous *Madonna del Duca Terranova*.

However, I recall Wilhelm von Bode once telling me in his unforgettable way that Waagen was prouder of the 121 pictures he had banished to the storerooms than of the more than a hundred new acquisitions he had been able to hang in their places.

III

If Waagen was still of the generation of the late romantics, Wilhelm von Bode, born in 1845, belonged to that of the impressionists. Nearly the same age as the painter Max Liebermann (1847–1935), he resembled the latter in being full of nervous energy, always accessible, and with a gift of vision that disposed him to feel most warmly toward the Dutch painters of the seventeenth century, although he considered the Italian paintings highly important for the collection in Berlin.

A striking instance of the fact that even the art historian tends to see with the eyes of his own generation is that it was Bode who rediscovered the true greatness of Frans Hals, who had been all but forgotten during the rococo and classical periods. Velázquez too, underestimated by the eighteenth century, was discovered by the French impressionists to be the most painterly of painters; it was under Bode's direction that the museum bought two of his works, the first of which was the portrait of the painter's wife usually called the *Countess Olivarez*. Each generation also has its own judgment of the past, a change of emphasis from that of the preceding generation. A newly gained insight is likely to be closer to the truth than a rejection based on ignorance.

Despite the addition of the New Museum on the west side of the Museum Island of Berlin, the buildings of Schinkel's period and that of his immediate successors soon ran out of space to house the bulk of the new acquisitions for the various divisions of the state museums. Bode therefore worked out his plan for two new building complexes: the Kaiser Friedrich Museum, his greatest achievement, completed in 1904, and the Deutsches Museum, intended to provide room for the other collections and further the acquisition of German art.

By founding the Kaiser Friedrich Museum Association, in company with the leading collectors and art lovers who supported him, Bode obtained large financial resources independently of the state prior to the erection of the building. Giotto's *Madonna of Glatz,*

Schongauer's Christmas painting, Geertgen's *John the Baptist in the Wilderness*, and the 1962 acquisition of Johann Liss's *Satyr with a Peasant Family*—all of which are reproduced in this volume—were purchased with funds donated or raised by this association. The recrudescence of the Kaiser Friedrich Museum Association in our own time testifies to the vitality of the tradition that Wilhelm von Bode left as a duty to the state museums of Berlin.

Until his death in 1929, Bode, who was even more of a connoisseur than Waagen, who died in 1868, worked tirelessly to expand the gallery. His "didactic universalism"—in the apt phrase of its longtime director Müller-Hofstede—gave the Berlin collections their international stamp.

From the 1870's on, Bode was decisively involved in nearly all the gallery's acquisitions. It was due to his initiative that the Rembrandts transferred from the royal residences to the museum in his time increased from eleven to twenty-six. Today, only Leningrad has more Rembrandts than Berlin, and only one more at that; the other European museums lag far behind. When the greater part of the best German private collection of seventeenth-century Dutch painters—the Suermondt collection in Aachen (Aix-la-Chapelle)—made its way into the Berlin museums back in 1874, Wilhelm von Bode, then a young assistant in the sculpture division, took a passionate interest in it. He had, after all, written his doctoral dissertation—decorated with an etching of the *Malle Babbe* by Frans Hals (Pl. 122) —under the tutelage of Suermondt himself, who eventually had been forced to sell his treasures in order to pay off the debts of a relative. Some of the prize possessions of the Berlin museums derive from his collection, among them Van Eyck's so-called *Madonna in Church* (Pl. 34), the *Man with a Pink* (Pl. 35), attributed to Van Eyck, and *The Pearl Necklace* (Pl. 140) by Jan Vermeer.

Berlin's indebtedness to Bode's initiative and to the vigor with which he dominated the international art market is incalculable. Back in 1884 it was thought monstrous that the sum of 100,000 taler should have been paid for Dürer's *Portrait of Hieronymus Holzschuher* (Pl. 59); today Berlin's success in acquiring an entire group of the Nuremberg master's works, beginning with the portrait *Elector Frederick the Wise* (Pl. 58), is appreciated as the remarkable achievement it was. It is no less astonishing that to the single Albrecht Altdorfer in the Berlin gallery that had come from the Solly collection, seven more works by that rare master (among them, Pls. 63, 64, 65) were obtained by the knowledgeable Max J. Friedländer, Bode's worthy successor as Director of the gallery (Bode continued as General Director), where he remained until 1933.

After 1871, the importance of Berlin as the capital of all of Germany encouraged the Prussian State as well as the three successive emperors to contribute to the museum's aggrandizement. But this was not enough for Bode. He fired the capital's upper middle class to an ever higher pitch of collector's mania. Collectors and art dealers who owed so much to his counsels became donors, and when they offered to thank him personally by the gift of a work of art, he passed it on to "his" museum.

A famous instance of this is the James Simon collection, the treasures of which fill a special room in the Italian section of what was once called the Kaiser Friedrich Museum and is now known as the Berlin-Dahlem Gallery. The contents of that room are among the most distinguished gifts ever to be received by the museum. It contained, among other works, a *Madonna* by Mantegna (Pl. 17).

IV

This is not the place to describe the disasters that befell the museums of Berlin during the Second World War. Thanks to the foresight and efforts of museum officials, most of the art treasures on the Museum Island opposite the palace were saved, even though the rescue operation was long delayed by the heedlessness of the leaders of the dying regime, despite the pleas of the experts. Except for the great altar paintings, which could not be moved out of Berlin, the principal holdings of the gallery were hidden in West German mine shafts and gradually returned to Berlin after the war.

Bode himself had caused a stately building to be erected in Dahlem, Berlin, by the well-known architect Bruno Paul, to house the collections of eastern Asiatic art and the research materials of the museum. Today it also shelters the anthropological museum, whose own building had been destroyed. New plans for extensive additional construction will assure dignified quarters for the museum departments now temporarily housed in Dahlem.

The original aim—to represent the gradual evolution of Western art—remains the informing principle that determines the museum's structure, groupings, and further growth.

Today the art collection is in the Dahlem museum; a large new building, presumably to be erected near the southern end of the zoological gardens, is being planned for it. Its future growth is assured by the Foundation for Prussian Cultural Property, established by the federal government and the states of Württemberg-Baden, Berlin, North Rhine-Westphalia, and Schleswig-Holstein. The foundation administers the former state collections, libraries, and archives centrally, as a unit. The present publication was prepared on the occasion of the art gallery's bicentennial, in 1963.

Note on the drawing on page IX: Enlargement of a woodcut by Adolf von Menzel, showing Frederick the Great of Prussia in the art gallery of Sans Souci, which he built.

The Paintings

6

15

26

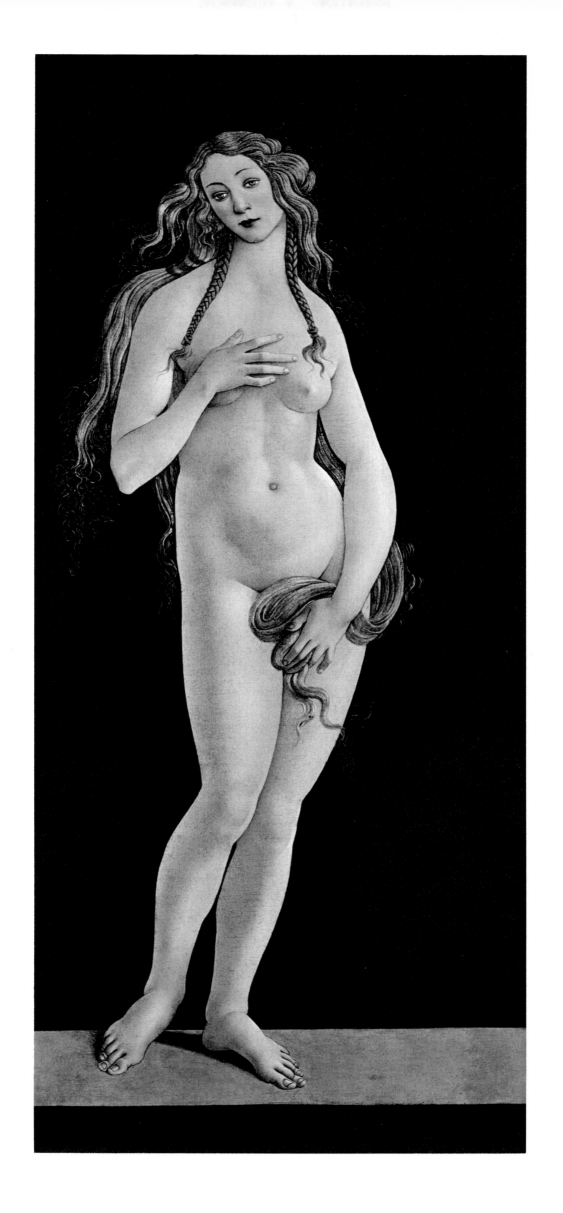

30

37

44

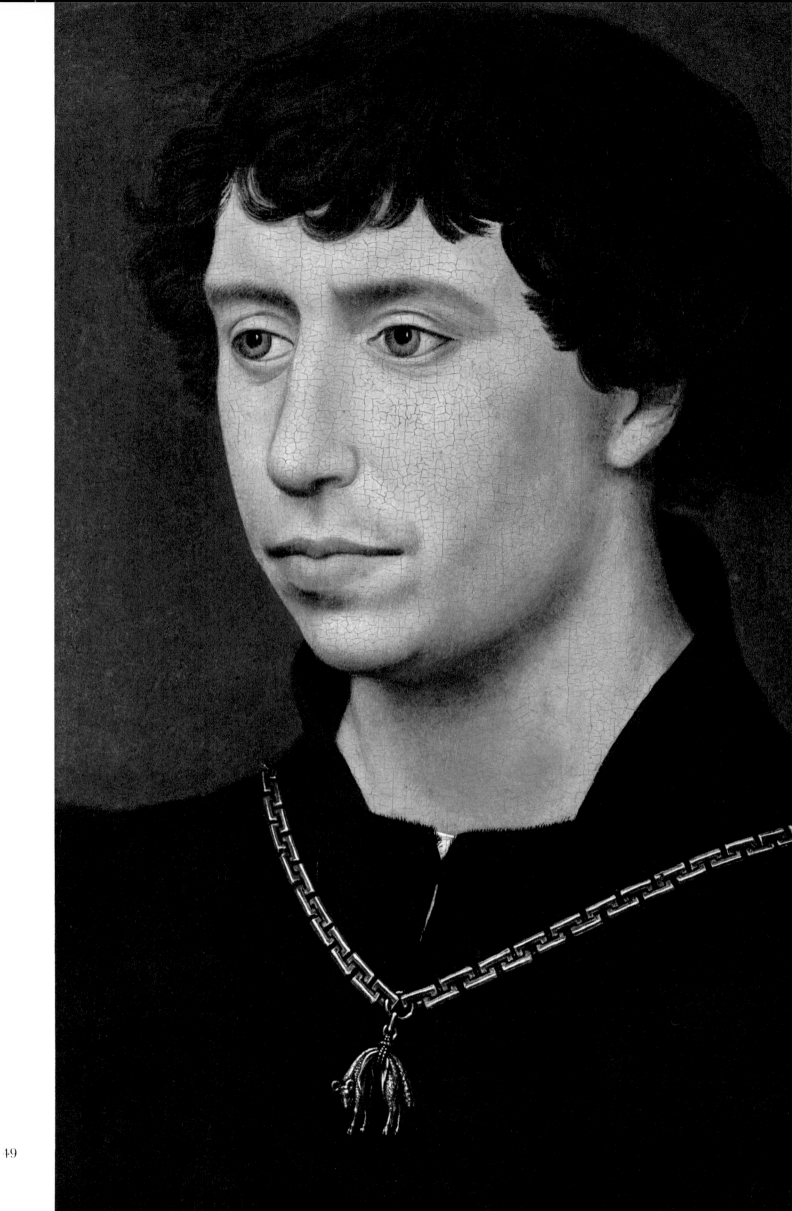

52

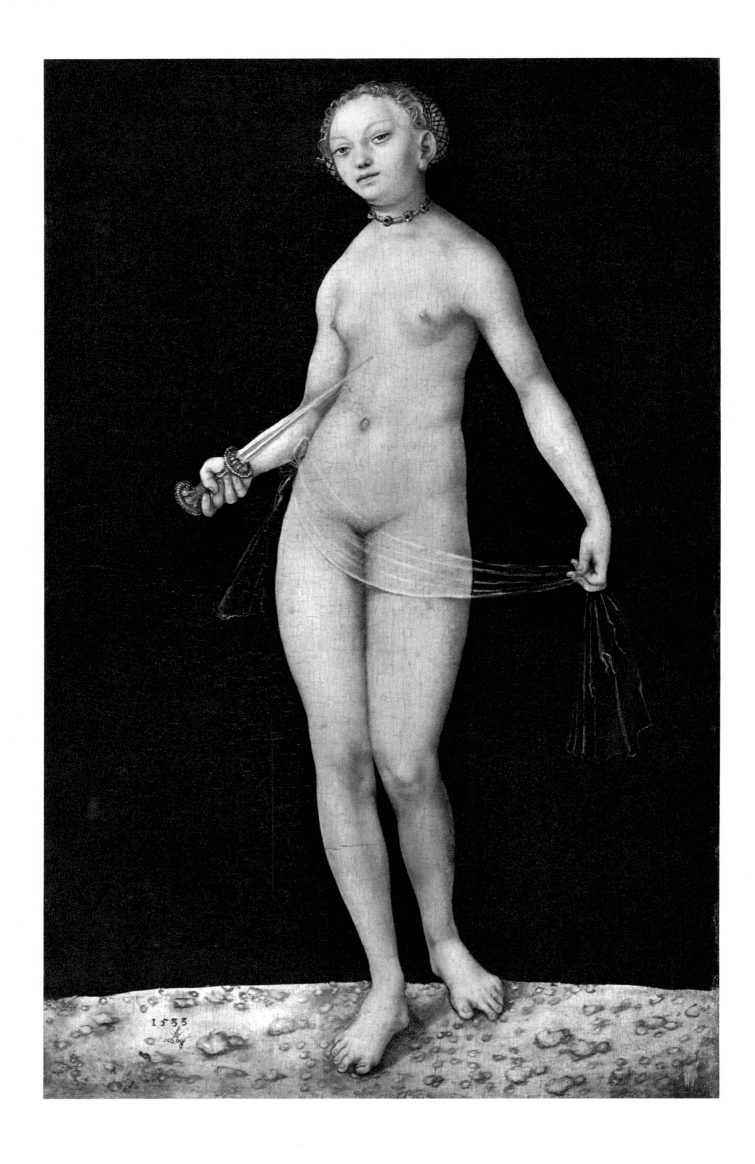

68

71

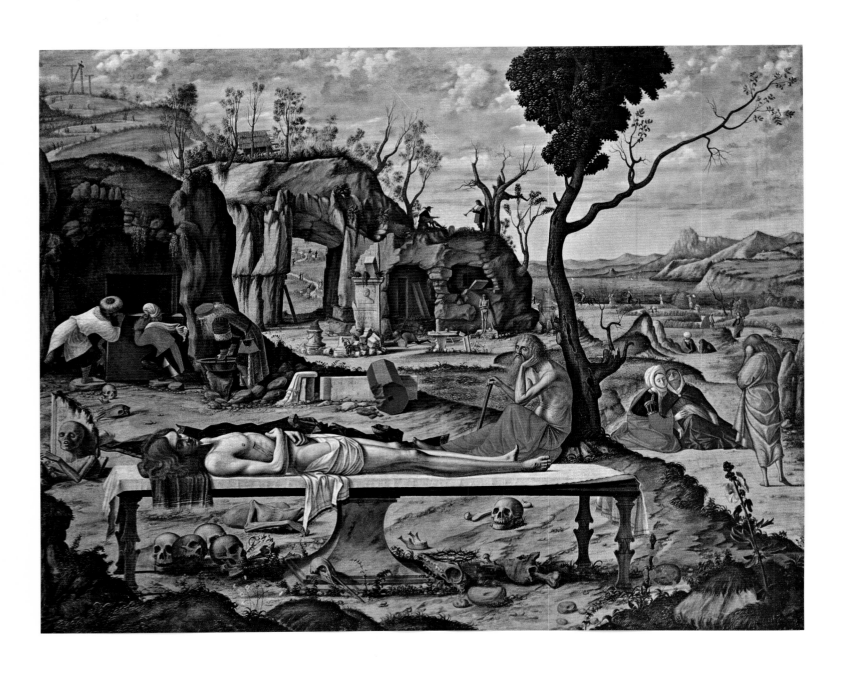

114

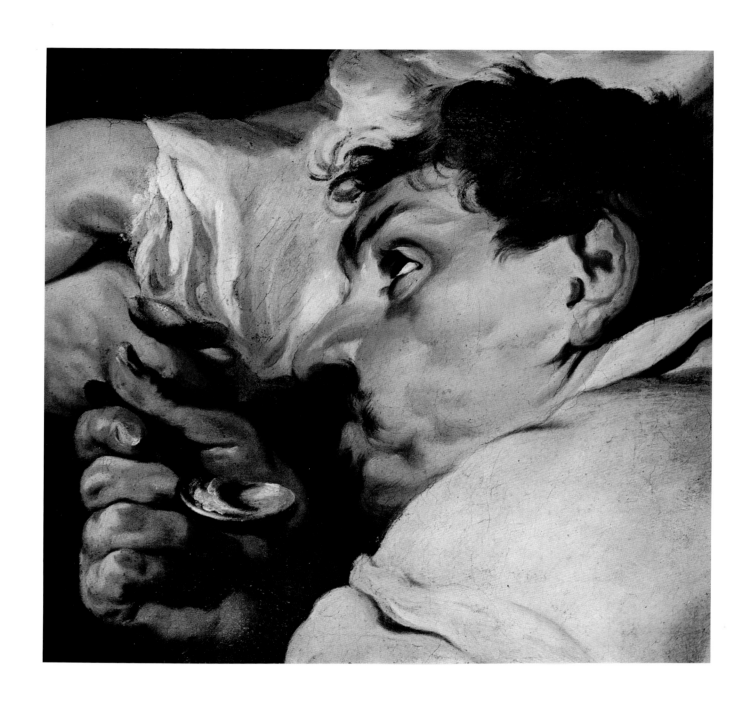

121

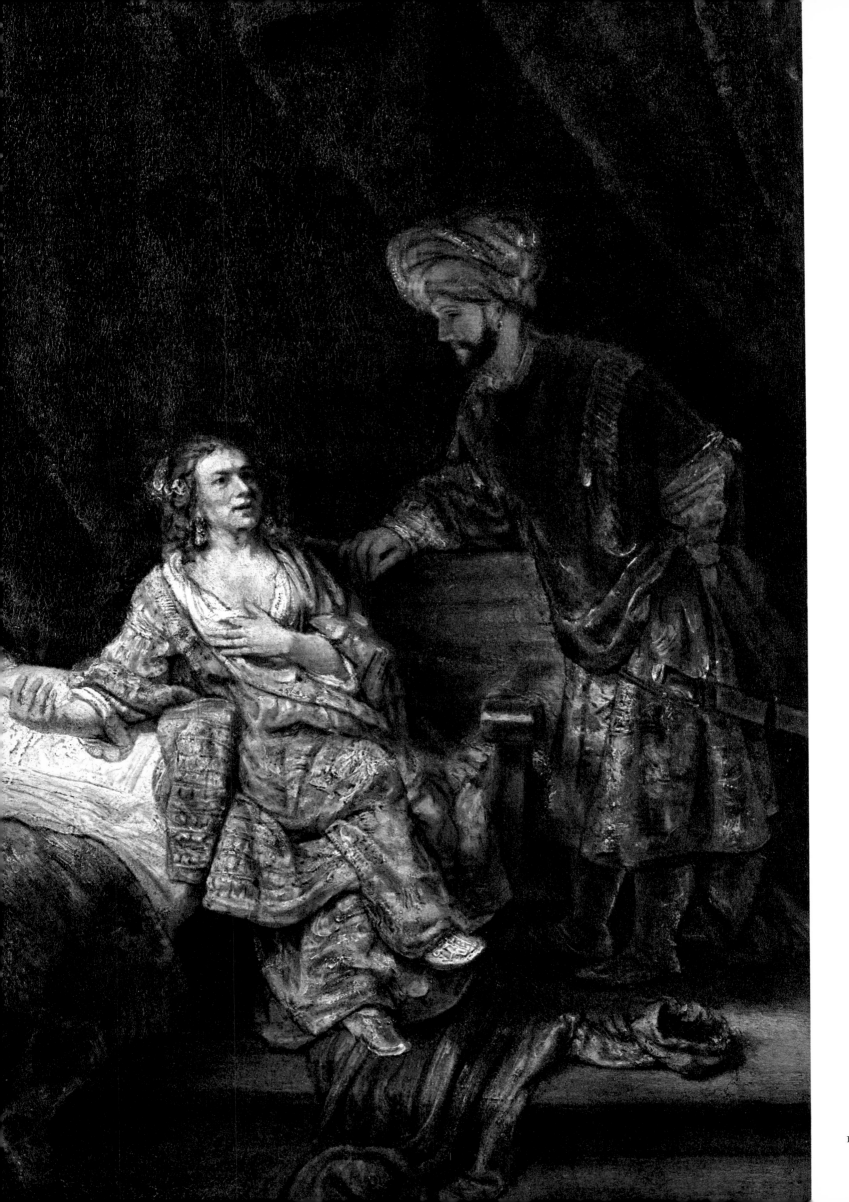

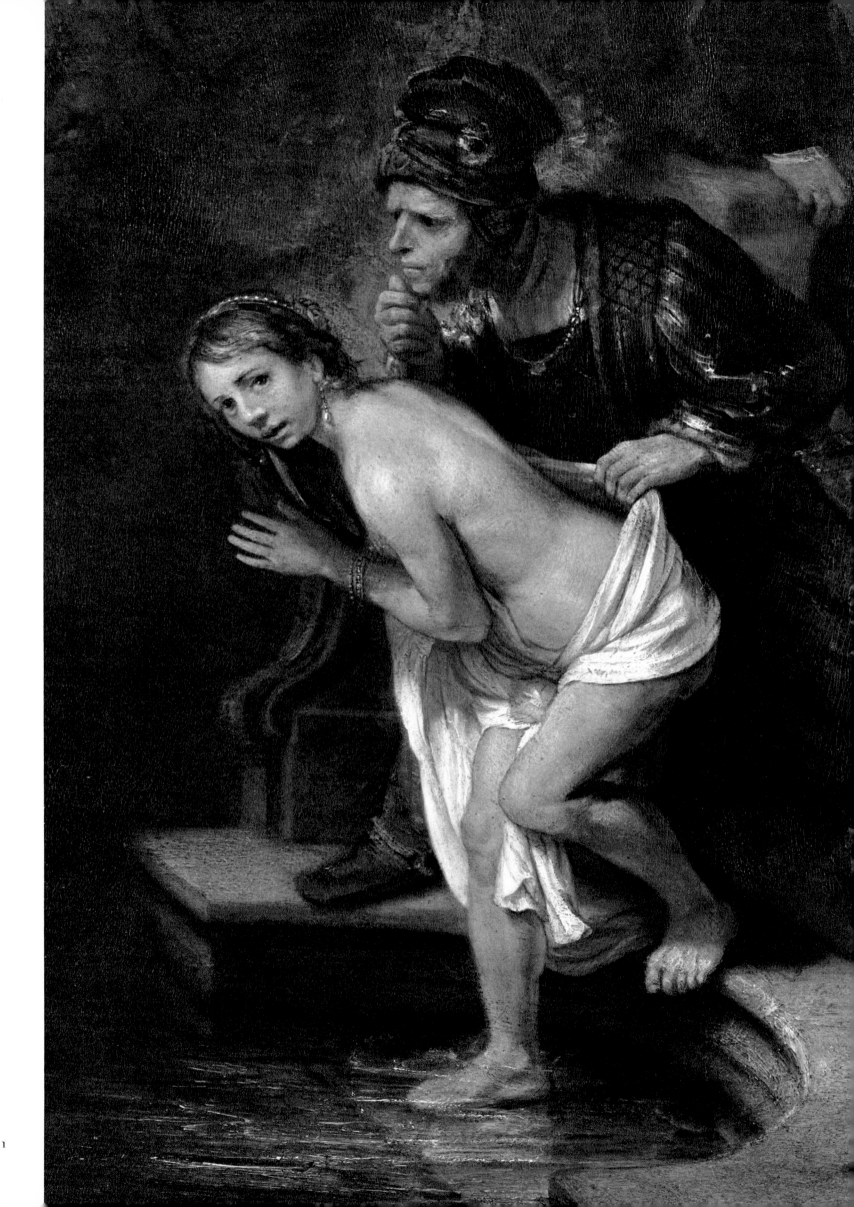

146

147

149

Catalogue of the Artists
and the Paintings

Unknown Master of Westphalia or Cologne

Before 1250

Mural painting had come into full flower in the Rhineland and, branching out from there, in Westphalia. The names of the painters who decorated the Romanesque churches with murals, painted the earliest panels, or illuminated prayer books with their delicate brushes are rarely known. Their work was done to serve God; it dwarfed the personal element.

Tradition is more likely to have preserved the name of a goldsmith such as Roger of Helmershausen or Nicolas of Verdun, who worked in Cologne toward the end of the twelfth century and whose *Altar Screen of the Three Kings,* which had once stood on the high altar of the cathedral, became the great model for many subsequent panel paintings and wood carvings by other artists. The gold grounds of the panels and the gilding on the sculptures suggest that their prototypes were made of precious metals. Medieval panel painting is rooted in the art of the goldsmith, the fresco and miniature painter.

JOHN THE BAPTIST

Detail from an altarpiece

Tempera on oak. 71 × 120 cm.

PROVENANCE: *Acquired in 1862 from the Wiesenkirche in Soest.*

1   In the early part of the second millennium A.D., altars were decorated only with a facing of precious metals on the front panel (antependium) or with finely embroidered cloths. When it became customary to set the painted decoration upon the altar as a back panel, the task at first fell to the fresco painters, who tended to give the altarpiece an architectonic framework and paint it in a monumental style.

One of the most splendid examples of the kind of work that shows the derivation of medieval panel painting from fresco painting is the altarpiece from the Wiesenkirche in Soest, with its sculptured half columns and triple rounded arch giving it a clearly architectonic form. The oaken frame and panels are richly gilded. The center panel shows the Trinity in the form of the Seat of Mercy: God the Father enthroned, holding a crucifix, above which a dove is flying. The left-hand panel shows Mary lamenting; the right-hand panel, John the Baptist (Pl. 1). The latter figure especially shows the master's style to perfection. John the Baptist's inner turmoil is suggested by the sharply angular movement of the folds of his garment, which are drawn in an abstractly ornamental way. This panel is an example of the Romanesque style in which each form is given a life of its own. The red cloaks of the three figures stand out in glowing con-

trast to the gold background. Recessive bluish-white, dull green, and brown tones leave the red-gold note fully dominant.

No doubt this altarpiece originally came from a much older church and was later transferred to the Gothic Wiesenkirche in Soest. Stylistically similar work, also suggestive of the murals in the Church of St. Nikolai in Soest, can be seen in a fresco of the Church of St. Cunibert in Cologne. There, on a wall already overarched in the Gothic manner, is a crucifixion group showing close kinship, especially in its conception of St. John, to the panel we have just described. The expressive figures, the restless, jagged lines of their garments, and the dark-rimmed halos are alike; however, the Cologne fresco seems to be gentler and far less monumental than the panel picture. While the Cologne fresco was painted around 1247, the Berlin painting is usually considered to be of later date (1250–1270). But Georg Dehio, whose *Geschichte der deutschen Kunst (History of German Art)* ranks as a classic, favored a much earlier date, around 1220. This, to be sure, would mean too great a gap between it and the frescoes of Cologne and Soest; yet it seems closer to the truth to date the Berlin panel before the middle of the thirteenth century and thus earlier than the fresco in Cologne.

With two other altarpieces of the Berlin museum, this panel marks the beginning of German panel painting. And like so many pioneer works of an era, the first efforts to solve a new problem, this painting has an air of overwhelming grandeur.

Giotto di Bondone

THE ARTIST: Giotto was born about 1266 in Tuscany, in Colle di Vespignano, near Florence. He was said to have been a pupil of Cimabue. Toward the end of the century, he worked in Rome, mostly for the old Church of St. Peter, the razing of which also meant the destruction of his frescoes. From 1305 to 1307 Giotto decorated the Arena Chapel in Padua with a fresco cycle of the Old and New Testaments that is still well preserved.

But the main theater of his activities was Florence, where he created the frescoes in Santa Croce. Until about 1322, he contributed to the design of the Church of St. Francis in Assisi. From 1330 to 1333, he worked in Naples, then returned to Florence to become the chief architect of the city-state. He planned the decoration of the cathedral's facade and began the building of the Campanile, the relief decorations of which stem partly from his sketches. He died in 1337 and was buried in the cathedral in Florence, where a monument was erected to him.

We now stand on the threshold of modern times: Dante and Giotto, both instrumental in the rise of the Renaissance, were at the peak of their productiveness at the beginning of the fourteenth century. Acquainted with each other's works they strove to bring a new reality, based on their own experience of life, to the religious faith and the world view of their time. In the plastic arts, this led to the transcending of the two-dimensional formulas of the Byzantine style. With Giotto, it became the great task of art to show the oneness of man with nature, the reality of the physical and spatial world.

His contemporaries were aware of this forward movement of his art, and Dante states it in the *Divine Comedy*:

> *Credette Cimabue nel pittura*
> *Tener il campo, oggi a Giotto il grido.*
>
> Once Cimabue thought he held the field
> In art; now Giotto's all the rage.

With Giotto, whose art is primarily that of the fresco painter, panel painting began to be a leading form in the Italian Trecento. Whereas in the Netherlands the panel picture was influenced primarily by miniature painting, Italian altar painting owes its style to the monumental frescoes that, beginning with Giotto and continuing through Masaccio, Mantegna, and Ghiberti to Raphael and Michelangelo, remained the painter's noblest task.

ENTOMBMENT OF THE VIRGIN

Painted about 1315–1320

Tempera on poplarwood. 75 × 179 cm.

PROVENANCE: *Painted by Giotto presumably for the Ognissanti Church in Florence. Vasari saw it in that church around the middle of the sixteenth century, but by 1568 it was no longer there. The picture subsequently made its way into the collection of Cardinal Fesch, and when his collection was sold at auction, the panel was acquired by the Davenpoort-Bronley family of Wooton Hall (later of Capesthorne). It was bought in 1914 by the Kaiser Friedrich Museum Association.*

2, 3 Next to Giotto's *Madonna in Glory* in the Uffizi in Florence, still thought to be clearly influenced by Cimabue, looking as it does like the painted front of a choir stall in a Gothic church, the panel reproduced in this volume showing the entombment of the Virgin is the most important example of the relationship of panel to mural painting.

The work gives the impression of a fresco that has been pried from a wall and given the form of a gable to make it serve in the construction of an altar. It illustrates the transition from a wall painting to an altar painting and so marks the beginning of an epoch in which the panel painting, placed within an interior space and therefore involved in the creating of space, becomes the characteristic form taken by painting.

According to Lorenzo Ghiberti, the chronicler of Florentine art, a work of Giotto's representing the *Death of the Virgin* existed in the Ognissanti Church on the bank of the Arno. The *Maestà (Madonna in Glory)* of the Uffizi

previously mentioned also comes from the same church. It seems reasonable therefore to assume that the painting in Berlin, so entirely a Giotto in style, is the one mentioned by Ghiberti.

The grouping is still strict, almost rigid. The painter is forced to adapt himself to the triangular shape of the panel, a restriction new to the fresco painter. The striking difference between the two halves of the painting shows that the painter gave up the schematism of the right-hand half, with its serried ranks of heads and halos, for a greater freedom of execution on the left. Here the figures in the forefront clearly emerge as the leading characters, while those behind them, who might be compared with the chorus of a Greek drama, are limited to a single row. While the background figures in their echelon formation are reminiscent of Giotto's early work, such as the frescoes in the Arena Chapel in Padua, the brightly robed principal figures bring to mind the master's frescoes in Santa Croce in Florence.

Action and movement are concentrated on the side where the head of the Virgin is resting. The usual title, *Death of the Virgin*, is misleading. Mary is not represented on her deathbed; she is shown, rather, in death, being lowered into a sarcophagus, ornamented with Cosmati work, by two angels holding her shroud with the help of the apostles Peter and John. Christ, standing behind this group, but understood to be in heaven, is holding her soul, which is shaped like an infant, in both hands—a motif belonging iconographically to the scene of death. The presence of the angels, especially those holding the mortuary candles, shows that it is not a deathbed scene that is represented, but the parting of the soul from the mortal frame, to take shelter in the hands of God.

The work's relationship to Giotto's mature style appears in the treatment of color, such as the way in which he obtains three shades of red by adding white: a strong red in the robe of the apostle behind the corpse's head, an intermediate red in the robe of Christ, and a very light shade on the sides of the panel. The way the figures seem to float rather than stand firmly on the ground is characteristic of Giotto. The angels' wings, with their scale-like, rounded feathers, suggest that the painter was influenced by the sculpture of Giovanni Pisano.

Bohemian Master
About 1350

THE ARTIST: Unidentified by name, he is likely to have been a member of the *Malerzeche*, a "round table" of painters founded by the Emperor Charles IV, to whom the donor of the painting was closely attached. It was in 1349, two years after his accession to the throne, that Charles collected this group of painters, thus giving a strong impetus to the flowering of the arts that brought the so-called Bohemian school to prominence around the middle of the fourteenth century.

The artists were summoned to Prague from various places; German and Italian names appeared among them. In 1354 the name of Nicolas Wurmser of Strasbourg is mentioned, for one, and Theodoric of Prague is known to have painted the chapel of Karlstejn Castle in 1365. But the *Madonna of Glatz* cannot be attributed to any known painter, and it only possibly may be the work of the so-called Master of Hohenfurth, a distinguished painter then working in Bohemia, with whose style this painting shows a strong affinity.

MADONNA OF GLATZ

Tempera, poplarwood on canvas. 186 × 95 cm.

PROVENANCE: *Originally from the Church of the Minorites-on-the-Sand, at Glatz (now Klodzko, in southwestern Poland). Bought by the Kaiser Friedrich Museum Association in 1902.*

4, 5 The master who created the Madonna of Glatz, seated in state upon a throne monumental with the architectural elements of a Gothic cathedral, must have seen pictures of the Queen of Heaven as she was painted by Cimabue, Giotto, or the Gothic masters of Siena. We have here the same combination of figures schematized almost as in the old icons, with ornamental architectural forms, together giving a visionary grandeur to the appearance of the Madonna. The angels and lions in the canopy-like structure around the Virgin's head and the two angels gracefully holding up the curtain behind the throne are drawn so small in proportion to the Mother of God that she appears to be raised to unearthly sublimity.

The figures are flat, two-dimensional as in the icons; a certain spatial effect is aimed at, but without knowledge of perspective. The slender upward movement of the columns, arcs, and vaultings gives the elaborate throne the appearance of a cathedral choir. The contrapuntal effect of the rising architecture of the throne as against the descending folds of the Madonna's garments emphasizes the Gothic elegance of the composition.

The painter, delighting in ornamentation, decorated Mary's crown and scepter with golden leaves. The white head scarf, framing the Virgin's face almost like the silvery halo on an icon of the Eastern Church, is an unusual touch. The direction of the Christ Child's gaze connects the heavenly figures with the tiny one of the donor kneeling at the steps of the throne. He is scarcely larger than the angels bearing attributes and swinging censers on both sides of the throne; he even seems smaller than the two heavenly messengers holding up the curtain and the angel who appears to be setting the crown on the head of the "Empress of the Angels," as she is called in a hymn of the period.

The crowning of the Mother of God is an element lightly touched on; yet because of it, the fact that the lions, whose presence legend requires at the throne of Solomon, are placed above Mary's head instead of at her feet is all the more surprising. However, it suits the solemnly decorative composition, which suggests a church window but does not rival the translucent brilliance of colored glass. Instead, with its predominance of gold and silver and the delicate gradations of bright hues, it is the enchantment of the Gothic goldsmith's art that suffuses the painting and enhances its air of the supernatural.

The *Madonna of Glatz* occupies a special niche as a historical document among German and Bohemian works of art.

About the middle of the fourteenth century, Charles IV of Luxembourg—a grandson of Emperor Henry VII, of whom Dante had sung—who had inherited Bohemia from his mother, developed Prague into a city of considerable importance as well as a center of European culture by gathering in great artists from Germany, France, and Italy.

The donor who commissioned the painting, Bishop Ernst, son of a royal captain of Glatz, who styled himself Pardubice after a fief bestowed on him, was born toward the end of the thirteenth century (1297). He was a man of the world, had studied in Padua and Bologna, and when he visited the Pope in Avignon as Bishop of Prague, the Pope raised Prague to an archbishopric. This is confirmed in the painting: not only do the Bishop's insignia lie before the throne, but we also recognize the patriarchal cross of his high station, leaning against its pedestal. It may be surmised that the subject of this portrait, whose appearance is known from a miniature, donated this painting of the Madonna to his hometown soon after his promotion to Archbishop. This makes the picture a historical document of high rank, in addition to its importance as an exemplar of the religious mysticism of fourteenth-century art. It incidentally gives evidence of a likable personal trait of the donor's: tradition has it that Archbishop Ernst of Pardubice humbly laid down the insignia of his dignities when he prayed at the altar. His high office, he used to say, was nothing to him compared with the love of God. This special touch, expressing the humility and self-surrender of mysticism, makes the painting deeply moving to the beholder.

Bohemian Master
About 1360

This artist also is unknown. He clearly belongs to the Bohemian school that arose in Prague in the middle of the fourteenth century but was international rather than local in character. The similarity of the angels in this painting to those on the *Madonna of Glatz* suggests a close relationship between the artists.

The style strongly resembles that of the Master of Hohenfurth, and the painter of the Crucifixion panel in the Berlin museum may certainly be ranked with the

173

creator of the nine-panel altarpiece that was painted around the middle of the century and can still be seen today in the gallery of the Hohenfurth Chapter. The Crucifixion was most probably painted by someone in the circle or workshop of the Master of Hohenfurth—possibly by the Master himself.

CHRIST ON THE CROSS BETWEEN TWO THIEVES

Tempera, originally on wood covered with canvas; now transferred to canvas. 60 × 29.5 cm.

PROVENANCE: *Gift of the art dealers Paul Cassirer and F. W. Lippmann of Berlin and H. Helbing of Munich, in 1918.*

6 Upon the narrow panel that comes to a gable-like point in the Gothic manner, the painter has crowded together everything he or his client could have had to say about the Crucifixion.

An abundance of story elements is represented: the agony of martyrdom, the handing up of the vinegar-soaked sponge, the opening of the wound in Christ's side, the torture of the thieves—Dismas at the right of the Savior and redeemed by him, while Gismas, at his left, is unrepentant and therefore damned. At the right of the cross, led by St. John, is the group of the four Marys, one of whom, Mary Magdalen, embraces the instrument of the Lord's martyrdom. On the other side, the mercenaries are casting dice for the garments of the Crucified; behind them is the captain on his horse, with a companion and two knights following him. Longinus is pointing upward, having realized the injustice of the verdict. Overhead two angels swing their censers like their siblings in the *Madonna of Glatz.*

The master, whose art combines the religious sentiment of his period with the new skills of the school of Prague, seems close to the altar of Hohenfurth in both conception and form. Something new, however, is the attempt to show foreshortening on two heads; it may be due to the influence of Italian art by way of Avignon. Another difference is the profusion of forms, the crowded composition, reminiscent of the painting by Simone Martini that follows (Pl. 7). Nevertheless, the relationships to the *Madonna of Glatz* and the altar of Hohenfurth are so pronounced that we are justified in considering this a painting of the Bohemian school, which reached its apogee in the work of the Master of Hohenfurth. However, in comparison with the other paintings, this Crucifixion has greater dramatic intensity, more contrast in the juxtaposition of grief and love with brutality and greed, and greater variations of type and expression even among the executioners.

The whole brings to mind the words of *The Golden Legend*—its scholastic interpretation of the Scripture was undoubtedly known to whoever commissioned this painting: "Once that was deepest anguish which now is boundless glory."

Simone Martini

THE ARTIST: Simone Martini was probably a pupil of Duccio, contemporary of the somewhat younger Giotto. Duccio was born about 1255, Simone Martini about 1283. The principal scene of his activities was Siena, where Gothic art was flowering, not least in the works of both these masters.

About 1317, Simone Martini accepted a summons to Naples from King Robert of Anjou. He worked in Pisa from 1320 to 1321, then again in Siena. He is known to have painted the St. Martin frescoes of Assisi in 1333 and 1334. In 1339, the highly productive artist moved to Avignon—an event of decisive importance for the development of art north of the Alps—where he died early in 1344.

Ever since Giotto in Florence and Duccio in Siena, Italian art had been moving toward the humanization of the great figures of sacred history and their actions and passion. Like these predecessors, Simone Martini is shown by his style to have been a fresco painter. As Giotto knew Dante, so Martini knew Petrarch; like Giotto, he also painted in Assisi; and, like Petrarch, he was summoned by the Pope to Avignon, where he worked chiefly in the monumental style. This monumentality is evident in the rhythm of movement and the compactness of the composition, even in the small picture in Berlin, a late work presumably painted in Avignon.

THE BURIAL OF CHRIST

Tempera on poplarwood. 22 × 15 cm.

PROVENANCE: *Center panel of a triptych, painted presumably in Avignon between 1339 and 1344. Bought in Paris in 1901 by E. Pacully for the Kaiser Friedrich Museum.*

Lamentation turning to ecstasy, grief deepening to **7** despair, the boundless love of the mother who embraces her dead son once more, the devotion of the disciple passionately kissing Christ's hand—such are the themes depicted here. The master, more sensitive than forceful, more of a lyricist than a dramatist, renders the tragic scene of the last parting from the dead as a song of lament. On the small panel, no more than a hand's breadth in height, twenty-four mourners are gathered around the body. Seven of these—the mother, the two Marys, the Magdalen, Peter, John, and Joseph of Arimathea, handing the pot of unguents to one of the disciples—are distinguished by ornamented halos; the other figures appear crowded together like a Greek chorus led by the passionately lamenting woman with upraised hands.

Expressive as the individual heads are, the master, painting in the medieval spirit, was not concerned with merely characterizing individuals; he painted grief itself in all its subjective variations. Where Giotto (Pls. 2 and 3) depicts a sacred scene, the Sienese renders the ecstasy of grief and the surrender to mourning.

The composition, ascending from the lower right to the upper left of the panel, befits the picture's original function as centerpiece of a triptych. The two complementary panels are today in Antwerp and London. If it were possible to see the altar screen as a whole, the enamel-like brilliance of coloring would really come into its own. One would see how the shimmer of beauty comes to rest even on this painting so tremulous with grief, a beauty characteristic of all the Sienese master's works and owing much to his technique in blending his colors with the utmost care. His cinnabar reds and golden yellows are brought to their highest luminosity by contrast with the blues and greens, with the opening chords lightly struck in the blue, red, yellow, and orange, all lightened by white, of the four figures kneeling before the sarcophagus. The stronger colors of the upper half must be imagined against a ground of gold—which unfortunately was painted over later on, much to the detriment of the originally intended effect—with the landscape of four trees and the sky darkening toward the top.

Tommaso di Ser Giovanni Guidi (Masaccio)

THE ARTIST: Fifteenth-century Florentine painting begins with Tommaso di Ser Giovanni Guidi, called Masaccio. Born with the century in 1401, in Castello San Giovanni on the Arno, near Florence, he was said to be a pupil of his older friend Masolino, who, however, was also clearly influenced by him. From Florence he went to Pisa in 1426, then to Rome in 1427. Invited to paint some murals in San Clemente, he worked there until his early death in 1428. His principal works are the frescoes begun in 1423 in the Brancacci Chapel of the Santa Maria del Carmine Church in Florence; they were widely influential and are considered to have determined the course of Florentine painting of the Quattrocento.

"The whole power lies in expression!" These words are the climax of Stendhal's hymn to Masaccio, whom he glorifies as the initiator of the Renaissance. With the instinct of a poet, the Frenchman, who was obsessed with the art of Italy, saw that Masaccio's greatness lay in his capacity to do justice to the inner content of a motif, to heighten its expression by spiritual means. But if the painter of the frescoes in the Brancacci Chapel had been asked what his art aimed at, he would probably have said something quite different. He was a friend of the great Filippo Brunelleschi (1377–1446), architect of the octagonal ribbed dome of the cathedral in Florence, a structure that appears to be wholly liberated from the law of gravity, probably the most

beautiful of its kind in the world. From Brunelleschi, Masaccio learned about the art of perspective. And as a friend, too, of the boldly original sculptor Donatello (1386–1466), Masaccio was aware of far more concrete aims: the rendering of space by means of relating the figure to the environment; the use of movement and grouping in such a way that his figures would stand out in silhouette like the statues in Donatello's reliefs. Even the undulating landscape of Tuscany that forms the background for his *Adoration of the Magi* tends to move forward in a sculptural manner.

In form and feeling, Masaccio stands midway between Giotto and Raphael, in whom this realistic tendency in Italian art found its perfection, but also its end. Masaccio is regarded as the founder of realism south of the Alps, just as the art of the Van Eyck brothers is regarded as the victory of realism in northern Europe. And yet Stendhal's conception of the nature and value of Masaccio's art is the more profound one; there is historical insight in his statement about Masaccio's work when he says: "Here we stand at the cradle of expression."

ADORATION OF THE MAGI

Tempera on poplarwood. 21 × 61 cm.

PROVENANCE: *Part of the predella of the polyptych mentioned by Vasari. Masaccio painted it as commissioned by the notary of San Giusto, Giuliano di Colini degli Scarsi, for the Del Carmine Church at Pisa. According to Vasari, the predella consisted of five pictures on three panels, with the* Adoration of the Magi *as the center panel. The entire altarpiece had vanished from the Del Carmine Church by 1570. It was purchased in 1880 for Berlin, from the collection of the Marchese Gino Capponi in Florence.*

Even on so small a panel as is this *Adoration of the Magi,* **8, 11, 14** the originality and profundity of Masaccio's art find full expression.

The composition, in the style of a relief, lines up the figures as in a frieze, with the center of interest at the left in the mother holding the child and, kneeling before them, reverently kissing the foot of the newborn infant, the venerable king. In the center stands the youthful king, the third of the Magi, who represent the three ages of man and the three then known continents of the world. Near them, stationed somewhat in front of the main scene, is the donor with his son.

Masaccio prefers intense colors on his panels: a bright red in the cloaks of Joseph, the third of the Magi, and his companion; a darker red in the clothing of the other Magus and elsewhere; the yellow in Joseph's cloak; the rich ultramarine in the garments of Mary, Joseph, and the young king approaching in prayer.

Although the donors stand in the front rank, the eye passes over them, for their garments are done in somber blacks and grays. The background landscape is in green and red-brown, with blue for the distance. The legs and feet of the men standing and stepping forward are rendered with a compelling vigor; the rhythm of the verticals and diagonals combines most expressively with the rhythm of the horizontal shadows.

Within a small space, this picture, which might be a sketch for a large fresco, holds great riches of color harmony, plastic vigor, and spatial effects.

Fra Filippo Lippi

THE ARTIST: Born five years after Masaccio, under whom he is said by Vasari to have studied, the Carmelite monk Fra Filippo Lippi continued the work of the great initiator of the Florentine Renaissance in his own way, contributing his particular warmth of feeling and humanity to the representation of sacred subjects. He was far more of an innovator than is obvious at first glance. In concept, psychology, and spatial composition, he developed an art more secular than ecclesiastical, the lifelike concreteness of which brought a new fulfillment to the spirit of the Quattrocento.

Born in 1406 in Florence, he worked also in Padua, Prato, and Spoleto, where he began a series of frescoes for the cathedral in 1467. He died in 1469.

"A first-rate mind is a gift from heaven, not a beast of burden!" said Fra Filippo Lippi to Cosimo Medici, who had locked him up in the Palazzo Riccardi so that he would not interrupt his work on a commissioned painting. Fra Filippo, of course, tore his bed sheet into narrow strips and let himself down into the street, in pursuit of a gay adventure.

The life-loving monk's statement, however, was more than a witty rejoinder. It applies to his art as well, which was also a gift from heaven. In his paintings, he shows himself straightforward and gay of heart, unburdened with calculations of linear perspective and spatial construction; he has a bold, instinctive grasp of the relationship between figure and space and a storyteller's gift for grouping the figures in a painting in the most meaningful way. One might call him a naive painter by comparison with those who take pride in their intellectual approach and conscious techniques—Pollaiuolo, for example, whose spatial composition in his *Annunciation* (Pls. 22, 23) is more a matter of calculated architectural painting than of religious feeling. Born nineteen years after the Dominican Fra Angelico, whose art has something of the unearthly raptness of Gothic mysticism, Lippi does not bring his holy figures down from heaven as a visionary; rather, he is able to portray an earthly figure in such a way that his art transfigures and elevates it. The portrait of the young novice he abducted from her convent and made the mother of his son (Filippino Lippi, who inherited his father's artistic gifts) becomes his image of the Madonna. And the city of Florence recognized the exceptional status of this exceptional spirit, this "first-rate mind."

Robert Browning, though English and of the nineteenth century, had a very special feeling for the human element in the Florentine Renaissance. He dedicated a monologue in verse to the splendid monk, imagining him being caught out at midnight by the guard on a Florentine street and saying:

Yes, I'm the painter, since you style me so.
What, brother Lippo's doings, up and down,
You know them and they take you? like enough!

THE LEGEND OF ST. AMBROSE

Tempera on poplarwood. 28 × 51 cm.

PROVENANCE: *Painted presumably in 1441 as the left-hand panel of the predella for Lippi's* Crowning of the Virgin *in Sant' Ambrogio (now in the Uffizi). Property of the Kaiser Friedrich Museum since 1905.*

We know that Fra Filippo Lippi frequently crossed the Arno to see the Masaccio frescoes in the Brancacci Chapel upon which he modeled his own work. The little painting shown here, a predella to a large altar painting, shows Lippi's indebtedness to Masaccio and the grand Florentine style of painting far more than does his popular Christmas painting, the *Adoration of the Child,* also in the Berlin gallery, but more reminiscent of the influence of Fra Angelico.

We see a room clearly structured in the manner of the early Renaissance, permitting the eye to roam over the landscape visible through the center door and an adjoining window. At the right there is a crib with a one-step base, and in it is the child with golden rays emanating from his head in token of his sanctity. Eleven women crowd into the room, four of them kneeling or sitting beside the crib.

The painting apparently was done for the altar of the nuns of Sant' Ambrogio in Florence and represents a miracle during the infancy of St. Ambrose. The story is related in *The Golden Legend* as follows. Ambrose, son of the prefect of Rome, was once put into the courtyard of the palace, asleep in his cradle. Suddenly a swarm of bees came down and settled on the baby's face, covering it entirely, with the bees going in and out of his little mouth as though it were their hive. Then the swarm took off, rising so high in the heavens that no human eye could fallow it. When the father saw this, it frightened him, and he said: "If this child lives, it will have a great destiny."

Lippi does not show the scene with the bees, nor even their ascent heavenward, but only the moment when the miracle has been made manifest, when the infant, illuminated by rays from heaven, is endowed with the aura of the saint. Four women and a small child clinging to its mother surround the crib, gazing in wonder on the manifestation; three other women, center and back, approach in gentle adoration; and on the right, a servant is seen entering hurriedly.

But the most impressive group, and the one most inspired by the style of Masaccio, is not the one directly participating in the miracle. It is that of three women standing to one side and discussing the event they have seen. It is a conversation among women such as one might see any day on the streets or in the marketplaces of Florence—but Lippi has given it a grandeur and a beauty that suggest the Three Graces of antiquity.

The woman facing forward and the one seen in profile have expressions that seem to reflect the sacredness of the occurrence; the bearing of all three figures, their garments falling in rich folds, has a sublimity that might be said to surpass even Masaccio. In other respects, the painting points toward Ghirlandaio.

Unknown Master of Northern Italy
In the Style of Pisanello

THE ARTIST: Stylistically, this painting might be ascribed to either of two masters or their circles. Domenico Veneziano, to whom it is attributed—with a question mark, to be sure—in the catalogue of the Berlin gallery, handles his composition, colors, and light very differently and much more freely. More convincing is the attribution of this painting to the school of Antonio Pisano, called Pisanello—the Little Pisan—because he was born in Pisa (about 1395), but he actually grew up and spent most of his life in Verona. He was active in many Italian cities, however: Venice (1420–1424), Padua (1430), Mantua, Ferrara, Rimini, and finally Naples and Rome, where he died in 1455.

ADORATION OF THE MAGI

Round panel of poplarwood. 84 cm. in diameter.

PROVENANCE: *Painted about the middle of the fifteenth century. Acquired in Paris in 1880 (previously in the Barker collection in London).*

12, 13, 15   Before the manger in Bethlehem, in which the ox and the ass are resting, sits Mary holding the Christ Child, whose hand is raised in blessing toward the kneeling king, bent low to kiss the infant's foot. Behind him stand the other two kings in gorgeous array. They are presenting as their gifts precious golden vessels; that of the old king prostrated in adoration is being held by Joseph.

In the composition within its round frame, the principal subject of the painting seems to play a role subordinate to the splendor of the knightly entourage. It is as though the subject served only as a pretext for showing off the gentlemen of the court, just as the famous frescoes in the chapel of the Palazzo Riccardi in Florence painted by Benozzo Gozzoli around 1460 display the Medici with their court.

The nobles are most painstakingly portrayed, not only their features but even their clothes and horses. As though this were not enough, their heraldic mottoes are shown in letters of gold, further identifying their bearers. Two of the knights are wearing their devices embroidered around the edges of their tunics across the hips. One of these reads: "*Grace fai die*" ("God gives Grace"); the other shows the beginning of the phrase "*Ainsi va le [monde]*" ("Thus goes the world"), the word *monde* not being spelled out but represented by a globe. The harness of one horse bears the inscription "*Omnia bona in tenpore*" ("All good things in time"). Part of the same saying (here, too, with the word *tenpore* instead of *tempore*) appears on the headgear of the horseman behind this horse. All this is quite in character with the playful romanticism of the decadent knighthood around the middle of the fifteenth century at the courts of northern Italy, under French and Burgundian influence. The science of heraldry might enable us to identify the families whose arms bore these mottoes, and thereby one might learn the name of the person who commissioned the painting and even the name of the painter. Attempts to identify him on the basis of his style have not yet led to a conclusive answer. Before the painting was bought for Berlin in 1880, it was attributed, without reason, to Fra Filippo Lippi. Wilhelm von Bode, much more plausibly, considered it a work by Pisanello, who had been active at the courts of Ferrara, Rimini, Milan, and, above all, Mantua, as well as Verona. It undoubtedly stands in some relationship to Pisanello's art, which developed in the courtly culture of northern Italy.

Antonio Pisano's famous fresco in the Church of Sant' Anastasia in Verona, *St. George and the Princess*, showing St. George setting out for his combat with the dragon, seems in many respects to be the model for the unknown master of our *tondo*, or circular panel, who adapts the style of the fresco in Verona to his panel. We see the same delight in profile presentation characteristic of Pisanello—who also created sharply contoured portrait medallions—and the same tendency to group minor figures together, but not without painstakingly reproducing all the facial traits and the clothing. The rear view of a white horse with a braided tail occurs frequently in the work of Pisanello, even on his medallions, and in the aforementioned Verona frescoes it most closely resembles the representation in our *tondo*. In the frescoes, too, one finds the gallows seen in this panel (Pl. 13). But the technique of our unknown master is more that of the miniaturist; he paints with a pointed brush, yet without the sharp pointedness of Pisanello.

Bode's persuasive attribution of the work to Pisanello (at least in regard to the general tendency) has recently been disputed. The name of Domenico Veneziano has been suggested, without convincing anyone, though it got into the museum's catalogue. It is true that there are paintings with a tendency to show profiles by this Venetian turned Florentine. But the little panel in the Berlin gallery that comes from the predella of the Lucia altar in the Uffizi especially illustrates a lighting and a loose, free composition that are quite lacking in the *tondo*—considering, for example, the profile portrait of a young woman so much more rightfully attributed to Veneziano (Pl. 21). Nor do Veneziano's paintings show any of that highly detailed landscape painting which, together with his pleasure in painting animals—something he shares with Pisanello—characterizes the master of the *tondo*. The viewer's gaze roams afar over a landscape with a lake bordered on the one side by mountains, on the other by precipitous cliffs such as might be seen on the southern slopes of the Alps. The slender tree that was added subsequently, in order to divide the round area so unsuitable for a composition with so many figures, is more likely to be found there than in Tuscany. But the two falcons attacking a heron high in the air could have been observed by the painter more readily at a lake in northern Italy than in Florence.

The eye roams this landscape with pleasure. There is a castle, suggesting the nearness of Verona, and one enjoys the sight of the grazing sheep. This is probably the largest flock ever granted to the poor shepherds of Bethlehem. The train of followers escorting the Three Wise Men can be seen far into the distance. Another argument for the northern Italian locale is the fact that subsequent representations of the Adoration of the Magi in Veronese paintings suggest, by the nature of some of the details of their composition, that their creators were familiar with this round-panel painting.

That the minor motifs—the train, the flock, birds, gallows—that enrich the panel are rendered with so much delight in detail is characteristic of this painter's style. It distinguishes him from the grand style of Pisanello, who was trained as a fresco painter. Nevertheless, its close relationship to that master's work is so evident that we should like, following Bode, to call the style "School of Pisanello."

Andrea Mantegna

THE ARTIST: Born in 1431 in Vicenza, he became a pupil of Squarcione, who adopted him, in Padua. Donatello, and the nearness of Venice, profoundly influenced him. Mantegna married the daughter of the famous Venetian painter Iacopo Bellini in 1454. Beginning in 1460, he was connected with the ducal court of the Gonzaga in Mantua, but he also worked intermittently in other Italian cities—Verona (1463), Florence (1466), Rome (from 1488). He died in Mantua in 1506.

Andrea Mantegna was in the van of those artists who gave its special stamp to the Italian Renaissance in the fifteenth century. Following Alberti's rejection of the Gothic tradition, they strove to do justice to reality in a new sense of the term, searching for its inner laws and giving it form in the spirit of classical antiquity.

PRESENTATION OF CHRIST IN THE TEMPLE

Distemper on unsized canvas. 68 × 86 cm.

PROVENANCE: *About 1455, an early work. Once owned by Pietro Cardinal Bembo, who died in 1547, it made its way into the Solly collection and was acquired for Berlin in 1821.*

The figures, aligned like statues in strict vertical sequence, make an arrangement typical of Mantegna's frescoes. Even in his panel painting, the master retains that monumental, classical serenity that in itself generates a religious aura. In a relatively small space, and despite the characteristic crowding of the figures, the grandeur of Mantegna's style is apparent. The painting shows Mary, accompanied by Joseph, presenting the newborn infant to Simeon, the venerable priest to whom legend attributes the prophetic words uttered on this occasion: "Lord, now lettest thou thy servant depart in peace, according to thy words, for mine eyes have seen thy salvation."

Simeon, then, is the patriarch with the flowing white beard and keen-eyed gaze. Compared with him, Joseph, seen facing front in the second row, is a man in the prime of life. With Mary as a young woman and Jesus as an infant, this makes four generations, representing the course of human life, adumbrated by the mysterious words of *The Golden Legend*: "The old man carried the child, but the child ruled the old man." The expressive movement of the priest's hands suggests also that the child is to pass from the mother's care to that of the priest, who has a premonition of the child's mission.

A particularly impressive structural aspect of the painting is the way in which Mantegna uses the hands and arms as a horizontal base to support the sharply vertical four figures, with the additional element of the cushion on which the feet of the infant are resting. The correspondence between the lavish velvet brocades in the garments of the mother and the vestments of the priest is another means of achieving a unified effect.

As the placement of the Joseph figure indicates, the picture has a background space from which, smaller and more distant, two heads look outward. The male head (Pl. 19) is clearly a self-portrait of the artist, as comparison with the portrait bust of Mantegna shows. The female head on the far left is that of his wife, who served as the model for his *Madonna* of 1455 (Pl. 17) as well. The presence of these portraits lends a touch of personal warmth to a picture that is otherwise austere.

MADONNA WITH SLEEPING CHILD

Distemper on canvas. 42 × 32 cm.

PROVENANCE: *Painted about 1455, also a work of Mantegna's early period. Formerly in the collection of the Conte della Porte in Vicenza, it was eventually bought from an English art dealer by James Simon, who gave it to the Kaiser Friedrich Museum in 1904.*

17   Like the preceding panel, this is also considered an early work of the master, done when he was about twenty-four years old. Born in Vicenza, Mantegna grew up in Padua. He came to know Giovanni Bellini of nearby Venice, who was almost exactly his own age, and married Bellini's half sister Nicolosia in 1454. The depiction of the youthful mother pressing the sleeping infant to her bosom surely testifies to the artist's own conjugal happiness. Both the paintings in Berlin—the *Madonna* and the *Presentation of Christ in the Temple*—apparently represent the expression of the artist's delight in the birth of his first child, which would also account for the newborn baby portrayed in both cases.

The coloring is subdued, more a matter of the interplay of light and shadow by means of shadings of color rather than of any particular color emphasis. The dark blue of Mary's dress, together with the black background, sets off the golden tones framing the mother and child and glinting in the brown hair of the virginal young woman. Delicate touches of red animate the two faces, in effective contrast with the gray veilings of shadow around them.

PORTRAIT OF LUDOVICO CARDINAL MEZZAROTA

Tempera on poplarwood. 44 × 33 cm.

PROVENANCE: *Painted about 1459. Received in exchange from the Solly collection in 1830. Formerly in the collection of Francesco Leone in Padua.*

18   To capture the individuality of a person clearly and evocatively was one of the aims of the art of the Quattrocento, animating sculptors and painters alike. In this respect, the portrait of Ludovico Cardinal Mezzarota is one of Mantegna's triumphant achievements. Long influenced by Donatello, Mantegna here achieves the same kind of plastic vigor in the strong lines of the features and the interplay of light and shadow as did the sculptor. To this he added something beyond the sculptor's province: the glow of color—especially in the red collar circling the neck as it emerges from the white of the alb; the red gleaming in the silken cloak, harmonizing with the dark green of the background; and the healthy red tints in the face, adding warmth and life to it. The onlooker senses the vitality, the energetic man's love of life; the Cardinal was a soldier, a distinguished human-

ist, and a gourmet who took such an aesthetic pleasure in the delights of the table that he was nicknamed Cardinal Lucullus. The sitter was a generation older than the artist; born in Padua in 1402, Mezzarota died in Rome in 1465.

Stefano di Giovanni (Sassetta)

THE ARTIST: Sassetta, who was born about 1392 in Cortona and died in 1450 in Siena, became a member of the Sienese painters' guild in 1428. He was influenced by the brothers Lorencetti, themselves heirs of Duccio, Lippo Memmi, and Simone Martini.

Compared with the creative power of the austere Florentine school, that of Siena is characterized by a lyrical tenderness, from Duccio to Simone Martini and from Lippo Memmi to Sassetta, who painted the Madonna on a golden ground, crowned by angels and blessed by God the Father. As late as the middle of the fifteenth century, Sassetta was still painting as though he were living in the early fourteenth century, more than a century earlier, and before Siena's tragic year, 1347, when the Black Death raged in the narrow streets of the hill city and destroyed the flower of a whole generation. The dawn of Siena's art was followed by an early sunset. The city clung to the ancient form of the cult image at a time when the rest of Italy had moved into fifteenth-century realism; it was for Siena—"City of the Virgin," as it called itself—a way of keeping alive the memory of its springtime.

In the Berlin gallery, the master's art can be seen in its two aspects: as glorifier of the Holy Virgin on little altar panels, in the manner of the goldsmiths of the Gothic period, and also as an original narrator of sacred legends, dressing their protagonists in the costumes of his day. His special manner is most evident when he is telling a story; it is naive rather than archaic. Significantly, our own time, one of whose modes of expression is surrealism, has rediscovered the freshness and originality of Sassetta.

VIRGIN AND CHILD, CROWNED BY TWO ANGELS

Tempera on poplarwood. 47 × 25 cm., with raised center.

PROVENANCE: *Presumably acquired with the Solly collection in 1821.*

This little altar of the Madonna, only a hand's breadth wide but twice as high, in accordance with the Gothic taste, shows with what delicacy the master could capture religious sentiment. He enlivens his treatment   **20** by contrasting the dreaminess of the mother with the infant's carefree joy in movement. The way the baby's feet are held by the mother's hand while his little fingers go into his mouth illustrates Sassetta's original touch. Strongly in the tradition of the Trecento are the hovering angels holding the crown above the head of the Mother of God.

Sassetta's characteristic mood is reflected in the coloring: the deep-blue—indeed, much darkened—cloak of the Madonna richly contrasts with the unusual bright-red wrapper from which the child has kicked free, and the red-patterned pillow seat. The halos, the crown, and the ornamental frame are outlined in points of gold beaten into the golden background; gold gleams in the belts of the angels, in the border of Mary's cloak, and even in the pattern of the carpet. The traditional art of the goldsmith in which so many painters were trained is manifest throughout.

Domenico Veneziano

THE ARTIST: Neither the year nor the place of his birth is known. He was demonstrably active as a painter from 1438 on, and he died on May 15, 1461, in Florence. Since he signed two of his paintings "Dominicus de Veneciis," it is assumed that he was born in Venice. Stylistically, however, his work belongs wholly in the Florentine tradition. From a letter of his to Piero de' Medici, we learn that he was working in Perugia in 1438, but we do not know how long he stayed there or what works he created in that period.

PORTRAIT OF A YOUNG WOMAN

Poplarwood. 51 × 35 cm.

PROVENANCE: *Acquired for Berlin in 1894 from the collection of the Earl of Ashburneham in London.*

21   The rare paintings of Domenico Veneziano, known for their bright hues, their silvery lighting, hang in the Uffizi, in London, and in Berlin, diffusing the brilliant sheen of Venice among the heavier-toned panels of the Florentine masters of the early Renaissance. One wonders at the fact that the art of the master who created them is generally treated as of secondary importance and that even one of his most typical works, the *Portrait of a Young Woman,* has repeatedly been listed as the work of other painters. In 1815, when the history, and particularly the criticism, of art was still in its infancy, this painting, then in the Massias collection in Paris, was attributed to Cimabue; later, those who sensed the artist's closeness to Piero della Francesca, who was his pupil, attributed it to the latter; and at various times it has been ascribed to others, such as Baldovinetti and

Antonio Pollaiuolo. But Pollaiuolo's more incised, metallic style is not nearly so close as that of the *St. Lucy Altarpiece* in the Uffizi, known to be by Veneziano, the predella panel of which was acquired for Berlin in 1841 by the gallery's excellent director, Gustav Friedrich Waagen.

In all three of these paintings, we see the same preference for light colors, among them a bright carmine contrasting with green, and this master's characteristic way of letting white sing out as a color. In all three there is the same preference for profile presentation, which could make the *Adoration* (Pl. 12) a possible Veneziano. Something of the grace and feminine nobility of the portrait is also seen, in rarefied form, in the *St. Lucy Altarpiece.* The altarpiece, painted for the Church of Santa Lucia dei Bardi in Florence and signed "Opus Domenici Veneciis," must have been created in Florence, but in this portrait, the balcony railing, the blond coloring of the lady, the pattern of her dress, and the sky that bespeaks the nearness of the sea all cry Venice.

At the same time, the relationship of his art to that of the painter and medallionist Pisanello, who also favors the profile, is evocative of Verona.

Regardless of its place in the history of art, however, the finely proportioned lines of the profile and the nape of the neck and the contrast between the tender uses of light in the modeling and the rich colors in the velvet brocade of the dress add up to a masterwork that manages to capture even the psychology of its subject by purely painterly means.

Piero Pollaiuolo

THE ARTIST: Born in 1443 in Florence, he died, presumably in Rome, in 1496. He was a pupil of Andrea del Castagno, and worked with his brother Antonio, who was active as a goldsmith, painter, and sculptor, chiefly in Florence. Pollaiuolo lived for a time in San Gimignano and probably also in Rome. Both brothers were much concerned with perspective and spatial effects, and their inclusion of landscape in the context of their subject was of decisive importance. In their paintings distance achieves spatial value.

The longing for space, the movement to unheard of distances, realized toward the end of the fifteenth century by its bold seafarers and discoverers of new continents, also found expression in the new sensibilities of the painters. Like the Van Eyck brothers, the Quattrocentists of Florence and Venice were also born before Amerigo Vespucci, Christopher Columbus, and Martin Behaim (the German traveler and cosmographer). It was the creation of space by the architects and the painters that gave mankind an entirely new sense of life. Now the golden background of the Madonna ceased to be felt as a vision of the beyond and became constricting. The eye, seeking the freedom of distance and depth, demanded the clear lines of a geometrically constructed perspective for guidance. No subject of religious painting indicates this new sense of space more dramatically than the Annunciation painted in the new style. For the medieval painter, the archangel Gabriel, as the Lord's messenger, had come into the house from the regions of the sky, his wings suggesting the accomplished flight. The Virgin's alarm and surrender, the angel's message and adoration were the painting's mystic content. But now the figures of Mary and the angel seem to have become mere accessories to what appears to be the painter's principal interest: the representation of space. Competing with the architect in the invention of structural and decorative forms in the style of the early Renaissance, he coaxes yet a third dimension from his flat surface.

ANNUNCIATION

Poplarwood. 150 × 174 cm.

PROVENANCE: *Acquired with the Solly collection in 1821.*

22,23   The style is entirely that of the young Piero. Antonio is likely to have modeled the figures in a more energetic way, being more of a sculptor than a painter, but his influence on his much younger brother is evident in the bronze tones of the painting. The opalescence of carefully modulated mixed tones of yellow, brown, red-brown, olive, and gold makes for brilliant color effects in combination with the bright blue of the Virgin's cloak. The overabundance of ornamentation is held under control by the mood of the color tones. The paint is laid on thickly; the media appear resinous, even oily: the techniques of oil painting are being developed.

This relatively large panel is one of the best and most important among the many paintings of the Annunciation in fifteenth-century Italy, extraordinary in its mastery of perspective, its riches of ornamentation, and its chromatic unity. Here panel painting begins to escape from the domination of traditional fresco painting and to presage new possibilities through the use of perspective as a way of representing space: by giving the illusion of depth, it brings a new vision reaching far into the distance.

Like many other paintings of the Annunciation in the Quattrocento, Pollaiuolo's panel is divided midway into two sections—probably an echo of the times when this scene was frequently painted on two wings of an altarpiece. Behind the angel there is a kind of vestibule, with pilasters supporting a coffered ceiling, and a marble floor. The scene is so constructed that the viewer seems to be looking in from the left. The Virgin is sitting upon a richly jeweled chair; she has put the little prayer book she was reading on her knee and has turned toward the angel, her hands crossed on her bosom in a gesture of obedience. The eye passes above the head of the messenger through the double-arched window and far into the distance, where Florence, with its domed cathedral, the winding Arno, and the hills of Tuscany, can be seen. The peacock so beloved by the painters of the Quattrocento is perched on the railing of a balcony that leads the eye toward the intersection of the lines of perspective, rather high up in the left window. The lines of foreshortening in Mary's window also converge toward the same point. Her bed with its pillow is visible in the upper-right corner of the room.

At the left of Mary's head is the door to another antechamber, in which tiny angels are seen kneeling and making music. The effect of distance the painter appears to have been striving for here does not come off as well as the linear perspective constructed by him or his brother Antonio, who is thought by some critics to have plotted this painting. Florentine contemporaries must have seen the work as a marvel of perspective. It represents the fulfillment of a principle laid down by Leon Battista Alberti, who paved the way for the Renaissance: "The painter of a picture must, at the outset, be familiar with the laws of geometry and the theory of optics."

Sandro Botticelli

THE ARTIST: Sandro di Mariano dei Filipepi, called Botticelli, was a Florentine. Born about 1444, he died in his native city in 1510. He began as an apprentice in his father's goldsmith shop and then studied with Fra Filippo Lippi. His art transfigured the Florence of Lorenzo de' Medici and thereby the entire period of the early Renaissance, which was inspired by the ideals of humanism.

Botticelli worked in Rome in 1482 and 1483, commissioned by Pope Sixtus IV to decorate the Sistine Chapel. After his return to Florence, he painted the *Primavera*. But in the 1490's, profoundly shaken by the fate of Savonarola, he became a painter of deeply religious subjects. The Berlin gallery has six of his paintings, and the collection of copperplate engravings in the same museum includes the greater part of his pen drawings for Dante's *Divine Comedy*.

MADONNA WITH CHILD AND SINGING ANGELS

Tempera on poplarwood. Round panel, 135 cm. in diameter.

PROVENANCE: *In 1824 the Polish Count Edward Raczyński, one of the great collectors in Berlin, bought this painting in Paris for 2,500 francs. It had come to Paris as a loot from Italy during the Napoleonic wars. From 1884, it hung in the Berlin museum as a "permanent loan." After the erection of the Kaiser Friedrich Museum in 1906, it became one of the most popular works in the collection. When the heirs of the former owner succeeded in reasserting their rights to it, the painting was purchased in 1954 with the aid of the federal goverment and its constituent states.*

24, 25 To the eye, the circle is the most perfectly self-contained form there is. In his treatise on painting, which became fundamental to all Renaissance theory of art, Leon Battista Alberti, the creator of the facade of Santa Maria Novella in Florence and the leading architect and theorist of the early Renaissance, described the act of seeing as follows: perception takes place through a cone-shaped form, with the point of the cone at the pupil of the eye and its circular base formed by the area perceived, a kind of "pyramid of vision." Accordingly, the so-called *tondo* was, he felt, the picture shape most suited to the natural functioning of the eye, and it became the fashionable form of panel painting and even of sculptural relief during the Quattrocento, an era dominated by humanist theories of art.

This fashion soon waned, however, for human vision, regardless of theory, accommodates itself to the upright posture of the human figure, the horizontal expanse of the landscape, or the depth of a room. It is, in short, determined not only by the structure of the eye but also by that of the visual object.

The popularity of the *tondo* during the Renaissance has also been rightly attributed to its suitability for private devotions. Bocchi's old description of Florence, confirmed by Vasari, tells us that *tondi* were used in the churches to decorate the chapels. The *Madonna* of Sandro Botticelli in Berlin is thought to have originated in this manner.

The strict symmetry of the composition and the spatial effect created by the suggestion of the glory of heaven above the Madonna's head, over which a crown is held by hands reaching from the clouds, suggest the ceremonial of worship in the house of God. The group at the right is apparently singing the Magnificat from the book around which it is clustered, while the angels on the left, dark-haired in contrast to their blond companions, quietly rejoice in the presence of the Christ Child. The child is turning from his mother's breast to gaze toward the beholder, as does the handsome angel at the far left.

The Mother of God, tinged with melancholy like all of Botticelli's Madonnas, gazes pensively into the distance and holds the Christ Child with overly delicate but sheltering hands. White lilies irradiate the blue of the sky.

The coloring is low-keyed, as befits the devotional feeling of the painting. The delicate tones of blue-gray and rose-violet in the choirboy albs worn by the angels contrast effectively with the unbroken blue of the Madonna's cloak and even more with the red of her dress patterned in gold. Over all this discreet play of color, the golden ornaments shed an unobtrusive glow. The gold on the Madonna's veil, in particular, seems almost unearthly, a glory sent down as a blessing from heaven. The perfect beauty of the composition, the forms and colors, and the slender, narrow heads characterize this as an early work, created in the brilliant Florence of Lorenzo the Magnificent about 1475, when Botticelli was still a young man.

ST. SEBASTIAN

Tempera on poplarwood. 195 × 75 cm., rounded on top.

PROVENANCE: *Acquired with the Solly collection in 1821. The painting belongs to Botticelli's early period. It was created about 1473–1474 for the Church of Santa Maria Maggiore in Florence—according to Vasari, for the elder Lorenzo de' Medici.*

The saint is shown life-size, standing on two sawed-off **26** branches of a tall tree trunk to which his hands are tied behind him. Pierced by six arrows, he acquiesces in his fate. Only Botticelli could have given the martyr's eyes this expression of mingled self-surrender and faith.

Nevertheless, the painter was probably not too much concerned with the subjective religious element, profoundly as he had grasped it; he was in fact competing with the other Florentine painters and sculptors concerned with the representation of the human body. It was beauty he was after, and that elongated body with its relatively small head stated his conception of the harmony and the proportions of the human figure. Hence we have a work oriented toward classical antiquity yet entirely in the spirit of its own century.

The painter here has an advantage over the sculptor: he can relate the figure to the surrounding space, and he can endow the whole with the living glow of color. A landscape stretching to the far horizon juxtaposes depth and horizontal layering against the steep verticality of the foreground. Figure and space are interrelated and chromatically unified by the light hues of yellow and brown throughout. The delicate green in the landscape and the pale blue of the sky with its white clouds, combining with the fading blue of the distance, set off the figure in the foreground.

The abundance of detail in the background signalizes this as an early work. The careful execution in all particulars of rocks, trees, and towers expresses the delicate sensibilities of the early Renaissance. There is also a touch of the narrative flair of the period: among the mercenaries withdrawing in the middle distance, one is seen gaily aiming the last arrow in his quiver at a bird perched on a branch high above him.

VENUS

Tempera on canvas. 157 × 68 cm.

PROVENANCE: *Acquired in 1821 with the Solly collection. A variant, formerly in the Gualino collection, is now in the Galleria Sabauda in Turin.*

There are certain works of art that not only express the **27** period in which they were created, and which they helped to create, but go beyond it to achieve a timeless beauty and meaning. It is thus that in Sandro Botticelli's celebrated *Birth of Venus* in the Uffizi, the Renaissance proclaims itself as the triumph of beauty. The statuary aspect of this work, freed from allegory, was expressed a second time by Master Sandro in the *Venus,* one of seven paintings by him owned by the Berlin museum. Its sculptural quality is even more pronounced than that of the *St. Sebastian,* which preceded it by about five years. We do not know by what antique statue this was inspired. The famous *Venus de' Medici* that now stands in the center of the Tribuna in the Uffizi was unearthed in Rome no earlier than the sixteenth century and arrived in Florence about two hundred years after Botticelli had painted his *Venus.* But this type of marble statue, echoing the work of Praxiteles, was considered at the time a representation of the ideally beautiful female figure.

Botticelli was not an eclectic; he invoked classical antiquity, but he had his own idea of beauty. His figures are more slender than the classical; and as a master of the Quattrocento, he loved sharpness of contour. The head of his Venus is exceptionally small in relation to the length of the body, and her golden hair flows around her like an aureole.

He gave his Venus the features of Simonetta Vespucci, the most beautiful woman of Medicean Florence in its springtime. She wears the two braids she has made out of her abundant hair as a blond ornament draped forward over her shoulders. In this graceful Genoese lady, the mistress of Giuliano de' Medici (who was murdered in 1478), Florence saw the incarnation of beauty itself. She was born in Portovenere, where, according to legend, Venus landed in Italy. The hint of melancholy in her gaze seems appropriate in one fated to die young, and in character for the painter whose ideal of feminine beauty she was.

Carlo Crivelli

THE ARTIST: Crivelli was born in Venice in 1430 and died in Fermo in 1495. His art is in the tradition of The Marches, even though he always designated himself as a Venetian on his altarpieces. The Venetian element in his art is only one of many; Vivarini of Padua, the painters of Murano, and the works of Donatello and Mantegna also exerted a strong influence on him. He left Venice early in his career, presumably because a love affair with a married woman brought him a taste of the severity of Venetian justice in the form of a jail sentence. To the detriment of his art, he lost touch with the great current of development in Venetian painting, becoming a provincial leader in art who was kept busy in the southern Marches, first in Ascoli and then in Fermo. But on his pictures he kept proudly signing himself "Carlo Crivelli of Venice."

Carlo Crivelli's style might be characterized as having a certain grandiosity rather than the inner grandeur of a Mantegna, his contemporary. Grandiosity is so much of his essence and expresses itself—he is unique in this—with such naiveté and religious seriousness, despite his full awareness of the means employed, that his art continues to arouse controversy. Misjudged during the period that defined beauty in accordance with derivative, classicist tenets, he began to be appreciated at last by the generation whom expressionism had taught to value purely painterly effects.

Although Crivelli's art is in the tradition of Venice, it shows no trace of the atmosphere of that city of lagoons. At most one might find reflected in it the golden shimmer of the San Marco mosaics—intensified by his reveling in the splendors of the liturgical vestments and vessels at the altar during the rituals of worship. Few painters have so combined the showpieces of the goldsmith's art with embroideries and tapestries into a polyphonic harmony to set the mood of an altarpiece. Preserving the Gothic tradition, he consciously fashioned his panels to blend with the gilded frame of carved wood in order to retain an over-all effect of gold. His creations must be understood as cult objects, as an art wholly and inextricably of the church, and not as isolated paintings in a museum.

The panels impinge on the realms of architecture and sculpture not only with their opulent frames; the halos, jewels, and precious vessels depicted on them are painted as if three-dimensional, like a sculptured relief. All this is in the tradition of the Gothic masters of Venice and Murano, such as, for example, Antonio Vivarini. Vivarini's influence on Crivelli became greater in Padua, where the Renaissance of Donatello and Mantegna excited Crivelli's receptive imagination.

MADONNA IN GLORY WITH SEVEN SAINTS

Tempera on poplarwood. 191 × 196 cm.

PROVENANCE: *Purchased in 1892, when the collection of the Earl of Dudley was put on auction in London.*

The style of this panel, showing the influence of **28, 29** Padua (and thereby that of Donatello and Mantegna) rather than that of Venice, is sculptural rather than painterly. It was painted in 1487 for 100 gold ducats and represents the ripest fruit of Crivelli's fourteen-year sojourn in Ascoli. It bears the inscription, in large letters, "OPUS CAROLI CRIVELLI VENETI," at the bottom center. This work may be considered a high point in the master's achievement. Soon after its completion, he moved to Fermo, where other commissions awaited him.

It is an unusual scene that, predictably, this fifteenth-century eccentric has depicted on this panel: the key, and therewith the founding of the papacy, is given to St. Peter not, as ordinarily, by Christ, appointing the apostle his vicar on earth, but by the Madonna, enthroned as Queen of Heaven with a backdrop of Renaissance architectural ornamentation.

One may assume that Crivelli, bringing his art to the remote little town on the northern slope of the Apennines, had considerable freedom in choosing the content and form of his altarpieces and found patrons whose special wishes he was willing to accommodate in return for their willingness to let him try a new, dramatic arrangement in lieu of the conventional schematic portrayal of the saints flanking the throne. Something new was to be created here, sumptuous and exciting in form, profound in meaning. Since the Madonna was to be the center of the picture, the painter let the symbol of the papacy, the two keys—the golden one could open the gate of heaven—glide from the elegantly poised hand of the Lady, through the infant's hand, into that of St. Peter, dressed in papal robes and with the gold and silver of the papal tiara glittering beside his knees.

The other six saints all stand in some special relationship to Ascoli. The Bishop holding the book at St. Peter's side is the patron saint of the town, St. Emidius. Behind him, closest to the throne, is St. Francis, recognizable by the stigmata on his hand. At the extreme left, holding the banner, stands St. John of Capistrano, conqueror of the Turks and therefore protector of Ascoli's harbor. On the right, opposite the Bishop, stands St. Louis of Toulouse, identified by the fleur-de-lys pattern on his blue cape. Behind him, and corresponding in the daring foreshortening of the head to the figure of St. Francis, is St. Bonaventure. And to the far right, as patron saint of the Franciscans and The Marches, is St. Giacomo della Marca, with a monstrance full of blood.

Typical of the master is the way the three-times-three figures of the painting are crowded together around the structure of the throne, on the entablature of which sit two *putti* playfully holding a garland of heavy, shiny fruits above the crowned head of the Madonna. Testifying to Crivelli's love of the still life, an ear of corn from the entablature above the head of St. Peter and a red-cheeked apple lie upon the steps of the throne.

Crivelli's tendency to exaggerate gesture and expression and to overdo decorative accessories may have been partly due to his move to the provinces and the resulting loss of contact with the mainstream of development in the arts. He thus fell into mannerism, while Mantegna achieved true greatness. The Berlin panel illustrates the perils but even more the special beauties of his work.

Hubert and Jan van Eyck

1370–1426 and 1390–1441

THE ARTISTS: These two Flemish painters, brothers, derived their name from their birthplace, Maaseik. The elder brother, Hubert, died around 1426, when the work on the altar of Ghent, which they had begun around 1420, was still in progress. Jan, the better known of the two, completed this celebrated altarpiece in 1432. After a brief period of activity in The Hague, he entered the service of Duke Philip the Good of Burgundy in 1425, traveling to Spain and Portugal on his behalf. In 1430 he settled in Bruges, where he died in 1441.

CHRIST ON THE CROSS BETWEEN MARY AND JOHN

Transferred from wood to canvas. 43 × 26 cm.

PROVENANCE: *Here attributed to Jan van Eyck. Presumed to have been painted before the completion of the Ghent altarpiece, about 1430. Bought from an English dealer in 1897. Property of the Kaiser Friedrich Museum Association.*

The figures and the landscape, the forms and the space have not yet been blended into a unity in this painting, just as there is a certain disjunction between figure and space in *The Madonna in Church* (Pls. 32, 33). The figures are reminiscent of late-Gothic wood carvings, which tend to render expression realistically in the same way. The effect is one of three carved wooden figures in front of a Gobelin. This, in addition to the noticeable relationship of the *Madonna* to miniature painting, indicates an essential difference between the two paintings. It helps to explain the statuary size of the figures and the ornamental quality of the landscape—the way its various elements are lined up side by side—as well as the tendency to a certain grandeur, evident even here despite the small format, a tendency that decisively informed Dutch painting of the fifteenth century after the altarpiece of Ghent, until it was perfected by Hugo van der Goes.

In the Crucifixion by Konrad Witz (Pl. 30), as well as in the one attributed to the Master of Flémalle, which hangs next to the Van Eyck in the Berlin-Dahlem Gallery, the body of the Crucified looms high above the horizon. In the Van Eyck, however, the landscape occupies nearly three-fourths of the panel, although in the foreground and center its function is only to fill the spaces between the figures. But it achieves importance in itself in the background, with its towering buildings and mountains ranging far into the distance. The city of Jerusalem is presented as an architectural frieze, beginning at the left with a delicately painted tall, leafless tree with birds. At the right, a group of southern trees, an umbrella pine and three cypresses, in naive togetherness with a Dutch windmill, juts above the horizon. The southern character of the buildings and trees casts doubt on the view of some critics that this is the work of Hubert, the elder brother; it rather supports the opinion of those who ascribe the work to Jan, on the trip he made to Portugal in 1428 for Duke Philip of Burgundy, to paint a portrait of the Princess who was the Duke's chosen bride. There he saw the trees he put in his Palestinian landscape, and the domed buildings of his Jerusalem also seem to be the fruit of travels in southern Europe.

If we consider the three figures in relationship to the art of the Netherlands, we realize how much of the Gothic tradition is contained in this painting, presumably an earlier work than the altarpiece of Ghent. The body of Christ has a Gothic line, though the attitude of a new era expresses itself in the realism with which

Christ's martyrdom is represented: a particularly moving aspect of the picture is the way in which the blood streams from the wound in his side and down the lower part of the cross into the ground. This corpus Christi does not rise up high, like that of the Master of Flémalle, but rather hangs down, with his hanging hair and down-flowing blood, from the heavy crossbeam stretching almost from side to side of the painting and emphasizing the horizontal together with the clouds, mountains, and buildings behind it. In contrast to this, the two figures at the sides of the cross rise high up from the ground, the mother at the right, the disciple at the left of the Savior. The two trees overtopping the horizon near their heads further emphasize this ascending movement.

The massive, heavy folds of their garments strengthen the sculptural effect. It makes the visible grief of Mary and John all the more moving: the mother with lowered head, wringing her hands; the disciple weeping bitterly, physically so broken by his sorrow that his posture disturbs the balance of the composition and by this very fact makes the horror tangible.

The coloring widens the range of emotional expression: Mary, in a white cloak over the fall of the blue dress, appears as though turned to stone by grief, while the red-with-violet of John's garments gives the effect of an outcry.

The monumental realism of the early Netherlanders, the plastic strength of their figures, the importance of the landscape, destined to become more spacious and to strive for a greater effect of perspective—all were going to become typical of fifteenth-century painting. Equally significant—but not as transmissible, since it is a spontaneous expression of creative intensity—is the deep emotion with which the painter was able to express that anguish the sanctification of which is the meaning of the Christian religion.

THE MADONNA IN CHURCH

Oak panel. 31 × 14 cm., rounded on top.

PROVENANCE: *Ascribed to Hubert van Eyck. Painted soon after 1420. Purchased in 1874 with the Suermondt-Aachen collection. The picture is only one wing of a diptych, the other panel of which shows the kneeling donor, upon whom the Madonna looks down in blessing. This painting was copied twice as the left half of a diptych: in 1499 (Antwerp Museum) and early in the sixteenth century (Rome, Galleria Doria).*

34　If one considers the architectural background of this panel, one sees that the Gothic church north of the Alps no longer has any wall surfaces upon which mural painting can develop, as it continued to do in Italy. Accordingly, while panel painting in Italy was an outgrowth of fresco painting and retained the monumental approach of the latter, it developed in the north, especially in the Burgundian cultural realm, out of miniature painting. This is particularly well exemplified by *The Madonna in Church*. For their wood-panel paintings, the brothers Van Eyck developed the technique of oil painting, which gave the painter opportunities to enrich his art and to make the representation of light an element of style.

This little picture therefore represents in content and form the beginning of a crucial development. In content, the divine, of which the medieval conception had been a supernatural one, is here humanized and gains in reality. Technically, it reveals the possibilities of the new medium, in which the colors, not bound with glue and egg white but with oil and resins and applied with glazes, retain their translucence.

In brilliance and transparency, these colors can now compete with those of shrines and reliquaries covered with gold, jewels, and enamels; and in luminosity, with the glass windows of the cathedrals. Also new is the realization of the problem of how to make a new unity of figure and space, form and perspective, even though it has not yet been solved realistically. The painter uses the interplay of light and shadow to give form to his principal figure and to the figures of the Crucifixion group in the rood loft and takes great pains with his perspective. But his principal figure remains disproportionately large, and his lines of perspective are not in perfect alignment. Delighting in his new possibilities, however, the painter represents the sunlight by bright spots on the floor, light from the windows.

Like the architecture shown—undoubtedly a representation of a church well known to the painter and the donor—which glorifies the Gothic heritage, the pose of the Madonna, too, recalls the concept of beauty and grace of the vanishing Middle Ages. The blue of her cloak, with the ornamental lines of its golden border, emphasizes the sculptural feeling, while the painter has taken obvious pleasure in the distribution of his red. It appears in Mary's dress, in the glittering rubies of her crown, in the background, in the finely drawn, miniature-like group of singing angels in the choir—reminiscent of the wings of the Ghent altarpiece—in the foreground window, and as a calculated accent in the pointed arch of the choir window above the crucifix.

If we compare *The Madonna in Church* with the Crucifixion painting, we would hardly be inclined, at first, to believe that the same painter could have been involved in both. However, the crucifix, derived apparently from a wooden model, does suggest a connection between *The Madonna in Church* and *Christ on the Cross*. Though the question of which brother painted which picture may never be resolved, we do feel justified in assuming that the *Madonna*, with its evident debt to miniature painting, was the earlier work, while the landscape in the Crucifixion appears to owe much to Jan van Eyck's much later journeys to Spain and Portugal. If we are to give Hubert a share in the series of the panel paintings, it is far more likely that he painted the panel of the *Madonna* than that of the Crucifixion.

MAN WITH A PINK

Oak panel. 40 × 31 cm.

PROVENANCE: *The painting was bought by the collector Suermondt at the Engels auction in Cologne in 1867 and became the property of the Berlin museum in 1874.*

35   Among the innovations brought to fifteenth-century painting by Jan van Eyck's sense of reality, in contrast with the otherworldliness of medieval painting, not least is the sharp individuality seen in his portraits, which in fact helped to make portrait painting a major branch of art. The history of portrait painting begins with Jan van Eyck and north of the Alps. Even the heads of saints now begin to appear as portraits, direct and realistic images of living people.

One can see that the subject of *Man with a Pink*, despite a certain coarseness of his weather-beaten features, is a gentleman by his costume, in the fashion of the third decade of the fifteenth century, and by the insignia of the Brotherhood of St. Anthony, founded in Holland in 1392. He is wearing a fur-trimmed mantle that allows the rich brocade of his collar to show, and the tall Burgundian fur hat. St. Anthony's cross with its pendant bell hangs on a twisted silver chain; its wearer is duty-bound to contribute to the care of the sick. He appears to be well along in age, yet the three pinks in his hand bespeak his engagement, just as the young merchant George Gisze in Holbein's portrait is shown with three pinks symbolizing his betrothal (Pls. 72, 75).

But the personality of the subject, whose name and circumstances we do not know, is irrelevant. The great significance of the painting as a work of art is that, together with the two other portraits by Jan van Eyck in the Berlin gallery, it inaugurates a new era in Western art that is dominated by realism north of the Alps.

The model's lack of charm is compensated for by the attractiveness of the painting. The warm flesh tones, the vigorous red of the brocade collar and one of the flowers glow in contrast to the grays of the mantle and the dark brown of the fur framing the face. The dark green of the background heightens the colors and enhances the harmony among them. It is as though the freshness of the colors was meant to triumph over the withering of old age. A border painted in yellow tones makes the highly sculptural head appear to retreat behind the frame, thus suggesting the third dimension of depth.

Jan van Eyck's portraiture represents the beginning of a great development, opening the way for Rogier van der Weyden and Hans Memling and preparing for Dürer, whose portrait of Holzschuher (Pl. 59), painted after a journey to the Netherlands, shows the effects of Flemish realism.

Konrad Witz

THE ARTIST: Konrad Witz was born during the first decade of the fifteenth century in Rottweil, Swabia, and he worked there and in Constance. He painted in Basel from about 1431 and in Geneva from 1444. One documentary source refers to him as dead in 1447. In his strong realism, saturated with emotions and in the way he uses light for modeling his forms, he shows a kinship with the Master of Flémalle.

The generation born around the turn of the fifteenth century was full of vigor and made its influence felt upon the plastic arts for a long time. These men countered the "soft" style of mystic surrender to emotion with a hard realism of their own, a reaching out for the earthly in form and space. For Germany, Konrad Witz and Hans Multscher represent the new era; it seems to be no coincidence that they are of the same generation as Johann Gutenberg.

CHRIST ON THE CROSS

Transferred from wood to canvas. 34 × 26 cm.

PROVENANCE: *Acquired in 1908 from private ownership in London.*

The slightly diagonal position of the cross adds depth **30** to the scene, and the asymmetrical grouping, with four figures positioned under the right arm and only one under the left arm of Christ, also characterizes the originality of Konrad Witz's painting compared with older depictions of the Crucifixion.

For medieval art the cross was a symbol, and as such it stood directly in the center of devotional paintings, in strict symmetry. For Konrad Witz to present it not as a symbol but as a part of reality was a daring innovation. There are few works that more clearly show the irruption of realism into art in the fifteenth century than this moving little panel. The medieval symbol has become an experience; it takes place not in an unearthly distance, before a golden background, but in the real world, here on earth. The cross is placed in a familiar landscape; the figures in the landscape, the ships on the lake belong to the present time, that of the painting. The scene, a fortified town and a towering castle on the shore of a vast lake, was probably well known to the donor, who is shown kneeling in the foreground. It may well be on the shore of Lake Leman, where Witz died sometime after 1444. Some experts, however, consider this one of his early works, a view that has yet to be proved.

The painter has consciously placed his figures in contrast to the landscape, in which the horizontal lines are strongly emphasized, an emphasis echoed by the horizontal bands of clouds. This effect is strengthened by the slant of the crossbeam.

In coloring, the landscape is subdued in tone, while the holy figures, the donor, and the cross stand out vividly against the background. The three shades of red, echoing delicately in the background, the rooftops of the town, accentuate the colorful effect of the whole.

THE QUEEN OF SHEBA BEFORE KING SOLOMON

Oak panel. 84.5 × 28.5 cm.

PROVENANCE: *Purchased in 1913 from a dealer.*

32, 33   The unrest of the times also had a creative effect on religion. This made itself felt particularly at Basel in the fourth and fifth decades of the fifteenth century, when the flames of the Reformation were lit at the great Church Council (1431–1449), never again to be extinguished.

This atmosphere of religious and intellectual ferment must have had its influence on Konrad Witz, who moved to Basel in the first year of the Council, 1431, there to create one of his principal works, the *Mirror of Salvation* altar. In accordance with the prevalent brooding on religious themes, this work attempted a juxtaposition of the events of the Old Testament with the New Testament's story of salvation and may have been the outcome of long consultations between the donors and the painter.

Of what is left of the altar, eight side panels are now in the Basel art museum and one can be seen in Berlin. We see it here out of context, as an individual painting, *The Queen of Sheba Before King Solomon*. Here the master, whose boldness in the representation of space we have seen, has retained the Gothic golden background, richly ornamented with a pomegranate pattern, to stand for a wall in the royal palace.

It depicts the well-known story from 1 Kings 10 that tells how "the Queen of Sheba heard of the fame of Solomon (and) she came to test him with hard questions." She kneels before the King, in homage to his wisdom and power. The vast quantity of presents reported by the Bible, the 120 talents of gold, the spices, the precious stones, are here symbolized by the one golden vessel she is offering him. As for the throne of Solomon, with its twelve lions upon six steps, the painter apparently did not consider this essential. What he does show is an encounter of two people that is in itself an event captured with uncanny vividness. Something of Burgundian splendor and worldliness is caught in the statuesque grandeur and dignity of this meeting. Dijon is not far from Basel; an affinity between Konrad Witz and Robert Campin is detectable, and it is as though something of the sculpture of Dijon has entered into the monumental realism of Witz's painting. But the decisive and unifying element remains a profound inwardness, more felt than planned.

The Master of Flémalle

THE ARTIST: Step by step, the realization has gained ground that the so-called Master of Flémalle, long declared to be a "primitive" on the basis of Roelof Huysman's ecstatic description of the paintings found in Flémalle, is identical with Robert Campin. Anyone contemplating this Crucifixion painting might be in doubt as to whether it should be attributed to the Master of Flémalle—which is to say, to Robert Campin—or to his pupil Jacques Daret, the painter of two altar panels in the possession of the Berlin gallery. In any case, the name Campin places it as to style and as to the time it was done, from 1430 to 1440.

Robert Campin was born about 1380 at the latest; he is mentioned as a master in Tournai as early as 1406. Rogier van der Weyden and Jacques Daret, who followed him by about a generation, were his pupils. Campin died in Tournai in 1444.

Jacques Daret was born in 1404 in Tournai. He lived for eleven years in the household of his master, Campin, so that he painted entirely in his manner and occasionally perhaps with his help. Daret was a master of the guild in Tournai from 1432 on and is also known to have worked in Lille, Bruges, and Arras until 1468.

CHRIST ON THE CROSS

Oak panel. 77 × 47 cm.

PROVENANCE: *Painted between 1430 and 1440. Purchased in 1892 at the auction of A. Hulot, Paris.*

In his principal works, particularly the altar panels   36, 37 now in Frankfurt that are said to be from Flémalle, as well as the Mérode altarpiece (in New York), for which Campin used to be called the Master of Mérode, Robert Campin appears more intense and monumental than he does in this panel. *Christ on the Cross* lacks the inner cohesion to be found in the panel by Jan van Eyck (Pl. 31) or even in that by Konrad Witz (Pl. 30), a contemporary. The Crucified appears smaller than the mourners surrounding him; detached from their group, he looms up before the landscape in the background. The dominant motif of the painting is the fivefold variation in the expression of grief in the faces and gestures of the holy women and the disciple John.

The hands, clearly done in Daret's sensitive manner, are most expressive. The mother is embracing the cross close to the Savior's feet; from her mouth issues a text by St. Bernard: "*Fili dignare me attrahere et crucis in pedem manus figere. Bernardus.*" She is praying, accordingly, to be held worthy to touch the cross and the feet of the Son with her hands. The inclusion of such a scroll is typical of Campin's early period (Dijon museum). Such an inscription customarily appeared on a golden ground, which should probably be restored. The gold background was crudely painted over later with the somber sky and the merest suggestion of a landscape.

The Savior's mother is supported by a matron, probably that elderly relative known as the mother of two disciples, while the woman who has collapsed in front of John—a married woman to judge by her head-dress—is not Mary Magdalen, as some have thought, but the mother of John. The figure of John, tall like those figures of the Master of Flémalle, towers behind her; he has turned away from the cross, so that four of the mourners are facing from left to right. The corresponding figure on the left is that of the youthful Mary Magdalen, whose attire recalls Daret's habit of signalizing characters from Scripture by dressing them in garments reminiscent of the Orient. The angels surrounding the cross—originally, when the gold background was still there, they served to complete the framework in the upper part of the picture—are characteristic of those found in the paintings of Daret (see the Thyssen collection, Lugano).

The color scheme indicates a clear preference for contrasting red and green tones; this too recalls Daret. The strongest color accent is in the carmine of John's voluminous cloak; this recurs in the sleeve of the Magdalen, while the mother's cloak is a vivid blue. The interplay of yellow with dark blue and of green with lighter or more violet-toned reds recurs in the robes of the angels.

Rogier van der Weyden

THE ARTIST: Rogier van der Weyden was born around 1400 in Tournai, a then flourishing town, where he became the pupil of Robert Campin, one of whose relatives, Elizabeth Goffaerts, he later married. He must have moved to Brussels, where he was nominated to the post of municipal painter in 1435. But he also did some work for Bruges, and for Middelburg he painted the famous altarpiece named after Peter Bladelin, who commissioned it and who was treasurer to the dukes of Burgundy. It is today one of the most prized possessions of the Berlin museum.

In 1449 and 1450, Rogier was busy executing commissions in Italy (Milan, Ferrara, Rome). His feeling for posture and expression, related to the courtly style of Burgundy, also made him one of the leading portrait painters of his time, preserving the images of a number of Burgundian notables for posterity. He died in Brussels in 1464.

BLADELIN ALTAR

Centerpiece

Oak panel. 91 × 40 cm.

PROVENANCE: *One of the master's principal works, painted about 1450–1452 for the main altar of the church in Middelburg. Acquired from private ownership in Brussels in 1834 for Berlin.*

The *Bladelin Altar* comes from Rogier's middle period, when his style had fully matured, and is one of his outstanding works. As the gift of Peter Bladelin, the treasurer to the dukes of Burgundy, it is connected with the splendid dukedom between France and Germany that was then rising to power. The donor is accordingly depicted by Rogier, portraitist of so many of the great figures of the country, on the center panel, in Burgundian dress of aristocratic simplicity. The highly individual features of the donor—with his fine nose, unusually deep and wide-set eyes, prominent cheekbones, sensitive mouth, and narrow chin—make an unforgettable impression on the viewer. One may safely say that the same man posed for Rogier's *Portrait of a Gentleman,* which is one of the treasures of the Thyssen collection in Lugano. This *Portrait* has been thought to represent the Comte de Charny, who, however, as a leading noble of the court of Burgundy, would have had to wear the Order of the Golden Fleece, a distinction to which the bourgeois chamberlain Bladelin was not entitled. Thus the painting in Berlin provides a good clue for the proper identification of the portrait in Lugano.

In the group of three angels hovering rather too near the roof of the manger, the Bladelin altarpiece preserves a final memory of Rogier's teacher, Campin, the Master of Flémalle, who was fond of this motif. But the unity of the composition and the mastery of the spatial structure are characteristic of Rogier's mature style, which probably benefited from his visit to Italy in 1449–1450.

This masterpiece of Rogier has its place somewhere between the art of Jan van Eyck and Hugo van der Goes. The principal figures stand out rather expressively: in the center, the blue-white dress of the young mother is softly luminous; at the left, the kneeling Joseph in bright red holds a little candle; his figure is balanced on the right by that of the donor, sunk in prayer. At the head of the infant lying naked before his mother, three devout little angels complement the lyrical mood of the painting. The manger has been put up in the ruins of a vaguely Romanesque building. The dark structure in mid-stage heightens the spatial effect needed by the altar painting in the church—an effect still maintained there by a copy of the work.

This altar is not only a devotional painting but also a historical document, for above the head of the donor one can see the handsome buildings of Middelburg, a town much indebted to him. The donor undoubtedly gave much thought to the plan of the altarpiece, in which he wanted to give a symbolic representation of the significance of the birth of Christ for mankind: the left panel symbolizes this meaning for Western man by showing the sibyl of Tibur directing the gaze of the Emperor Augustus toward the Madonna enthroned in glory; while on the right panel, the Three Wise Men from the East recognize the miracle of the divine birth through the apparition of the Christ Child in the sky.

ALTAR OF JOHN THE BAPTIST

Oakwood. Each of the three panels is 77 × 48 cm.

PROVENANCE: *From the artist's middle period, about 1440. Purchased in 1850: two panels from the collection of King William of the Netherlands in The Hague; the third from private ownership in England. A smaller variant is in the Staedel Museum in Frankfurt am Main.*

44, 45   In his most outstanding work, which may have been painted during the lifetime of Jan van Eyck (d. 1441), Rogier van der Weyden combined harmoniously two opposing styles: the architectural-sculptural, stemming from the Gothic tradition, and the pictorial-realistic of the postmedieval development, beginning with the brothers Van Eyck.

The Gothic legacy was handed down through sculpture, and it was probably owing to the fact that Rogier had begun as an apprentice to his father, a sculptor of stone, even before he entered Robert Campin's workshop that this tradition was so strong in him. In the painted architectural framings in his early pictures, one can detect painted sketches of the stone sculptures that were used to decorate cathedrals. Like the Twelve Apostles of the *Altar of John the Baptist,* these figures seem to be free inventions rather than replicas of previous works.

The three narrow panels, showing a stone structure like the triple portal of a cathedral, lose more than two-fifths of their surface to the gray-on-gray hues of the painted stone. The principal figures in the scene, which is reminiscent of a mystery play, have very little space in which to enact their story, which takes place in front of the painted architectural backdrop. This very fact gives them a vivid immediacy and lifelikeness. A space is created in front of the portals in which the figures, like the wood carvings of an altar, create the sculptural effect that the painter sought to achieve. The painted altarpiece possesses the monumentality of a sculpture.

The three main stages in the career of John the Baptist are clearly shown: birth, baptism by Christ, and decapitation. On the left wing, Mary is shown, as a relative of the woman in labor, presenting the newborn John to Zachary, his father, who as a priest must register the infant's name. Behind this group, a vista opens upon what might almost be called a genre scene, which anticipates the seventeenth-century interiors painted by Jan Vermeer and Pieter de Hooch. In the tester bed with its red coverings and white linen lies Elizabeth just after labor, cared for by a maid smoothing the sheets. Further back and to the left, coming through a narrow passage that ends in a view of the landscape, a visitor, followed by her servant, is approaching. The observer has a sense of the comfort of the main chamber with its Gothic wainscoting, upon which, close to the door, there sits a little carved lion, that brings to mind the decorations on the throne of the Frankfurt Madonna by Jan van Eyck. Near the window, the lower wooden shutters of which are closed, stands a sideboard; the two tankards standing on it between two silver vessels were clearly painted by Rogier in his shop, for although the light falls on them here through an open door, the reflections painted on the vessels show the window as seen by the painter at home.

The coloring is strong and rich: carmine for the tester bed, green tones in the servant's dress and the garment of Zachary, luminous blue in Mary's cloak, and red again in her brocade dress. The cool grays of the portals serve to intensify the gleam of the fabrics and the warmth of the flesh tones most effectively.

There is much to be noted in this altar panel besides the flowers in the foreground and the finely drawn tree in the distance. On the portal are the four slender figures of apostles, and above them six more sculptural groups: Zachary in the temple before the angel; Zachary, silenced by God, leaving the temple; the marriage of Joseph and Mary; and on the other side, from top to bottom, the Annunciation, the encounter of Mary with Elizabeth, and the birth of Christ in the manger.

PORTRAIT OF A YOUNG WOMAN

Oak panel. 47 × 32 cm.

PROVENANCE: *We know that Rogier van der Weyden was married before 1426, when he was about twenty-five years old. We also know the name of his wife, Elizabeth Goffaerts, and that she was a native of Brussels. We think we know what she looked like, for there is good reason to believe that she is the subject of a portrait in the Berlin gallery, for the style is clearly that of Rogier. We must admit that we have no proof of this, because the coat of arms on the back of the painting is no longer recognizable. The portrait is usually dated around 1435, for no very definite reason. But if this is indeed a painting of the artist's young wife, it must have been done about ten years earlier. Once owned by the Grand Duchess Soltikoff of St. Petersburg, it was purchased about 1908 from an English art dealer.*

This portrait was painted with particular care; even   46 the three rings, one of which is on the second joint of the ring finger of the folded hands, seem to have been very familiar to the painter. This portrait is not likely to have had a companion piece: the subject is seen in three-quarter profile turning left, which means that she would have been shown sitting at the right of her husband if he had been portrayed with her. But this would have run counter to custom, which decreed that the man must sit at the right—as, for example, in the Arnolfini wedding picture painted by Jan van Eyck in 1434.

The effect of intimacy results from the great simplicity of the color scheme. The almost black blue of the background sets off the many subtle gradations of white in the linen coif held together with pins, the symbol of the married woman. The quilted dress with the wide sleeves is painted a thin gray that allows the red ground to shimmer through. The rosy flesh tones of the round young face glow in the white frame of the headdress; with her blue eyes, oval face, and fresh young mouth, the plump young woman appears to be a real Fleming. The many shadings of the headdress, with its folds fresh from the iron, and not least the transparency of the linen that lets the forehead be seen through it, constitute one of the special charms of this painting.

The picture breathes a repose that expresses its period and also the character of the subject.

CHARLES THE BOLD, DUKE OF BURGUNDY

Detail

Oak panel. 49 × 32 cm.

PROVENANCE: *Painted about 1460. Acquired with the Solly collection in 1821.*

49   The culture and life-style of the waning Middle Ages north of the Alps were influenced by Burgundy far more than the following centuries recognized. Under her dukes, who sprang from a branch of the French royal family of Valois, knighthood once more knew greatness and splendor—though the greatness was repeatedly purchased by faithlessness and the splendor came to be ostentatious display. In this realm between France and Germany arose a political power complex—reaching from Burgundy to Brabant, Holland, and Luxembourg, finally coveting Lorraine, and threatening Switzerland— that made its dukes the masters of immense riches until the last of them was undone by his vaunting ambition for a royal crown.

What is left of Burgundy's ancient honor is the works of art created by Claus Sluter in Dijon and by the splendid series of Flemish painters who flourished in Ghent and Bruges, Brussels and Antwerp. They tended to express the rise of a bourgeois culture whose vitality survived the hazards of knighthood's decline.

The last Duke of Burgundy was Charles the Bold, born in Dijon in 1433, a proud and increasingly powerful ruler until he was defeated by the Swiss in 1476 at Morat. He died in the retreat from the battle of Nancy; whether he was killed by the enemy or by his own mercenaries is not known.

The portrait in the Berlin gallery is a great and historically significant work of art. Rogier van der Weyden painted Charles the Bold as a young man, when his father, Duke Philip the Good, was still alive and Charles, as heir, bore the title Count of Charolais.

Duke Charles, whose hubris ended the dream of Burgundian greatness, has an arresting, nobly proportioned head, with thick dark hair, reddish in tone. The intelligent but cold gray-blue eyes betoken a strong will; the features are mobile, nobly handsome except for the suggestion of excessive sensuality in the mouth and the unevenness of temperament and lack of self-control

hinted at in the receding chin. A certain knightly pride unifies the expression despite the inner disharmony. Destiny is written on that face.

Hugo van der Goes

THE ARTIST: The Dutch town of Goes, in Zeeland, is thought to be his birthplace; the date, somewhat prior to 1437. In 1457 he was accepted by the painters' guild in Ghent and by 1475 he had nearly finished his most famous work, the Portinari altarpiece (in the Uffizi). The donor of this altarpiece was in charge of the Medici settlement in Bruges and was close to Burgundy's Charles the Bold. When Hugo van der Goes had completed the painting reproduced here, he entered the Red Cloister of Soignies, near Brussels, in 1476, as an Augustinian brother. There he was visited by the future Emperor Maximilian, who married Charles the Bold's daughter, Mary of Burgundy. He died in 1482 in the monastery, a victim, it is said, of melancholia. Two of his principal works are in Berlin.

The art of Hugo van der Goes takes the inwardness, the clarity of structure, and the balanced color scheme of Rogier van der Weyden a step further. Especially the large-scale altarpiece *The Adoration of the Magi*, in Berlin, together with the Portinari altarpiece, represents a high point of Dutch art in the second half of the fifteenth century. If one compares the figures of Van de Goes with those of Rogier, the representative of the third generation appears to be a revolutionary, although he does regain for the art of the Netherlands something of the greatness and monumental effect of the Ghent altarpiece. But the fourth generation, that of Memling and Gerard David, brings back something of the delicacy of a Rogier and the restraint of a Dirk Bouts. It is as though the art of the Netherlands were echoing a law of life according to which it is not successive generations but those of grandfather and grandson that resemble each other.

THE ADORATION OF THE MAGI

Center panel of a winged altarpiece.

Oak panel. 147 × 242 cm. in the original frame. The center part, about 9 cm. higher than the rest, was originally even higher than that, but was cut down.

PROVENANCE: *Painted about 1470. Acquired in 1914 from the Monforte Monastery in Spain. Free-style copies with the two lost wings (Birth and Circumcision) by the Master of Frankfurt are in the museums of Antwerp and Vienna.*

The composition is determined by the painter's having   **39, 40** moved the central group of Mary with the child between   **42, 43** two kneeling figures to the side. St. Joseph is kneeling left front, near the edge of the picture. The architecture of the background, with its pronounced foreshortening of perspective, adds depth, while the right-hand half of the painting is occupied by the adoring kings and other figures.

This moving to the side of the principal group—the triangular structure of which shows a close relationship to the style of the Italian Renaissance—seems to be a characteristic of Hugo van der Goes. Though the conception of the Madonna is full of inwardness and delicacy, the play of her hand as it holds the naked infant's little arm most moving, and the praying hands of the old man in the center full of devotional feeling, nevertheless Van der Goes' powers of expression manifest themselves even more in the secondary figures—for example, in the rich brocade mantle and the pointed shoes of the Moorish king, splendidly dressed in the Burgundian fashion (Pl. 43). Behind him, two heads appear in a small space, one of which might be a self-portrait of the painter. Hands in particular are used most expressively, their various positions and gestures from figure to figure tying the persons and the action together.

The principal figures are related through their shared devotion to the child; the others serve more the formal requirements of the composition. The bearded follower in the background emphasizes the rising line in the middle; behind him, two youthful figures, looking like two Burgundian page boys, gaze forward in line with the diagonally placed wall that gives the scene its depth of perspective. The thrust and counterthrust of forces expresses a deep excitement. The painter combines a sense of reality, a sense of form, and an ecstatic vision into a harmonious unity. The development of landscape painting, still life, and flower painting in the Netherlands of the seventeenth century is also prefigured here. The two faïence vessels in the niche to the left of the Virgin's head constitute a still life in themselves, and the columbine in the foreground is reminiscent of the well-known aquarelle by Albrecht Dürer.

The two landscapes, one of which is shown in detail (Pl. 40), seem to be meant as fillers. The artist evidently did not care about the two horizons being at odds with each other. However, the scene of a town on a hill, with the horses of the kings, is a delightful picture-within-a-picture.

If we compare this painting with the same artist's *The Adoration of the Shepherds*, we see that Hugo van der Goes tends to separate the sides of his horizontal paintings from the center, to gain concentration. Here the vessel in the hand of the Moor and the wall behind Joseph give the effect of separating the two sides as though they were altar panels; if the original height of the center had been retained, the painter's effort to balance the horizontal spread through vertical structuring would be even more evident.

Petrus Christus

THE ARTIST: Petrus Christus is thought to have been born in Baarle, near Tilburg, Holland, at the beginning of the fifteenth century. He migrated to Bruges, where he probably studied with Jan van Eyck, and became a citizen in 1444. He died in 1473. His art is closely related to that of his great forerunner and fills the gap between the epoch of Van Eyck and the work of Hans Memling, who came to Bruges about a quarter of a century after Jan van Eyck's death.

PORTRAIT OF A YOUNG LADY

Oak panel. 28 × 21 cm.

PROVENANCE: *Painted about 1446. Acquired with the Solly collection in 1821. The Van Eyck scholar Waele speculated that the subject might have been Lady Talbot, first wife of Edward Grimeston, as stated in the last descriptive catalogue of the Dahlem Gallery (1931). Max Friedländer did not agree with this supposition.*

The arresting effect of this portrait owes as much to the model as it does to the painter's art. With her slanted eyes and the pallor of her rather stony face, she is certainly no beauty. Although the gaze of those almond-shaped eyes does meet the eyes of the onlooker, it seems to go beyond him into empty distance. The lips are beautifully curved, yet the line between them—straight, as though drawn with a ruler—is haughty, unfulfilled.

The subject is richly and elegantly dressed, and the painter has brought out the pale skin tones most effectively in contrast with the black headdress and chin band. The triple-strand necklace with its pearls, the gold-and-pearl border of the hat, and the transparent shoulder scarf underneath which the blue sleeves can be seen were lovingly done with a very fine brush, and the brown paneling and the gray-brown of the wall set off the luminosity of the delicately pale face.

The artist, who is known to have inscribed on a frame that has long since disappeared the words "Opus Petri Christophori," was following in the footsteps of Jan van Eyck, whose pupil he is said to have been. But the comparison between the vigorous realism of Van Eyck's portraits and the subjectivity here—both psychological and in terms of painting—seems to suggest that in the new generation a keen sensibility was taking the place of creative power.

The effect is a lessening of the painter's religious works (he is represented by six paintings in the Berlin gallery, almost a third of his known production). A connoisseur as cautious as Max Friedländer has called him "parasitic." Yet this first epigone of Dutch painting was enabled by his sensitivity to capture the special charm

47

and character of this particular sitter with unique impressiveness.

Understandably, there has been much speculation as to the identity of the model. She seemed so different from the Flemish and Dutch ladies of Van Eyck and Rogier van der Weyden (Pl. 46) that she was thought to be Lady Talbot, of whom there is a portrait in the collection of the Earl of Verulam of Gorhambury painted by Petrus Christus and dated 1446 by the painter himself. But the two portraits are too dissimilar in format to have been a true pair; the direction of their gaze is wrong—that is, it contravenes the established conventions for such matters in paired portraits. The *Portrait of a Young Lady* in Berlin seems destined to pose a permanent riddle, and, like the *Mona Lisa,* it has been widely reproduced.

Jean Fouquet

THE ARTIST: Fouquet worked primarily as a miniature painter for his patron Étienne Chevalier, treasurer to the King of France, and for the Duc de Berry. Born in Tours about 1415, he lived in Italy from 1443 to 1447, then returned to his native city, where he died in 1480. As early as the middle of the century, he anticipated the Netherlanders by including architectonic motifs of the Italian Renaissance. His affinity with Italy also expressed itself in his imaginary portraits for Boccaccio's *Famous Men and Women* (Munich, Bayerische Staatsbibliothek). His panel paintings show his inclination to portraiture.

Jean Fouquet belongs with the line of miniaturists, connected with the courtly culture of the widely branching house of Valois, who were active in France, Burgundy, and the Netherlands. In Italy, the art of his coeval, Piero della Francesca, strongly influenced him. With the great master of Tours, French painting takes its place as an equal in the development of art north of the Alps, hitherto determined by the Netherlanders at the time of the dukes of Burgundy. The art of miniature painting now reaches an apex that later enriches panel painting.

Fouquet painted for King Charles VII, who was living in the Touraine because of his war with England, as well as for other personages in the King's entourage. The treasurer to the King, Étienne Chevalier, particularly appreciated the master's value and commissioned manuscript illuminations and panel paintings that show his art at its peak.

Fouquet's early period coincides with the time when Joan of Arc, overcoming the King's indecision, led the French from victory to victory. With his brush he immortalized a second great feminine figure of the period, Agnès Sorel, the King's mistress. She was the first of the officially recognized—by the court and even by the Queen—*maîtresses en titre,* that line of *dames du coeur* who had such a great influence on French history and culture.

Fouquet's patron, Étienne Chevalier, enjoyed the particular favor of Màdame de Beauté (as Agnès Sorel was called for two reasons: because of her beauty and because the King had signed over to her his castle Beauté, a transaction in which his treasurer undoubtedly played a significant role). Agnès bore the King three daughters, but she died suddenly in 1450, at the age of twenty-eight. "Poisoned by the Dauphin," they said. The faithful Étienne was the executor of her will.

The painting by Jean Fouquet is one of the choice treasures of the Berlin portrait gallery.

ÉTIENNE CHEVALIER AND ST. STEPHEN

Detail

Oak. 93 × 85 cm.

PROVENANCE: *This is a detail of the left half of a diptych originally in the church at Melun; the other half, showing the Virgin and Christ Child with angels, is now in the museum at Antwerp. Chevalier commissioned this painting for the church of his hometown, Melun, where he was later buried. The altarpiece was torn apart at the time of the French Revolution, when so many treasures were lost to the churches. The panel with the donor and his patron saint was eventually acquired from French ownership by a brother of the German poet Clemens Brentano (a contemporary of Goethe), from whose heirs it was purchased for the Berlin museum in 1896.*

Fouquet's painting, which shows Chevalier kneeling, hands folded in prayer, beside his patron saint, St. Stephen, hangs in the Berlin gallery among the Dutch masters of the middle of the fifteenth century. In one way it seems to belong there; in another way it does not. It seems to belong through its powerful characterization of the two figures, especially that of the saint, represented in a manner entirely in accord with the art of portraiture developed by Jan van Eyck and Rogier van der Weyden. What makes it seem out of place is the cool stone architecture in the Italian style that composes the background.

The color scheme does not have the deep, rich luminosity of the Dutch school; it is cooler—perhaps also nobler. The characteristic tone is struck by the cold gray of the marble wall in combination with the dark blue of the deacon's cloak, accented by the cinnabar red of the book in St. Stephen's hand. Most unusual are the borders of wide braid, cut from precious brocade, decorating the saint's garment. They are patterned in gold-on-red, and the gold was not hammered on a specially prepared ground but was applied with the brush. The saint is decidedly the principal figure in this panel. The paleness of the flesh tones is emphasized by the gray background. The slim fingers curling around the book express Fouquet's characteristically French sensitivity.

But the picture is only half of a work created as a unity: the half showing the donor adoring, the saint

48

gazing with devotion at the Madonna, depicted on the other half (which is missing). Fouquet's Queen of Heaven is really a portrait of the King's mistress, whose favorite, Chevalier, commissioned it for his chapel.

The highly individual features of St. Stephen are rather aristocratic, in a sensitive-sensual way, and bear a certain resemblance to Fouquet's portrait of Charles VII in the Louvre. To be sure, St. Stephen looks more noble than the Louvre portrait of the tired, slumped figure of the King resting in a church pew. But the ear and the strikingly cleft chin are the same; the nose is similar to that in the Louvre painting, though there it appears thickened by age and drink. If the Berlin painting, with its missing portrait of Agnès Sorel, was done in the 1440's, one might assume that the Louvre portrait shows the King in later years, in any case after the death of Agnès Sorel (1450), to whom the weak ruler owed what poise and strength he possessed.

The recent supposition that the altarpiece may have had a third panel showing the wife of the donor seems highly dubious. There are enough examples proving that the diptych was a favored form of the altarpiece in the fifteenth century. For instance, the Berlin gallery owns half of a diptych by Master Michiel (Inventory No. 1722), who was Hans Memling's pupil in Bruges. It shows the Christ Child with the Virgin, who clearly has the features of Catherine of Aragon. The half with the portrait of the donor is now in the National Gallery in Washington.

Simon Marmion

THE ARTIST: Marmion gave Amiens, where he was born in 1430, a flowering of art parallel to that achieved in Tours by Fouquet. By 1454, however, he was demonstrably in Lille, whence he moved in 1458 to Valenciennes, where he worked until his death in 1489.

The art of Marmion, like that of Fouquet, is rooted in illumination. His best-known contribution to panel painting, the altarpiece of St. Bertin for the Abbey of St. Omer, was attributed to him because of its unmistakable kinship with attested manuscript illuminations done by him for Duke Philip the Good of Burgundy. Unlike Fouquet, Marmion was still deeply attached to the mystic religiosity of the Gothic.

What the novel is to us, the legends of the saints were to the Middle Ages. And the painter was free to invent and portray as he chose, or as his imagination dictated, a subject matter susceptible of great variation and untrammeled by any actualities.

For Simon Marmion, who, like Fouquet, transferred his narrative art from miniature painting and illumination to panel painting, it must have been a fulfillment to be commissioned by Guillaume Philastre, Abbot of the monastery of St. Omer and Bishop of Tours, to make an altarpiece for that church in 1453.

He was to represent—upon two broad but not high panels, a predella in format—the life of St. Bertin, the Benedictine monk who left the Luxeuil monastery to found St. Omer, where he taught and performed miracles.

ALTARPIECE OF ST. OMER

Two panels, showing the life of St. Bertin

Oak panels. 56 × 147 cm.

PROVENANCE: *This altarpiece was begun in 1453 and completed in 1459. Together with two little headpieces (Nos. 1302 and 1303 in the National Gallery in London), these panels originally formed the sides of an altar screen in the Abbey of St. Omer. In 1459 it was donated by the Abbot of St. Omer to the monastery church dedicated to St. Bertin, where it remained until the French Revolution. In the center, the altar shrine was filled, as far as we know, with sculptures and products of the goldsmith's art; the painter had been asked to execute only the two sidepieces. We have no exact idea of how the altar looked, the center part of which was a casualty of the Revolution. Yet the two panels with the story of the saint preserved in Berlin contribute much to our knowledge of fifteenth-century French art. On the back of the altarpiece, figures painted in grisaille can be seen in five niches that appear when the panels are closed.*

In the first half of the nineteenth century, the panels came into the collection of King William II of Holland; they were included in the list of his paintings to be auctioned in 1850. But the royal family withdrew them from the auction, and they came by inheritance to the Duke of Wied. They were purchased for Berlin in 1905.

The first panel of a cycle almost one and a half meters **50, 51** long, in the form of five adjoining pictures, shows the donor, above whom hovers an angel holding the former's coat of arms. Next is a painting of the saint's birth, his acceptance into the monastery, and how he was received, with his two companions, on the road. The left panel completes the history of the gift and shows the building of the new monastery, for the chapel of which the gift was destined.

The painter frames the series in a closed architectural scheme: the donor kneels in a Gothic structure; then there is the chamber in which the saint is born; in the center of the panel is seen the vestibule of the monastery, with Christ as Judge above the widened portal, through which the interior of the church and the rood loft can be seen. Next comes the open vestibule with the scene of welcome, followed by a view of the building of the monastery, with a fortress-like castle in the background, behind which a river makes a wide arc through a fine landscape. It is a picture quite in the style of the popular miniatures of the period.

The second panel, on the right of the altarpiece, begins out of doors: the saint is kneeling in front of a shed next to a wall; under the roof of the shed, wine casks are seen; unmasking a swindle, the saint separates water from wine. Above the wall, the unbelieving count, probably the lord of the proud castle close to the monastery, falls off his horse while out hunting. In the interior scene we see the same count entering the cloister, converted by his fall.

The middle picture is distinguished by a tall Gothic arch. It shows the noble couple making its vows while entering the cloister. The depth of the vista under the archway connects this picture with the previous one. Corresponding to the second picture on the left by its narrowness and intimate feeling, the next scene shows the good priest being tempted by an enticing enchantress. St. Martin of Tours recognizes the Devil in the woman wearing the Burgundian headdress, for under her bright-red gown he can see Satan's clawed foot. The final scene is the moving death of the saint, surrounded by kneeling, praying monks, as the noble patron approaches with a companion. The back of the panels, not shown, painted gray-on-gray, show Mark and Micah, John and Solomon, as well as the archangel Gabriel; on the right is the Virgin of the Annunciation, facing Gabriel, and beside her are David and Matthew, Isaiah and Luke.

Hans Memling

THE ARTIST: Hans Memling was born about 1433, probably in Seligenstadt, near Frankfurt, but made his way to the Netherlands. He was the pupil of Rogier van der Weyden in Brussels and then settled in Bruges (about 1466), where he died in 1494.

Memling clearly shows the influence of Rogier. He combines a sharp perception of detail with a delicacy of feeling that transfigures the conscientious realism of his paintings. He was exceptionally prolific. Besides his paintings on religious themes, of which one of the most notable is his cycle of the legend of St. Ursula in Bruges, he painted many portraits.

VIRGIN AND CHILD

Oak panel. 43 × 31 cm.

PROVENANCE: *This panel is thought to be the centerpiece of a triptych of which the two side panels in the Uffizi are considered to be the panel of St. Benedict and that of the donor. This dates the painting as of 1487, when Memling was at the height of his powers. However, there is a similar* Virgin and Child *in the St. John's Hospital in Bruges, a diptych with the donor on the other panel, also painted in 1487, which may be proof that the panel in Berlin also is half of a diptych. It was purchased for Berlin in 1862.*

52　　The small panel exhibits an incomparably balanced composition of vertical and horizontal lines, the rhythm of which makes for unity without a sense of constriction and achieves a harmonious synthesis of the formal and the spiritual demands of the subject.

It is hard to know what to admire most. The composition arranges mother and child in the form of a tall triangle, in the style of the Italian Renaissance, but emphasizes the horizontal at the bottom by the position of the half-recumbent child's legs, the pillow on which he is resting, and the interplay of the hands. In the landscape, a towering castle breaks the basically horizontal movement of river, woods, and horizon. Neither the vertical nor the horizontal movements are dominant; they are brought into equilibrium in such a way as to produce a sense of perfect peace and serenity. The striving for a harmony, an avoidance of contrasts, also makes for balance in the color scheme.

Few painters have known how both to brighten and to subdue like Memling, whose gentle lighting plays over his figures and landscapes. The flesh tones are veiled with a delicate gray, the blond hair shades to brown. The bright red of the dress, the deep blue of the cloak, and the blue tones in the sleeve pattern are applied in gradations in such a manner that the figure of the Virgin is framed in dark colors, and the red in the center lights up without disturbing the cool color harmony, though warming it as it does the greens of the landscape.

The interplay of the hands is extraordinary: the child is grasping from above at the apple, the symbol of the world, barely supported by the mother's slim fingers; his right hand is already lifted in the gesture of blessing.

The formal elements of the painting can be analyzed; its spiritual content, imbued with the master's tender lyricism, can only be felt.

Hieronymus Bosch

THE ARTIST: Hieronymus Bosch was born in 1450 in 's Hertogenbosch, in northern Brabant, in the third generation of a family of painters. Since his name is given in some documents as Hieronymus van Aeken, it is assumed that his family originated in Aachen (Aix-la-Chapelle). He lived and worked in his native town, where he died in 1516. A decisive factor in his life and art was his membership in the strict religious brotherhood of Our Dear Lady. His principal works were acquired by King Philip II of Spain; consequently his art is best represented in the Prado and the Escorial.

Bosch was an isolated figure in his own time, though he had posthumous followers in Pieter Brueghel the Elder and his son Pieter. In his art he combines two seemingly conflicting aspects: a demonic imagination or fantasy in which the medieval obsession with the Devil appears in a form we have learned to call surrealistic; and, on the other hand, a kind of landscape painting that was ahead of its time. The combination produces a mood, an inwardness, all his own. Contrary to the great figures who express their period, as do the brothers Van Eyck, Rogier van der Weyden, and Hugo van der Goes in the Dutch art of the fifteenth century, there are masters whose uniqueness consists in their being in opposition to the tendencies and inclinations of their own time. They tower like mountain peaks amid their surroundings and among the representatives of the prevailing culture, but because of their very originality, they are innovators, bringing something that may decisively affect human thinking and vision in the future.

Hieronymus Bosch, however, is not lacking in tradition: something of the Middle Ages comes to life again in his art. It is reminiscent of certain drolleries on the capitals and friezes of cathedrals and in the garland work of the miniatures. Once more a religious conception takes shape that acquires a sectarian flavor through its representation of infernal powers and gargoyles, images of terror at the impending Judgment.

Yet we recognize new themes too: in contrast to the courtly and patrician refinements of the declining fifteenth century, and the rather too submissive yet superficial dependence on Italian art, there now appears in the paintings of Hieronymus Bosch—anticipated in the shepherds of Hugo van der Goes—the peasant class. The holy personages are increasingly recognized and represented as companions of the poor. While the "Romanists" outdid themselves in modishness by piling on the marble pillars and round arches of the Renaissance, the spokesmen of an indigenous art rooted in the people of a locality showed the saints as inhabitants of their own world, with a background showing the town for which the painting was meant. Thus the last of the Gothics, artists like Geertgen tot Sint Jans and Hieronymus Bosch, became also the founders of modern landscape painting. The nature and significance of this development in art can be seen in the Berlin gallery in Geertgens' *John the Baptist in the Wilderness* and Bosch's *St. John on Patmos*.

ST. JOHN ON PATMOS

Oak panel. 63 × 43.3 cm.

PROVENANCE: *Purchased in 1907 in England. Formerly in the collection of W. Füller, Milan.*

54   At the lower right are parts of the signature. The back is painted in grisaille, showing scenes from the Passion of Christ in a circular arrangement around a *tondo* in the center of which are a steep rock with a pelican and a landscape with the Maas or Rhine River. The principal figure in the picture, a St. John filled with his vision of the Madonna and the newborn Savior and occupied with writing down the Gospel, is so like Martin Schongauer's engraving that this may be regarded as Hieronymus Bosch's model for his painting. But what has Bosch done with this starting point? The resemblance ends with the figure, in profile, of the saint, the heavenly vision, and the crown of the tree that balances the composition. Between the gazing saint and the remote vision of the Virgin and Christ Child, there now stands an angel with bizarre wings, pointing upward like the heavenly messenger in the mystery plays. This is the key figure of the vision now; the Madonna has been moved, in contrast to Schongauer's, to an immeasurable distance.

Preoccupied with his divine vision, the scribbling evangelist pays no attention to the devilish phantom behind him. The monster has a human head, small and senile, planted on an insect's body—"Leg of spider, gut of toad," as Goethe puts it in *Faust*—and is apparently plotting to hook the saint's writing utensils with his stick. But he fears the bird staring at him across the figure of St. John. Bosch scholars see in this bird the eagle of the evangelist, but since it is so small, they call it, with palpable uncertainty, a "falcon-like eagle."

In this case, however, the painter departed from the Schongauer model. He probably knew *The Golden Legend,* which relates that the saint kept a partridge as a pet, with which he played when relaxing from his labors. The posture of the feathered companion in the picture, with his humped back and retracted neck, is certainly characteristic enough of that bird, known to be a good companion to man when tamed. Our little partridge is keeping a sharp eye on the hobgoblin, who is thus prevented from doing mischief. In this little secondary figure, Bosch's special bent announces itself; it was destined to take on wild and demonic forms later on. The tense situation has for its background a wide landscape that counterbalances the upward movement of the figures. It is the landscape of the Netherlands, where the Rhine divides into two branches that widen between broad meadows as the river moves toward the North Sea.

Scholars have attempted to identify this landscape more exactly. It is thought to be the area around Nijmegen or Arnhem; but it could, more plausibly, be in the vicinity of 's Hertogenbosch, and thus the river would be the Maas, not the Rhine. The round tower in the city on the horizon is a bit of fantasy; such buildings were added when the painter wished to suggest the Holy Land, even in the midst of the native scene he was painting.

The beauty of the painting owes not a little to the color contrasts between the cool blues of the distance and the warm browns and olive greens of the foreground, setting off the luminous pinks of the Baptist's garment, with its careful Gothic folds, in the center.

Geertgen tot Sint Jans

THE ARTIST: According to Karel van Mander, whose *Schilderboeck* is one of the main sources of our knowledge of the Dutch painters, Geertgen van Haarlem—as he was originally called—died early—at only twenty-eight. Since his dates are not known, we must accept approximations: 1466 as the year of his birth in Leiden and 1495 for that of his death in Haarlem. With Albert van Ouwater, who is thought to have been his teacher, he stands at the beginning of Dutch painting but shows a certain relationship to the art of Rogier van der Weyden and Hugo van der Goes.

In the work of the master who marks the beginning of Holland's great period of art, the landscape plays a special role. Geertgen tot Sint Jans, who joined the Order of St. John as a lay brother and painted an altarpiece for its settlement in Haarlem, created, in his representation of John the Baptist, "the most memorable single figure of primitive painting, with its great simplicity, and its mysterious multiplicity of meaning," to quote Friedrich Winkler.

JOHN THE BAPTIST IN THE WILDERNESS

Oak panel. 42 × 28 cm.

PROVENANCE: *Formerly privately owned in England by the painter W. Cope. Purchased in 1902 from the collection of Percy Macquoid in London; property of the Kaiser Friedrich Museum Association.*

55 The subject was the forerunner of Christ, preparing himself for his mission in the desert. But instead of the desert, Geertgen painted a luxuriant landscape, so that the saint has been occasionally referred to, by those who overlooked the Baptist's lamb in the picture, as John the Evangelist on Patmos.

The upper half of the painting offers the delights of a background whose peace, joyfulness, and clear spatial structure make it the first of the great Dutch landscapes. It goes far beyond what Rogier van der Weyden and Hugo van der Goes did for the backgrounds of their altarpieces. Painted in 1490, it points toward the development of landscape painting by Hieronymus Bosch (Pl. 54) and Pieter Brueghel (Pl. 111).

We see gently undulating meadowland, with a brook winding through it, on the banks of which daisies and columbines bloom. Toward the back, tall beech trees gradually close in to form an ever denser wood, with deer grazing on its edge. There are rabbits, leaping and at rest, and two startled pheasants or partridges winging over the grass. A variety of birds enliven the scene. Behind the woods the roofs and towers of a city can be discerned, and beyond these the eye roams into a blue distance.

And so the master of Haarlem reveals himself as a landscape painter interested in the moods of nature and in the composition of space in nature. This became the new task of his art; in solving it, he was ahead of his contemporaries.

In contrast to the peacefulness of nature, we see the anxiety of the prophet, who has intimations of his future martyrdom. The saint's sorrowful absorption says something about the painter as well; a premonition of his own early death may have weighed on him. This might explain the austere look, the almost helpless submissiveness to fate of St. John's pose, but there is also a touching realism in showing the man of God on his long wanderings rubbing his tired feet together. The powerful expression of the mood, and possibly also the sense of a self-portrait, makes the onlooker feel that the artist is addressing him directly. Another notable innovation appears in the color scheme, with its effect of noble simplicity and solemnity: the avoidance of red, hitherto used in all religious paintings for accentuation. Amid the golden greens of the summer landscape, there are only the rich browns and blues of the saint's garments, the flesh tones of face, hands, and feet, the whiteness of the lamb; the delicate blues of the distance are subtly connected with the strong blue of the saint's cloak in the foreground by the widening of the brook at the upper left, where it reflects the blue of the sky.

Hans Multscher

THE ARTIST: Hans Multscher was born about 1400 in Reichenhofen, near Leutkirch, once a free imperial city on the Danube. He lived in Ulm from 1427 to 1467 as a sculptor, wood-carver, and painter. There is documentary proof that he completed this altarpiece in Sterzing (southern Tyrol), Austria, about 1457. A similar work of four scenes from the life of the Virgin and four from the Passion of Christ, in the form of altar panels from Wurzach, can be found in the Berlin museum. The shrine in the center probably held painted wooden figures. Multscher was the master of a workshop in which he employed many apprentices; but since his presence in Sterzing is attested, both altarpieces are justly attributed to him.

Like Konrad Witz, Hans Multscher stands for the monumental realism that the generation born around 1400 in German-speaking countries, in the Netherlands, and in Italy opposed to the "soft style" of declining Gothicism. Both are Swabian by origin, and both show the influence of the painters of the Netherlands, specifically those of Burgundy.

THE BIRTH OF CHRIST

From the Wurzach altarpiece

Deal panel. 148 × 140 cm.

PROVENANCE: *Dated 1437, the altarpiece—of which the paintings of the life of Mary on the outer panels and the scenes of the Passion on the inner panels are preserved, while the carved figures* once in the shrine must be regarded as lost—was apparently painted for the local church or the Cloister of St. Salvator in Wurzach, which is near the artist's birthplace. In the fourteenth century, the town was part of the domain of the counts of Waldburg, Lord High Stewards to the King. The altar came to be in their collection at the castle of Wurzach, but at the end of their regime it was auctioned off in England in 1803. In 1900, Sir Julius Wernher of London donated it to the Berlin museum.

The outer panels of the altar were four in number; the two lower ones were signed. The fourth panel bears the following moving inscription in minuscule lettering (the fifteenth-century orthography, with its child-like effect, is impossible to render in translation): "Pray to God for Hans Multscher of Reichenhofen, citizen of Ulm, who made this work in the year accounted MCCCCXXXVII."

56   The intensely lifelike effect of Hans Multscher's figures may owe a great deal to the fact that he was a sculptor and carver of figures, as his works in Ulm and his monumental Madonna in the parish church at Sterzing attest. It was through sculpture that he was enabled to break with the Gothic tradition and paint these scenes from the life of the Virgin and the Passion with a sharp realism and yet with a monumental compactness.

These scenes do not seem to be the product of the unaided imagination, however. In particular, the panel with the birth of Christ strongly suggests a scene from one of the popular mystery or Passion plays of the time. The onlookers crowding one another at the fence around the manger of Bethlehem—men and women dressed up for the occasion—look so much like real people that one must assume they were actual spectators at a mystery play, captured by the artist's brush. There are an older and a younger woman, two patrician daughters in pious devotion before the holy scene, an older and a younger burgher, with three servants craning their necks behind them. That this is a representation of the donor with his family and his servants is an idea hard to resist. That these are not meant to be shepherds is made clear by the separate scene of the Annunciation to the shepherds in the background.

Mary and Joseph are shown with dramatic gestures, as if miming the action; the child lies in its woven basket like a stiff doll. On the panel showing the Adoration of the Magi, which once adjoined this panel on the altar, the same manger roofed with straw that was set up for the performance is shown. Here the spectators, visible between the heads of the Moors, are crowding toward the scene from the other side, so that both scenes appear to be framed by spectators.

Multscher's work is noteworthy not only as the first great example of realism in the history of art; we see in it also a documentation of early German drama and acting, an important contribution to the history of the theater.

His color scheme is subdued—as one might expect, considering that the approach is more sculptural than painterly: blue-gray and white tones predominate, although the two principal figures are emphasized with a somewhat blue-tinged red in the dress of Mary and the cloak of Joseph.

Martin Schongauer

THE ARTIST: Martin Schongauer was born in Colmar, Alsace, in about 1440. His father was a goldsmith there, just as a generation later the father of Dürer was in Nuremberg. He was educated in the Upper Rhineland and in Augsburg, where his family originated, and was decisively influences by the art of the Netherlands. The main scenes of his activity were Colmar and Breisach, on the Upper Rhine. He died, to the regret of the young Dürer, who had been hoping to go to see him, in 1491 in Breisach, where his fresco of the Last Judgement in the cathedral testifies that this master of engraving and intimate devotional paintings was also desirous of achieving monumentality in his pioneering art.

ADORATION OF THE SHEPHERDS

Oak panel. 37.5 × 28 cm.

PROVENANCE: *This little devotional panel was once the centerpiece of a private altar, the structure of which provided the architectonic unifying framework for the picture crowded with figures and strongly emphasizing perspective through the contrast between the strong foreground colors and the fading colors of the background. Property of the Kaiser Friedrich Museum Association, it was acquired in 1902 in the London art market.*

The graphic character that occasionally makes German art of the fifteenth century and earlier seem somewhat narrow here lends intimacy to Schongauer's panel of the Adoration. The composition gives the effect of having been sharply and firmly engraved on copperplate, and there is a special refinement in the expressiveness of the faces and hands.   **57**

The composition is divided into two parts by a diagonal line that begins below the knee of the praying shepherd and progresses along the heads of the infant, the Virgin, and Joseph. The holy group that has the dark rock for a background is done in rich colors, while the group of the three shepherds, like the landscape behind them, is painted in more subdued browns and greens.

The hilly landscape with its winding river is a picture in itself, with sheep grazing in the distance beyond the diagonally ascending rock in the middle. The center foreground is occupied by the Christ Child bedded on white linen on a red-and-gold blanket (which is, however, full of holes), propped on a heap of straw. Above it are the heads of ox and ass, as well as the dark wooden supports of the thatched roof, which, with its dark beams and rotten straw, holds the divided composition together, even while the horizontal is emphasized below by the stick going through Joseph's bundle in the corner and by the baby's red blanket.

It is a complex composition, such as only a virtuoso draftsman could conceive and execute. But Schongauer's approach is painterly too: the effect of light and air in the distance pleasingly counterbalances the crowded richness of color and detail in the foreground.

All this is held together by the devotional element, the adoration with which Mary, Joseph, and the shepherds experience the miracle of the divine birth. There is a Gothic intensity in the hands: the strong, towering figure of Joseph in bright red has his fingers interlaced; the delicate long fingers of Mary, touching in prayer, suggest the form of a pointed Gothic arch; the clumsiness of the shepherd's hands is touchingly expressive.

The master of engraving achieved, in this small panel, a marvel of balanced form, in which he combined the new realism with the old piety. Painted about 1475–1480, it signalizes the transition from the Gothic to the modern period in art.

Albrecht Dürer

THE ARTIST: Dürer was born in Nuremberg in 1471, a free citizen of a free imperial city (that is, subject to no feudal lord, only to the Emperor), the son of a goldsmith. For a time, he was apprenticed to the painter Wolgemut, then traveled as a journeyman artist through the towns of the Upper Rhine. He married soon after his return to Nuremberg in 1494, went to Italy in 1495 and again in 1505–1507. There he came under the influence of Mantegna and Bellini; the one affected his graphic style, the other his striving for harmonious composition and brilliant coloring.

Emperor Maximilan I appreciated the master of Nuremberg and his art; he granted him an income, though when Maximilian died, Dürer had to journey to the Netherlands (1520–1521) to secure its continuance. In the Netherlands he was honored as an artist and as a representative of humanistic learning, and he attended the painter Patinir's wedding, also painting a portrait of the groom. He died in 1528 in his native city.

When the Elector Frederick of Saxony spent five days in Nuremberg in 1496, he may have been told—his interest in the arts being well known—that the town boasted a rising master of brush and burin, with which instruments he performed wonders. Despite his being only twenty-five years old, Dürer had already turned out copperplate engravings that surpassed those of the famous Martin Schongauer: the *Madonna on the Sickle Moon*, the *Death and the Lovers*, the *Prodigal Son*. His excellence as a portraitist was already attested by his portrait of his father, a noted goldsmith, and a self-portrait.

He had managed to do something as yet unknown in Germany: give so much expression to the hands that the sitter's character could be read in them; the way his father was painted holding the rosary and he himself the blue flower popularly called "man's faith"[1] was admirable. He had brought from his journey to Venice some amazing examples of his virtuosity and had already surpassed Wolgemut, his teacher in Nuremberg.

ELECTOR FREDERICK THE WISE

Distemper on canvas. 76 × 57 cm.

PROVENANCE: *From Dürer's early period, about 1496, and signed with his monogram at bottom left. Acquired in 1882, when the Duke of Hamilton's collection was auctioned off in London.*

The Saxon Duke, barely over thirty himself, but matured by the experience of his journey to the Holy Land by way of Venice, did not hesitate to commission a portrait by Dürer. The resulting painting belongs among the masterpieces of portraiture, as that genre came to reflect the new appreciation for the value and uniqueness of the individual personality, and is the first and foremost of those by Dürer himself. Some historians believe that the portrait was done from a drawing, and they date it, for no special reason, as a later work. But since there is no proof of either assumption, there is nothing to prevent us from believing that the lifelike portrait was done directly from the model. This would explain the unusual medium: only a few day's time was allotted for the Duke's visit, and, unlike oils, distemper dries quickly, making it possible for the painter to work far more rapidly. It is worth noting that the altarpiece the Duke ordered from Dürer later on for his church in Wittenberg was also painted in distemper.

The situation was dramatic: the young artist, already enjoying some fame but not yet honored with a commission from his city, suddenly coming face to face with the first great lord in his career, the German prince second in power and prestige only to the Emperor himself. The young painter was apparently so deeply impressed by the Duke's elegant appearance that he promptly adopted the same hair style—as can be seen in the self-portrait of 1498 in Madrid. Thenceforth, his hair was to fall in studied curls to his shoulders. This is a further bit of evidence that the Elector's portrait was painted before 1498.

But Dürer's understanding of his model went beyond the fashionable exterior. The subject, who had been the ruler of his lands for ten years, looks serious and firm of purpose. There is an effect of disciplined power, but a certain melancholy is also present, that is compatible with his love of music. His "singers" often had to accompany him on his travels.

[1] *Mannstreu*, probably the alpine bluetop eryngo or possibly the sky-blue eryngo. But, of course, the German name is significant in symbolizing the transition from the father's orthodoxy to the son's Reformist, humanistic "faith."

Almost three decades were to go by before the Duke sat again for Dürer. He had grown in power and prestige, had founded the University of Wittenberg, and was considered the mightiest protector of the Reformation. It was when Frederick was attending the Imperial Diet of 1522–1523 in Nuremberg that Dürer did his second portrait of him, this time in a grandly conceived drawing designed to be transferred to copperplate, which is now among the many treasures of the École des Beaux Arts in Paris. The comparison of Dürer's two portraits of Frederick is psychologically most interesting. The features of the older man show a new calm; the mannered insistence on his dignity and the earlier tension have yielded to an equilibrium that makes his sobriquet "the Wise" appear understandable. One can understand, too, that there was much regret when this man, who was assured of four out of the seven electoral votes when Maximilian I died, declined the imperial crown and instead helped to place it on the head of Maximilian's grandson, Charles V, King of Spain. Frederick III of Saxony was not attracted to power politics; he preferred to devote his energies to his own lands, his own house and family.

Black and gold, brightened by the healthily reddish flesh tones and the chestnut-brown hair, dominate the color scheme of the first portrait. Dürer, who was quite capable of using color abundantly in his altarpieces, under the influence of Venice, used a wise restraint here, corresponding to the mood of the sitter, and thus achieved a masterpiece in this early work. The treatment of the hands, highly original for the period, is also noteworthy. In his later portraits, the master relinquished the hypnotic stare, meeting the viewer head on, of this portrait; only his Hieronymus Holzschuher shows this intent, arresting glance, seeming to look straight at the onlooker.

PORTRAIT OF HIERONYMUS HOLZSCHUHER

Lindenwood. 48 × 36 cm.

PROVENANCE: *This picture is still in its original frame. The inscription on the upper-left corner reads: "Hieronim Holtzschuher · Anno Domini · 1526 · Etatis sue · 57." Dürer's monogram is at the right, on the blue background. Acquired in 1884 from the by then ennobled Holzschuher family, for the then high price of 100,000 talers.*

59 Dürer in this work so expressed the ideal of "manliness, inner strength, and steadfastness," as Goethe put it, that the model became, for posterity, a representative figure of the German middle class at its best: proudly patrician in its free imperial city of Nuremberg and spiritually alert in its humanism. Nor is this man lacking in sharply defined traits, such as egotism and obstinacy. Some have described him, not convincingly, as a sanguine, pleasure-loving sort. When Dürer, soon after the completion of this portrait, painted his most outstanding work, the two panels of the four apostles (in the Pinakothek, Munich), something of Holzschuher's look went into the strong-willed features of his St. Paul. This fact might well serve to characterize the City Councillor of Nuremberg and the willpower to be discerned in his face.

At a time when Titian was already painting suggestively with a broad brush, Dürer was still painting, with "painstaking conscientiousness," as Goethe said, every hair of the beard or the fur collar. He even captured the reflection of the window frame in the eye of his sitter. If the model were looking directly at the onlooker, the pupils of his eyes would be exactly where that reflection of the window is now seen in the irises. (No other portrait painter has ever been so exact—or so exacting toward himself.) But he is looking past the viewer, as this detail proves.

Dürer was at the height of his development when he painted his friend, who was two years older than himself. A special sign of this friendship appears in the inscription meticulously placed in the upper-left-hand corner in the master's own lettering; his monogram at the right is in itself a gem of the calligraphic art.

Lucas Cranach

THE ARTIST: He named himself for his native town, Kronach, in northern Franconia. He was born in 1472, a year after Dürer. In his youth he was one of the innovators, when he was living in southern Germany and Vienna. Even before Altdorfer, he gave special prominence to landscape in his paintings, even when dealing with traditional religious themes.

In 1505 the Elector, Duke Frederick the Wise of Saxony, summoned him as court painter to Torgau, and soon thereafter to Wittenberg. There he founded a great workshop and was held in high honor first as Chamberlain of the Council and then as Mayor of Wittenberg. A friend of Luther and Melanchthon, he became the painter of the Reformation. When John Frederick, Elector of Saxony, the third in the series of feudal lords whom Cranach had served in Wittenberg, was defeated by Emperor Charles V at Mühlberg in 1547 and lost his status as Elector, Cranach accompanied him to imprisonment in Augsburg, where he met Titian, and then went with his lord to Innsbruck. In 1552, when Weimar became the Duke's official residence—his domain had been reduced to the small duchy of Thuringia—the aged painter followed him thither, and there he died in 1553. Goethe, another famous resident of Weimar some two hundred years later, who greatly admired Cranach's art, never knew that the painter was one of his maternal ancestors.

Art lovers appreciate most those paintings of Cranach that were done when he was still young and with naive unconcern, turned his back on the conventions of fifteenth-century art and its thematic traditions. That was the period of Crucifixion paintings that showed an entirely new kind of grouping, which ended with the lighthearted *Rest on the Flight to Egypt,* with which the impressive series of Cranach paintings at the Berlin gallery begins.

REST ON THE FLIGHT TO EGYPT

Beechwood panel. 69 × 51 cm.

PROVENANCE: *Inscribed "LC 1504." Purchased in 1902 from the Konrad Fiedler collection in Munich. Previously in the Sciarra collection in Rome.*

60, 61 This painting must have had a very special significance for Lucas Cranach, for it is the first of his works that he signed and dated; he was then thirty-two. His monogram and the date, 1504, are painted as if engraved upon a small boulder lying in the shallow brook at the bottom of the picture. Later on he took to using his well-known insignia, a winged dragon holding a ring in its mouth, which he also placed on the coat of arms conferred on him by the Elector of Saxony in 1508.

Cranach's theme is not the hardships of the flight to Egypt. What he shows is an idyllic scene, recalling Altdorfer's discovery of the beauty of nature in the foothills of the Alps. The Holy Family is resting at the foot of a wooded mountain, under a weathered fir tree and in the shelter of a rock wall from which a miraculous spring was said to have gushed forth to slake the wanderer's thirst. Also shown is the second legendary miracle: a flight of angels descended from heaven to delight the infant Jesus.

Guarded by Joseph, standing in the center, Mary, dressed in brilliant red, is seated in the shade of the towering fir, holding the child. He stands naked on his linen wrapper, which has slipped down, and reaches for some wild berries offered by a cherub. Two older angels —one of them, not quite completed, is attired like a feudal lady of the period—are singing and playing the flute; a naked cherub looks at the notes, and another is waiting for his part to begin. A third cherub has caught a parrot and is taking it eagerly to the infant Jesus; the fourth is cathing water from the spring in a shell.

This picture, as compared with a pure landscape, has the charm of all those bright colors in happy profusion, against the background of green vegetation, brown rock, and blue distance. The painter, with his characteristic devotion to the "little things," gives us an abundance of finest detail, from the columbine on one side to the cowslip on the other, from the lichen on the fir tree to the withered tree beyond it. Yet everything is woven into a unity, and the realism of the physical details makes even the appearance of the angels and the luminosity around the head of Mary appear part of reality. It is truth as distilled by the fairy tale. In the words of Kleist: "Was ever a dream so rich as what is real here?"

CARDINAL ALBRECHT OF BRANDENBURG AS ST. JEROME

Lindenwood. 57 × 37 cm.

PROVENANCE: *Dated 1527 and bearing the symbol of the winged dragon. Acquired with the Solly collection in 1821.*

The Margrave Albrecht of Brandenburg was only 62 twenty-three, in 1513, when he became Archbishop of Magdeburg and Bishop of Halberstadt. A year later, Pope Leo X violated the custom of the Curia by giving him a second archbishopric, that of Mainz (Mayence), so that he became an Elector of the Holy Roman Empire, Lord High Chancellor, and Primate all in one. No prince of the church on German soil had ever had greater power than Albrecht, the Elector of Brandenburg's youngest son.

In his character and inclinations, he resembled the Medici Pope and patron of Raphael who had enthroned him. A humanist and friend of the arts and sciences, he admired Erasmus of Rotterdam and showed it by making St. Erasmus the patron saint of Halle, his capital city, having himself portrayed as St. Erasmus on the altarpiece of the cathedral he erected there. The painter who executed that portrait (now in the Pinakothek, Munich) had been summoned to Halle by Albrecht himself; he was none other than Matthias Neithardt, better known as Grünewald. But when Grünewald died in 1530, Albrecht of Brandenburg sought to enlist Lucas Cranach, of nearby Wittenberg, for his great enterprises.

With the exception of an earlier and far more impressively colored panel in the Munich Pinakothek showing the Cardinal kneeling before the crucifix, Cranach's portraits of Albrecht show the same rather effeminate features familiar from Dürer's engraving. Cardinal Albrecht, who loved having himself painted as a saint, appears as St. Jerome in no less than three paintings. Two of these panels show the pious man indoors; the most beautiful, though it is the smallest, shows him as a hermit in the woods writing in a tome, near the monastery of Bethlehem.

A great deal might be said about the sitter, whose life in no wise resembled the lives of his holy models. There was, for example, his princely ostentation, supported by the questionable trade in papal indulgence. But we are here concerned only with the way the artist dealt with his subject to create a picture. The portrait itself, not painted directly from the model, hardly plays a decisive role here. What is significant is rather the painter's narrative power, his original way with the landscape and the life of the beasts in the forest.

Next to this panel in the Berlin museum hangs a painting of St. Jerome that Cranach probably did several years earlier as a preliminary study. Here the bearded saint sits in ascetic nakedness at the rough wooden board propped on a tree trunk and a boulder: altogether an icon illustrating a legend.

On the panel commissioned by Cardinal Albrecht, on which the bearded old man has been replaced by the youthful prince of the church, then in his middle thirties, the painter renders the wooded landscape for its own sake. Between the pompous red of the Cardinal's hat, hung on a tree trunk, and the right shoulder of the seated figure, the background shows a clearing full of playful deer. In the extreme foreground, the lion is given the rightful prominence of a principal figure in the legend, lying peacefully between a hare and a badger painted with a hunter's keen understanding. Only Cranach, the friend and companion of the gentlemen of the Saxon court, who were devoted to the chase, could paint so authentic a portrait of a young roebuck, his head attentively on the board as though he were participating in the labor of translation with the saint. The slender antlers cut across the trunk of the cross, the crossbeam of which, markedly foreshortened, points to the background.

There we see the monastery and a peculiar scene: the lion of St. Jerome appears once more, driving the camels and riders of a caravan into the cloister. According to *The Golden Legend*, Jerome, whose name (Hieronymus) means "Sacred Wood," lived as a hermit near the monastery of Bethlehem, "a companion to the wilde beastes." We know the story of the lion he healed by extracting a thorn from his paw, whereupon "the lion grew so tame and home-loving that he dwelled with him like a house pet." Since the hermitage was near the cloister, the lion did duty watching the monastery donkey at pasture, its job being to carry the monks' wood from the forest to the monastery. But once, when the four-legged shepherd fell asleep, some merchants passing by in a caravan with their camels stole the donkey. This made the lion so unhappy that he could not rest until he had found the caravan and—as Cranach shows in his picture—had driven the merchants into the cloister, where he forced them to return the donkey and to pay a stiff fine in precious oils. Thus goes the legend of St. Jerome, who died in A.D. 420.

The painter of Wittenberg tells this story as a fairy tale. The only disturbing element here—especially to one who has seen the earlier Cranach picture of St. Jerome in Berlin—is the portrait of the Cardinal, whose features are far too obviously those of a worldly man of pleasure. However, the splendid red of the Cardinal's habit, the rich greens of the foliage and the grasses, and the golden brown fur of the animals all make for a fresh vibrancy of color, so that the painting looks as if it had just come off the easel.

LUCRETIA

Red-beech panel. 35.5 × 21.5 cm.

PROVENANCE: *Carries the insignia of the winged dragon and above it the date, 1533. Donated in 1917 by the heirs of the painter Ludwig Knaus.*

The representation of the human body for its own sake, to celebrate its natural beauty, is not seen in Western art until the Renaissance. The anecdotal framework, which was of paramount importance in the Middle Ages, now becomes a mere pretext. The new paintings, in which the painter and his patron openly admire the human body, are nudes, whether they are called Adam and Eve, Apollo or Sebastian, Diana or Lucretia, Venus or the Three Graces. A prince might commission a nude of his mistress in the role of a goddess or heroine of antiquity, and if the painter was a Titian, the result could be one of mythic grandeur.

Among the masters of the German Renaissance, none painted as many "nudes" as Lucas Cranach the Elder. Most are small in format, but he occasionally painted a life-size Venus or Lucretia. Comparison of these graceful figures shows them to be very much alike, regardless of differences in size or name.

Lucretia was a favorite subject of Cranach. While the Reformation emanating from Wittenberg shook the world and the new doctrine became the state religion of Saxony, while Luther was writing his hymn "A Mighty Fortress Is Our God" and his catechism, while Philip Melanchthon worked out the theoretical basis for the new religion in his house in Wittenberg, about thirty paintings of Lucretia were created in the course of ten years (1525–1535) not far from Luther's and Melanchthon's homes—though, to be sure, they constituted only a small part of the total production of Cranach's workshop. For the hanging of pictures in private homes had become fashionable, and many of the princes and great nobles of the courts probably ordered such pictures for their own rooms. They admired the beauty of the body painted by Cranach, in the traditional Gothic curve and with the Gothic sloping shoulders, and his unique and charming combination of winsomeness and reserve. The motif of the dagger might be interpreted in the sense that Lucretia was the patron saint of chastity. That to a Roman she was primarily the heroic figure whose suicide, after she was dishonored by the King, led to the founding of the republic was probably of less interest to Wittenbergers. Nor did Cranach, with the exception of two early, somewhat larger seminude representations, show the act of suicide. In our picture, at any rate, the dagger is only a kind of prop for the young creature with the lithe body, the by no means beautiful face, and feet characteristic of Cranach's women, the big toe of which one might be inclined to call a "foot-thumb." But the dagger may have represented, for Cranach and his client, the defense of the lovely young body, which emerges like a blossom from the dark background.

Albrecht Altdorfer

THE ARTIST: Born in Regensburg around 1480, probably the son of a painter, Albrecht Altdorfer was active in his native city from 1505 until his death in 1538. In 1511 he was in Vienna; in 1526 he was appointed municipal architect in Regensburg. When the town council offered him the honor of being Lord High Mayor, he declined because he was overburdened with work in his shop. He is called the father of German landscape painting and the leading master of the so-called Danube River school. The Berlin gallery owns nine works by this rare artist, among them his three earliest extant paintings, dated 1507.

In contrast to Patinir, who built his landscapes out of a mass of crowded details, almost in the manner of fifteenth-century artists, Altdorfer painted his landscapes far from observed reality. In his *Landscape with a Satyr Family,* dated 1507, the earliest known of his works, he appears more modern from that point of view, even though he was about five years older than Patinir, who is generally called the first landscape painter because of his *Rest on the Flight to Egypt* (Pl. 106). Altdorfer's choice of a subject from pagan mythology also characterizes him as a pioneer of the northern Renaissance. The religious or mythological trappings that he still needed when painting a landscape for its own sake can be disregarded even more than in the case of Patinir.

CHRIST ON THE CROSS BETWEEN TWO THIEVES

Lindenwood. 28 × 20 cm.

PROVENANCE: *Monogrammed "AA" at bottom center. On the back, a half-obliterated double coat of arms by the artist's own hand. Purchased in 1886. An old copy of 1528 is in the collection of paintings at Coblenz.*

63 The cross of the Savior and those of the two thieves are set by Altdorfer in the midst of a landscape typical of the Danube country in Upper Bavaria, in the foothills of the Alps. The height of the middle cross is emphasized by the tall ladder a mercenary has just used for putting up the insignia "INRI" ("Jesus of Nazareth, King of the Jews"), meant as mockery of the Crucified.

The incident in the Lord's Passion shown here was an unusual subject and Altdorfer underlined its uniqueness by showing the group of mourners in a new way: John, the mother, and her companion are turning away with Joseph of Arimathea, so that their grief is seen more in their postures than in their facial expressions. In the foreground sits Mary Magdalen, her back to the onlooker; with her long blond pigtails, she is evidently a young girl of the period and place in which the work was painted.

It is not primarily the narrative that predominates here; rather it is the lyrical, contemplative mood expressed by the mournful figure of the youthful Magdalen —the theme expressed two centuries later by Johann Sebastian Bach in the verse:

> I lived rejoicing in the world
> While Thou must suffer . . .

The group of the three crosses is also characteristic of Altdorfer: the victorious towering of the Savior, in contrast to the crushed attitude of the thieves, whose heads hang down brokenly. The gleaming inscription and the gloriole around the head of Christ intensify the contrast.

While deeply religious and thus traditional in subject, the painting was far ahead of its time in painterly approach and coloring. Color was intentionally used to carry the mood. The yellow of the soldier's tights gives the strongest accent. There is some red in the group of mourners and in the servant's jerkin, contrasting with the bright green of the rolling meadowland. In the precise center of the painting, the cross juts out against the background, dark against light-gray clouds that allow a glimpse of the gloomy sky above. The painter is a mystic of light, as his visionary treatment of the sky shows.

LANDSCAPE WITH A SATYR FAMILY

Lindenwood. 23 × 20 cm.

PROVENANCE: *Monogrammed "AA" at upper left. This painting was in the Kraenner collection of Regensburg around the middle of the nineteenth century. It was purchased by the Aachen collector Suermondt and was acquired for Berlin with his collection in 1874.*

The scene is the edge of a forest, where a satyr and his 65 family are camping. The trees are gigantic columns, partly screened by the rich green of tall bushes around them. The dazzling play of light on the leaves and the tips of the fir branches is done with a devotion to the wonders of nature that is the hallmark of the masters of the Danube River style: it glitters and sparkles, giving the natural landscape a touch of fairyland.

At the upper left, a high wall of rock reflects the sun between the tree trunks. On the right, an open vista with a strikingly low horizon suggests a great distance. Outlined against the cloudless blue of the sky is a castle built on a rocky eminence guarded by a river. In the lower right foreground—near enough to be watched with fascination by the family of satyrs—a naked man with a stick has just caught up with a woman in a red robe whom he has been pursuing—presumably Hercules capturing Deianira.

PRIDE GOETH BEFORE A FALL

Lindenwood panel. 28 × 40 cm.

PROVENANCE: *Monogrammed "AA" and dated 1531. Purchased in 1876 from the F. Lippmann collection in Vienna. Previously in the Develey collection, Munich.*

In this late work, Altdorfer achieved a perfect har- 64 mony of structure and mood between the scene and the figures in it. It is not simply a landscape with some figures painted in for decoration; every detail in the entire composition is aimed at illustrating the proverb of the title.

The central element in the panel is the arrogant couple, upon the end of whose enormous scarlet train squats a group of beggars with their hungry children. The two overdressed characters are moving toward steps that lead up to the courtyard of an opulent Renaissance palace. A cavalier, possibly the majordomo, awaits them with a drink of welcome in his upraised hand. To the left, another figure is draped over the balustrade in an attitude suggesting envy and a foreshadowing of evils to come rather than a welcome.

Altdorfer was an architect as well as a painter, although we know of his interest in architecture only from his paintings and etchings. Here he uses the fantastic castle, the pretentious residence of the approaching couple, to depict the nature of pride. The decaying castle in the middle distance is in deliberate contrast to this architectural confection, and it is subtly related to the group of beggars through the lines of a group of trees between them.

In the far distance, the painter is obviously free from the dictates of allegory and able to abandon himself to the creation of landscape for its own sake. The city on the broad waterfront, probably the Danube, is similar to the one in the Berlin painting of the Crucifixion, although the tower is taller here because of its compositional relation to the ruined castle. That tower is, incidentally, in the exact center of the painting, illustrating Altdorfer's painstaking deliberation. Below it starts the diagonal leading to the center of interest, while the opposing diagonal, beginning just below the initials and date on the tree trunk at bottom right, moves the eye past the old castle and the city to the rocky mountains on the horizon. This clear, balanced scheme is characteristic of the painter familiar with the laws of architectural construction.

The era of humanism delighted in all manner of apothegms and mottoes. Erasmus of Rotterdam collected Greek and Roman sayings; Agricola published his collection of German proverbs in 1529, two years prior to the Altdorfer painting; in 1494, Sebastian Brant published his *Ship of Fools*. Altdorfer, though a learned humanist and a man of the Renaissance, kept close to the life and thought of the common people. Hence the effect of his painting is not that of self-conscious allegory; rather, it has the kind of naiveté that later found poetic expression in the works of Hans Sachs (1494–1576), who described himself most aptly thus:

> I am a shoe-
> Maker and a poet, too.

Hans Sachs was made the central figure in Wagner's *Die Meistersinger*.

The mixture of learning and popular idiom gives Altdorfer's work its special charm; it is reminiscent of an old definition: "The proverb is a coin bearing the official stamp, but its art and its value stem directly from the people."

Three decades later, Pieter Brueghel the Elder of Holland illustrated a large number of Dutch proverbs in one huge painting in his own forthright, popular style. Like Altdorfer's panel, it is among the unique treasures of the Berlin gallery (Pls. 110–113). Brueghel's painting is blunt and unambiguous; Altdorfer's has the tender charm of a fairy tale.

Bernhard Strigel

THE ARTIST: Born in Memmingen about 1460, where he worked and died in 1528, the year of Dürer's death, Strigel was a disciple of Bartholomäus Zeitblom, the master of Ulm, and a representative of the Swabian school. With Albrecht Dürer and Hans Burgkmair, he was of the painters much employed by Emperor Maximilian. He worked briefly in Vienna, Nuremberg, and Augsburg, as well as in his native town. For a long time, his art was in eclipse and was not rediscovered until the 1880's.

His altarpieces, such as the high altar of Blaubeuren—most of them still painted with a gold background—show him to be a near-contemporary of Dürer, whom he preceded by about ten years. But the depth of his colors, the individuality of his heads and the realism in his representations of sacred history entitle him to a place of distinction among the shapers of the German Renaissance.

Strigel's power of characterization gave his work something of the quality of portrait painting, even when he was depicting scenes from the life of Christ. His art developed by clearly discernible degrees from the era of late Gothic to the Renaissance—and with a grandeur of conception all its own. Although he did not achieve the monumentality of a Dürer, his gift for realistic detail brought a new vitality to German religious painting and to the full-length portrait in the age of humanism. It is high time he received the recognition due him.

CHRIST'S LEAVE-TAKING FROM HIS MOTHER

Firwood. 86.5 × 71.5 cm.

PROVENANCE: *Painted about 1520. Companion picture to a* Disrobing of Christ, *held in storage, and to a* Crucifixion, *formerly in private ownership in Freiburg. Acquired by Waagen in 1850.*

This is a side panel of an altarpiece of the Crucifixion, hence it refers to the Passion of Christ, beginning with his leave-taking from his mother. Three groups are placed in a landscape showing the snowy Alps in the background between two clusters of tall trees: in the center, the mother breaking down in the arms of her son; at the right, the side adjoining the centerpiece of **66, 67** the altar, Mary's women companions; on the other side, farther back and smaller in perspective, three disciples waiting for Christ. The "whence" and "whither" of the central figure's story appear on both sides of the scene of leave-taking.

But both the scene and the secondary figures serve as a mere background to the representation of the mother's grief. We seem to hear the words of St. Luke the Evangelist: "Yea, a sword shall pierce through thy own soul also."

The effectiveness of the picture depends upon the ordinariness of the faces expressing the anguish and the urgency of the mission. The contemporary onlooker must have felt that the scene, together with the others of the disrobing of Christ before his flagellation and the Crucifixion, concerned him directly. And the painting has this effect even today.

Strigel's gift for capturing individual character gives him his modern quality, compared with the medieval conception of religious motifs by the Gothic painters. But he is more successful with the portraits than he is with the rest of this panel. His use of color cannot quite achieve the compositional unity that in his time was so perfectly mastered by a Dürer or a Lucas van Leyden; it fails to compensate for the structural weaknesses. And yet his colors are carefully chosen: the red in the clothing of the Marys and the apostles frames the center group, in which the deep blue of Mary's cloak and the violet-brown of the robe of Christ express the solemnity and grief of the occasion. A certain awkwardness in this painting of 1520, suggesting that the master was aware of his daring departure from convention, heightens its emotional impact.

Hans Baldung (Hans Grien)

THE ARTIST: Hans Baldung was born about 1484 at Weyerstein am Turm near Strasbourg (Strassburg); his parents came from Schwäbisch Gmünd. He was a pupil of Dürer in Nuremberg—indeed, the most prominent one—with whom he enjoyed a lifelong friendship. A lock of the master's hair was bequeathed to him at Dürer's death. From 1509 he worked in the free imperial city of Strasbourg as a painter, printmaker, and designer of stained-glass pictures. From 1512–1517 he worked in Freiburg im Breisgau, where he completed the great altarpiece in the choir of the cathedral in 1516.

The self-willed genius of Baldung deeply expresses the German humanism that shaped the cultural life of the Upper Rhineland.

MARY WITH THE CHRIST CHILD AND ST. JOHN

Lindenwood. 91 × 64 cm.

PROVENANCE: *Painted about 1535, according to C. Koch, author of a book on the drawings of Hans Baldung (1941) and*

other publications. Turned over to the gallery from the royal palace in Berlin in 1939.

In the great series of Madonnas in which Christian **69** painters have expressed their quest for beauty, this panel by Hans Baldung occupies a very special place. He painted not the Mother of God adored by the populace as intercessor and Queen of Heaven, but rather the Madonna of humanism, combining the spirit of Christianity with that of classical antiquity, and giving her the features of a Venus or Caritas.

This Madonna is a far cry from the medieval Christian ideal. Baldung's Mary is adorned with a diadem and precious necklace; her nakedness is shown as if she were a pagan goddess, with only a shoulder alluringly draped in glowing red velvet, to set off almost seductively the blond sheen of her flowing hair. This is not the "maiden pure" of Hans Memling, for example; it is the Venus of the Renaissance. Some historians have even gone so far as to argue that this painting is not a representation of the Madonna. But the drowsy boy in the background, holding the cluster of grapes symbolic of the Last Supper, is clearly the infant John. This makes the beauty, whose features and jewels are familiar from the artist's drawings, unquestionably the Madonna.

To judge by the style, the date of the painting is around 1535 or perhaps a bit earlier. It was at about this time that a great many Madonnas came to be painted in a worldly, an almost pagan, manner, as though it had suddenly come into fashion—possibly owing to the example given by Baldung in this panel. In any case, an order was issued against this practice by the town council of Strasbourg in which a quite forgotten painter under its jurisdiction was solemnly threatened with the destruction of his pictures if he should continue to paint the Mother of God in so unholy a fashion.

Baldung's panel, fortunately, has survived. It is a bold work in subject and composition. The juxtaposition of the sleeping infant Jesus at bottom left with the infant John diagonally opposite, drowsing behind Mary's left shoulder, is unusual. While Mary is here shown as *Maria lactans,* the nourishing mother, she does not primarily suggest a maternal figure. Her right hand seems unaccustomed to holding a child, compared, for example, with Mantegna's Madonna (Pl. 17). Baldung's Mary does not emanate sanctity, nor does she suggest a transcendence of the earthly being toward a heavenly glory. Instead, her fulfillment as a woman and the strong sense of her personality make her representative of the Renaissance ideal of the noble mistress.

In addition to his graphic style, Baldung's originality appears in a free, truly painterly conception and sensibility, illustrated in the movement of the hands here. His skill is evident in all the richly executed details, not least in the diaphanous floating veil that so delicately frames the composition.

Jan Gossaert (Jan Mabuse)

THE ARTIST: Jan Gossaert was born about 1478; he called himself Mabuse after his native town (French, Maubeuge). His early work was done in Bruges and Antwerp, until he entered the service of Duke Philip the Good of Burgundy, who took him along to Rome to see the art of classical antiquity. Later, when the Duke had been made Bishop of Utrecht, he employed Gossaert there too. Most of his work was done in Middelburg, where he lived close to the residence of his patron and where he died in 1533.

Gossaert painted a great variety of religious and classical subjects as well as portraits. After his return from Rome, he became a leading "Romanist," or proponent of the Italian Renaissance style in the Netherlands, with a decided leaning toward the emotionalism as well as the ornamental accessories in Renaissance painting, in contrast to the inwardness of his early works.

The use of contrasting lights and darks as a basic stylistic device, coming to its apex in the work of Rembrandt, evolved from several techniques. There was the *sfumato* of Leonardo da Vinci, a balanced modeling of figures and shapes by means of light and shade, brightening a dark color here, a somber area there. Another method was to depict a specific source of light, such as a torch, a lantern, thus creating dramatic lighting effects in the spirit of the baroque. An example of this is the night scene, with a basically dark ground on which exciting effects may be obtained by means of light coming from a specific source—in this instance, the moon and the comparative brightness of the sky. Among the religious themes from the Bible, the scene of Christ on the Mount of Olives was a favorite subject that had great emotional appeal and power. In Gossaert's painting, the darkness, broken by the visionary appearance of the angel in the moonlit sky, the metallic gleams of weapons, shields, and armor by which the approach of soldiers from the direction of the open city gate is barely discernible, provides a basis for ingenious contrasts of light and shades, making for a work of powerful impact.

CHRIST ON THE MOUNT OF OLIVES

Oak panel. 85 × 63 cm.

PROVENANCE: *From Gossaert's early period, about 1512. The painting was in the Winkler collection during the eighteenth century and was purchased for Berlin in 1848.*

70, 71 The composition is still basically fifteenth century, in the last quarter of which Gossaert was born. The principal figure is set clearly and decidedly in the center: kneeling under the bright moon, Christ towers above the sleeping disciples. His gray-blue robe, bordered in gold at the neck and hem, blends well with the cool nocturnal color scheme. In effective contrast to this are the red cloak and golden-red hair of John at the lower left, echoed by the gentler red of Peter's robe, while that of the angel above, left, is a rich, golden pink.

The Gothic zigzag of the garments' folds also heightens the tension. The Savior's spiritual struggle is seen in his despairing look at the cup, the symbol of what he must endure, set before him on a rock by the hand of the angel.

The head of this beardless Jesus is wholly, uniquely untraditional. This is no otherworldly Savior, but a young man of the painter's own time and race, which makes the despair in those still-boyish features the more moving. The contrast between the new generation—that of Gossaert, the slightly older Geertgen tot Sint Jans, and Hieronymus Bosch—and the primitive masters is here strongly apparent. One is tempted to deplore the Italian influence that made Gossaert one of the first Romanists among the painters of the Netherlands, as early as 1509.

VIRGIN AND CHILD

Oak panel. 46 × 37 cm.

PROVENANCE: *Purchased in 1821 with the Solly collection.*

On the frame painted around the dark-red ground of the picture, the following inscription appears, as if cut out of metal:

VERUS DEUS ET HOMO CASTA MATER ET VIRGO (TRUE GOD AND MAN CHASTE MOTHER AND VIRGIN)

76 Fifteenth-century paintings of the Madonna, beginning in the Netherlands with Van Eyck and continuing through Memling to Gerard David, are characterized by a combination of realism and piety. In the age of humanism and the Renaissance, Jan Gossaert, influenced by what he had learned in Italy, brought to this traditional subject a conscious formalism and, in content, an understandable underlying idea. His painting of the Madonna with the grapes clearly shows the transition to Romanism, the new fashion of the times, in the art of the southern Netherlands. Its symbolism—the grapes representing the Savior's sacrificial death—is clear. Gossaert's Madonna represents the new ideal of the times.

The special grandeur of the conception finds its formal expression through an unusual trick of perspective that makes appear as if the Madonna and Christ Child have come forward out of the frame behind them. At the same time, the table, with the lines of the pattern on the tablecloth creating a sense of depth, puts a mysterious distance between the Virgin and the beholder. Thus we have a devotional painting with realistic detail, expressing the master's inner tension most effectively. Tension is also produced chromatically through the contrasting of cold and warm colors, with cool tones surrounding the triangular form of the group. Lastly, a psychological tension is suggested by the image of the loving mother, who offers, simultaneously, the life-giving breast and those dark grapes signifying the sacrificial death. It is upon these that she bends her thoughtful gaze, while the healthy-looking child looks up intelligently at her beautiful face. The old mystic piety has here been replaced by formal and intellectual sophistication, signalizing a new era.

PORTRAIT OF BAUDOUIN OF BURGUNDY

Oak panel. 94 × 39 cm.

PROVENANCE: *This is a painting of Gossaert's later phase, between 1530 and 1540. It was acquired with the Suermondt collection in Aachen in 1874.*

77 Mannered as he is in his rendering of mythological subjects, Gossaert shows control and stature when dealing with reality and striving to give it significance, as in this portrait of a striking personality.

Here he was clearly striving to paint like an Italian. The activity of the hands, leading a life of their own in the picture, shows a kind of manneristic excess always wisely avoided by Dürer, his contemporary. Although Gossaert seems to be showing off his virtuosity as he revels in the splendors of the sitter's attire, the painting as a whole has a certain grandeur, expressing the character—or at least the pretensions—of the sitter in the fashionable Romanist manner. The shadow cast on the wall by the sitter's head is both a realistic touch and an uncannily, almost demoniacally ominous one.

The chromatic treatment is also extremely original. As in the painting of the Madonna (Pl. 76), cool colors take the center, bringing out the flesh tones of the face, also enhanced by the green background.

One cannot help wondering who the sitter might have been; his portrait surpasses in luxuriousness even those by a Raphael or a Sebastiano del Piombo. The motto on the dagger's sheath, "*Autre que vous (je n'aime)*" ("I love none but you") accords with Burgundian custom; and with the help of a later inscription on the back—copied from an older text—it has been established that this is the portrait of an illegitimate son of Gossaert's patron, Duke Philip of Burgundy, Bishop of Utrecht, probably born to his mistress, the beautiful Marquise van Vere, glorified by Gossaert as a Madonna (Brussels).

This son never attained the importance of his father, whose love of Italy, in the humanistic fashion of the time, helped to establish Romanism in the art of the Netherlands. Philip seems to have been one of the last exemplars of the Burgundian magnificence that ended with Charles the Bold.

Hans Holbein The Younger

THE ARTIST: Hans Holbein came of a family of painters in Augsburg, where he was born in 1497, and began as an apprentice in his father's workshop. At eighteen, he went to Basel, Switzerland; then to London for the first time, 1526–1528; then back to Basel, 1528–1532; and finally back to London, whence he returned only once to Basel, in 1538. In 1536, King Henry VIII appointed him his court painter. In his works, all the personages of importance at the court of the English Renaissance are portrayed with incorruptible clarity and truth. Holbein died in London of the plague in 1543.

When Hans Holbein left Basel for London for the second time in 1532, he was dependent for his livelihood upon the Stahlhof, the central office of the German merchants of the Hanseatic League, a number of whom commissioned portraits by him. Thus a series of portraits of German merchant princes living in England came into being. Holbein's ability to capture a sitter's character in an objective way that nevertheless expresses his personality continued the achievement of Dürer in his portraits, which reached a high point in that of Hieronymus Holzschuher.

PORTRAIT OF GEORGE GISZE

Oakwood. 96 × 84 cm.

PROVENANCE: *The sitter was the scion of a merchant family in Danzig; he was born in 1499 and died in 1562. Holbein painted his portrait in 1532. The first description of this painting occurs in the* Description des tableaux du Palais Royal *(Paris, 1727, 2nd ed.) of the Duke of Orléans' collection. Acquired with the Solly collection in 1821. From the catalogue of the auction held in the Galerie Orléans, April, 1733, where this painting was listed as No. 104, it appears that Solly bought it for 60 guilders.*

Holbein reached the summit of his powers for the first 72, 74, 75 time when he painted his portrait of the Danzig merchant George Gisze, showing his masterly handling of space and including elements of still life that make it more than a portrait. The artist had thus enlarged the scope of the portrait before, as when he painted, in 1528, the astronomer Nikolaus Kratzer surrounded by groups of instruments such as he must have used in his exploration of cosmic space. We may therefore assume that Holbein and his client Gisze agreed that this portrait should show to Gisze's family in Germany their son and brother as one engaged to be married, but seated at his desk, engaged in his daily occupations and surrounded by all the implements and appurtenances of a merchant prince.

The pinks in the graceful vase from Murano were the symbol of his affianced state. In this way, Holbein achieved a still life harking back to the tenderness with which flowers were depicted on the altars of the fifteenth century, but at the same time pointing to new directions for the art of a new era with its psychological realism.

It is characteristic of the humanist outlook that the picture reveals so much of the personal and that there are several inscriptions to tell us who is involved. A note is affixed with two drops of sealing wax to the wall above the sitter's head; it states:

This picture you see shows George as he really looks,
His features, the life in his eyes, the very shape of the man.

This statement appears in the form of a Latin distich, and underneath, also in Latin, one reads: "In his thirty-third year, the year of the Lord 1532."

Who "George" is can be learned by deciphering several other inscriptions, spelling his name now Gisze, then again Gisse or Ghisse, and the address on the letter, the seal of which he is just loosening with a little penknife. It reads: "To the honorable George Gisze at London in England, my brother." The original is in the sixteenth-century German of the north country.

The emotional value that all these inscriptions add to the picture is heightened by the motto the sitter himself had written on the wall beneath the shelf behind him:

Nulla sine merore voluptas
(no joy without sorrow)

However, numerous as these messages and objects are, they do not push the sitter into the background. Even though there are in addition two signet rings, a ball of string in a valuable casing hanging from the shelf on the side wall, and a round metal box with gold coins— as well as a valuable Persian rug that covers the table and serves as a basis for the composition—all depicted so artfully that the scene and the details almost seem to exist for their own sake, George Gisze towers above them. The young merchant's costly clothing—a black-velvet mantle over a red-satin camisole—matches his well-groomed appearance. His head is poised between the three-quarter profile and the frontal view, and this seems to intensify the glance that is firmly fixed on the beholder.

The many kinds of red in the patterned rug, the brilliantly painted sleeves, the cords and seals and sealing wax and bookbinding vigorously set off the healthy flesh tones. Shadows, rendered with quite a new sense of the atmospheric, set off the luminosity of the reds and golds. The emphasis on particular colors as developed in the fifteenth century is muted by a new understanding of aerial perspective. How Holbein intensifies the rare richness of his palette through the restrained use of colors is a secret of his art.

PORTRAIT OF A MAN WITH A LUTE

Oak panel. 23 × 23 cm.

PROVENANCE: *This painting was privately owned in England as late as the nineteenth century. It was acquired for Berlin in 1937.*

There is a difference of opinion about this panel, as a result of studies that enabled scholars to identify one of the men in the *Two Ambassadors* (the double portrait in the National Gallery in London) as Jean de Dinteville, a French *grand seigneur* who was King Francis I's ambassador at the court of Henry VIII until 1537. The lute player bears a certain resemblance to the Sieur de Dinteville, Holbein's client of 1533 and the subject of a drawing in Windsor Castle dated 1537.

The heads are indeed similar, but the most characteristic feature, an unusual double-lidded look found in both the portrait of the ambassador and the drawing, is missing here. I therefore incline to the view represented in the catalogue of the Berlin museum: that the sitter is unknown and that stylistically this seems to be one of the last, possibly the very last, of Holbein's works.

Several years after the completion of the Gisze portrait, Holbein entered the atmosphere of the English court, as a result of the many commissions he was executing for members of the leading social circles around it. This new phase begins with the famous painting known as the *Two Ambassadors*. As a combination of portrait with significant attributes of still life, it is a continuation of Holbein's earlier style. From both paintings, created in 1532 and 1533, a clear line of development leads to the *Man with a Lute,* which impressively crowns the series of five Holbein portraits in Berlin.

Holbein's progress as a painter from the portrait of Gisze, with its mass of detail, to the simple grandeur of this Renaissance portrait, is astounding. It is as though the great conception of the art of portraiture, born in fifteenth-century Venice, had been in part absorbed, in part even foreseen by him (see the painting by Lorenzo Lotto, Pl. 86). Even though one must consider the Gisze portrait a high point of achievement, Holbein seems to have reached a new plane of integration as a painter in his *Man with a Lute.*

Structurally, the painting shows a masterly control of composition. The squareness of the panel demands perfect balance between the horizontal and vertical components. Holbein emphasizes this by making the horizontal line of the table, paralleling the bottom edge of the picture, the base of the composition. At a right angle to this the neck of the lute rises in a strict vertical—a slender upward movement to the right. The sitter's body is slightly turned, a motion underlined by the diagonal of the open notebook before him. The head appears in three-quarter profile, although the angle of the body and the sitter's gaze is not pronounced. The drawing of the two hands is nobly beautiful; the elegant indoor attire is perfect in its simplicity. The folds of the curtain intensify the vertical movement, continued from the upright lute by a tie that provides a rich fall of drapery.

The color scheme is in harmony with this clear, firm composition: the noble red against the background of delicately shaded green, the pale skin tones of the serious man who finds consolation in his lute.

Giovanni Bellini

THE ARTIST: Giovanni Bellini, son of Iacopo, half brother of Gentile, brother-in-law of Andrea Mantegna, is the most outstanding of the painting family that was the glory of Quattrocento Venetian art. Born about 1430 in Venice, he lived there until his death in 1516. His long life was matched by the slow development of an art that began in the manner of Mantegna, then in about 1475 digested the influence of Antonello da Messina, and, anticipating such masters as Giorgione, Titian, Palma Vecchio, and Sebastiano del Piombo, perfected itself in the style of the Cinquecento. Even Dürer, who wrote from Venice in 1506 that Bellini was still "the best of the painters," came under his influence. It is his sense of beauty that, in contrast to the austerity of Mantegna, gives his paintings their splendor, their luminosity, and their harmonious charm.

The great task of religious art, to transfigure the human into something having the appearance of the divine, was solved by no one in fifteenth-century Venice as perfectly as by Giovanni Bellini. His Madonnas are Venetian women of the people, with a simple shawl covering their dark hair and their slender, lovingly sheltering hands. Their maternity, tinged as it is with a premonition of grief, elevates them into timelessness.

VIRGIN WITH CHILD

Tempera on poplarwood. 67 × 49 cm.

PROVENANCE: *Done probably between 1455 and 1462. A similar painting may be found in the Museo Civico in Verona. Acquired with the Solly collection in 1821.*

53   Among the paintings by Bellini owned by the Berlin Gallery, the panel of the *Virgin with Child*—the child standing on a balustrade—is the earliest, painted probably soon after the half-century mark, when Bellini was still strongly under the influence of Mantegna. The character of the landscape suggests that the work was done in Padua, in Bellini's early phase, which was marked by realism and an interest in characterization. But the youthful artist is already entirely himself in the emotional depth of his conception, seen in Mary's musing downward glance, in the child's bright upward look toward the light, and above all—however many Madonnas were painted at the time—in the unique grouping of the four hands, those of the mother tenderly protective, those of the child playful.

The color composition, too, is distinctive: the dominant chord is the luminous carmine of the cloak over the brownish-red dress. Bellini here departs from the customary blue of Mary's cloak in the Quattrocento, probably for the sake of the sharp contrast of the red against the rich background, the bronzed greens of the landscape, and the deepening blues of the distance, the linear emphasis of which adds depth to the towering verticality of the foreground figures. One might suppose that Bellini, who some think may have been born in Padua, was here assimilating impressions of the place and time in which his art came to maturity.

THE RESURRECTION OF CHRIST

Transferred from wood to canvas. 148 × 128 cm.

PROVENANCE: *Painted about 1479 as the centerpiece of an altar for the Church of San Michele in Murano, near Venice. This work was first attributed to Cima da Conegliano and only later to Giovanni Bellini. It was acquired for Berlin from an Italian art dealer in 1903.*

If some art historians fail to see the hand of Bellini   78, 81, 82
in this work, this may be owing to his having had to execute a commission—with the details prescribed, as they often were—in a dramatic style that was not really in accord with his more lyrical bent. He fulfilled the task in the spirit of his father, Iacopo, and his brother, Gentile, both of whom loved telling a story in their pictures. At the same time, he tried to conceive the theme in the spirit of his brother-in-law, Mantegna, superior to himself in forcefulness and intensity as well as in humanistic classical learning. A certain perplexity reveals itself in his not only imitating Mantegna in the costumes and weapons of his soldiers, but also copying an etching by Mocetto for one of the guards.

Compositionally, the interrelationship of figures and space, at least for the principal figures, Christ and the soldiers, is not completely successful. But a certain unity is achieved by the use of colors, in the harmony of the sky at dawn with the luminous vision of the Resurrected and equally in that of the muted brown tones of the hills and rocks with the warm sheen of the atmosphere. Color and light are the decisive factors in the creation of this truly paschal picture of the Resurrection.

Of great effectiveness are the deep ultramarine of the upper sky and the consonance of blue, violet, red, and white in the garments of the three Marys approaching in the middle distance: a picture-within-a-picture in which Bellini's subjective power richly fulfills itself.

Vittore Carpaccio

THE ARTIST: Carpaccio was born, at the latest, about 1460 in Capodistria and is thought to have been the pupil of Lazzaro Sebastiani in Venice. In his art, especially in its narrative aspect, he continued the line of Bellini and proved his own epic gifts in cyclical series, loosening the strict forms of conventional Quattrocento mural painting and carrying the naive pleasure in storytelling into the sixteenth century. He died in Venice in 1525.

As the Quattrocento, comprising the first phase of the High Renaissance, was nearing its end, the painters were using the same religious themes to the point of exhaustion. In the case of an original, inventive artist like Carpaccio, one senses the special delight he took in treating new, or at least unhackneyed, themes, such as his scenes from the life of St. Stephen, one of which is in the Berlin gallery, and his versions of the Passion of Christ.

BURIAL OF CHRIST

Canvas. 145 × 185 cm.

PROVENANCE: *Painted during Carpaccio's late period. On the pedestal of the table there is an inscription, added later and false: "Andreas Mantinea f [ecit]." In the catalogue of the Canonici collection in Ferrara, published in 1627, the painting is ascribed to Mantegna because of the false inscription. It was purchased in 1905 and is the property of the Kaiser Friedrich Museum Association. For the iconography of the subject, compare the listing for No. 73 in the National Museum, Stockholm, in the catalogue of the Stockholm exhibition,* Konstens Venedig (The Art of Venice), *published 1962–1963.*

79, 80, 83   Instead of painting the burial of Christ in the usual way, Carpaccio depicted the events leading up to it and the preparations for it. The corpse, naked but for a loincloth, lies stretched out on a low, rather elaborate table in the foreground. Lying on a sheet, with a blue cloth under the head, the Crucified's exsanguinated body is brought into relief by a dark-blue cloak on the ground behind the table. Presumably this had covered the body as it was carried from Golgotha, discernible in the distance (the three crosses on the high hill, upper left). No one is near except the gravedigger—or, rather, in this place where bodies are buried in rocky caves aboveground, the guardian of the graves with his spade —who sits leaning against a tree. Two rocky caves close off the middle ground; this is where the graves opened to surrender their dead when the earth trembled and the rocks were rent at the hour Christ died on the cross.

At one of the crypts—to the left of the passage through the rock that allows a view of the distance—Nicodemus is engaged in opening "his own new grave, which he had ordered to be cut into the rock" for the Savior's body. Beside him, Joseph of Arimathea lifts up a basin he will use in washing the corpse. To emphasize the horrors of the burial ground and the sinister effect of the open graves, skulls are scattered about and a corpse stands rigidly upright beside an open crypt.

Carpaccio adds a second theme to that of the preparations for the burial, like that of Bellini in his *Resurrection* (Pl. 82): the mother approaching with John and the two other Marys, the mothers of James and John. Far behind them, alone in her grief, comes Mary Magdalen, carrying the jar of ointment with which she once annointed the feet of the Lord. The mother of Jesus has fainted in the arms of one of her companions. At the extreme right stands John, in pale red. His back is turned, and he has covered his head in anguish. The tree where the guardian of the crypt is sitting cuts the right side of the picture off; the onlooker's eye moves from John back to Mary Magdalen and beyond to a lake surrounded by rocky hills. As is often the case with Carpaccio, one sees in his landscape men on foot and on horseback. They are part of the scenery, not part of the story. Their Oriental costume expresses this painter's love of color and variety.

On the second level of rock in this picture so rich in detail, Carpaccio has introduced an unexpected motif, independent of the subject: an idyll of two shepherds whose goats are grazing on the scanty grass. Unconcerned with the ghastly scene below, one of them is blowing on his flute as he leans against a withered tree. It is a picture-within-a-picture that, seen by itself, would hardly be connected with the art of the early sixteenth century. One might think of Callot or of some *chinoiserie* of the eighteenth century. It is in this kind of timelessness that the painter's originality is revealed.

Giovanni Busi (Giovanni Cariani)
(Attribution)

THE ARTIST: Giovanni Cariani, next to whose name the catalogue of the Berlin museum puts a question mark in connection with this painting, was born in 1480, probably in Venice; his presence there, as well as in Bergamo, is documented until 1547.

Giorgione, Morto da Feltre, and Giulio Campagnola have also been suggested as possible creators of this work, for the style shows affinities with Giorgione's circle and therefore also with the manner of Campagnola. Another possibility is Sebastiano del Piombo in his early Venetian period. Sebastiano was born in 1485 in Venice; he was a pupil of Giovanni Bellini and was influenced by Giorgione. Once in Rome, he came under the influence of Raphael and, later on, of Michelangelo, and his style changed. He died in Rome in 1547.

WOMAN RESTING IN A LANDSCAPE WITH A WHITE LAPDOG

Canvas on wood. 74 × 94 cm.

PROVENANCE: *Painted about 1510. Transferred to the gallery from the royal-palace collections.*

This painting poses a double riddle: What does it **84** mean? Who is the painter? The relaxation of the woman reclining in the foreground and the events going on in the far-flung landscape behind her are in sharp contradiction. The lower foreground is occupied by the youthful, vigorous figure of a woman of a type we have seen in pictures by Giorgione and Titian. Even the little white Bolognese at her back is something out of Titian. The beauty's posture—her body half-raised on an elbow, one leg crossed over the other, and one hand on the raised knee—is one of repose, in marked contrast to the dramatic goings-on in the background.

At the far right, we see a city in flames; right center, a troup of Turkish lancers is galloping forward; on the left, a decaying castle and a domed building seem to be threatened by lightning from the thunderclouds above them.

There is a certain oddity in the structure of this landscape. From the row of flowers with two trees in the foreground, there seems to be no transition to the middle ground behind them; there are waterfalls at about the same level as the castle on the other side; a river flows through the center; a second castle rises near the bridge across the river. The horizon is higher in the center than it is behind the burning town. Despite this patchwork effect, however, the eye is led most effectively to a distant mountain range topped by clouds.

One is inclined to think that the picture must be based on a story well known to the artist's contemporaries—an account of the doings of knights and a lady or perhaps a tale of classical antiquity. A castle under a spell, a city destroyed, enemy troups, even the lady's coolness would all seem to be part of the story.

Even though we lack an explanation of the subject, the painting manages to make a strong statement. Fire, war, and storm threaten the earthly paradise, the crowning glory of which is the youthful beauty of the reclining woman in the foreground. Then, too, the painting may be saying: What good are youth and beauty when life is encircled by threats of war and other calamities? That this picture poses a riddle is not the least of its charms.

The riddle we should really like to solve, however, is the identity of the painter. The attribution to Cariani offers itself simply because we have no very clear conception of that artist. None of the works attributed to him has the melodic unity of painting and poetry to which this work owes its magic appeal. It seems to be closer to those mysterious pictures that are associated with Giorgione and his followers. This painter's touch and the type of female figure here shown, however, differ from the style of Giorgione, who tends to combine figure and space, man and nature, into far more of a unity.

Fortunately, one need not search too long in this collection (at present housed in the Dahlem Gallery in Berlin) to find a master associated with the great Venetian Sebastiano del Piombo, with whose work this may be profitably compared. For although the woman reclining before a threatened landscape must be an earlier work, the type of woman and the stylistic treatment show a certain resemblance to that artist's *Portrait of a Roman Woman*.

Sebastiano del Piombo was about seven years younger than Giorgione. He left Giovanni Bellini to study with Giorgione and worked so closely with his master and friend that he is said to have completed paintings that had been left unfinished at Giorgione's early death.

This reclining woman shows a striking similarity to those in Sebastiano's early works, especially in the modeling, which boldly subordinates the details to the whole, curves the lips outward, and gives plastic form to the chin. There is also a decided likeness to the so-called *Roman Woman* in the Berlin gallery, a somewhat later painting; but our *Woman Resting* is far closer to Sebastiano's early works. It is interesting to compare it with the Magdalen in the altarpiece of St. John Chrysostom in Venice, a well-known early work by this mercurial artist, created under the eye of Giorgione.

Pending further study, there is much justification for considering Sebastiano as the possible creator of this painting, even though the treatment of the landscape speaks more strongly for Cariani.

Cima da Conegliano

THE ARTIST: Cima da Conegliano occupies a notable place among the followers of Giovanni Bellini. He was born about 1460 in Conegliano, a town at the southern tip of the Alps, and lived in Venice from 1492 until shortly before his death. There he came under the influence of Vivarini and Mantegna, as can be deduced from internal evidence.

Cima's decided penchant for landscapes is clearly discernible in the backgrounds of his altarpieces and devotional paintings. It became more pronounced in the course of his further development, just as his paintings also gained a greater brilliance and freshness of coloring, thus coming closer to the style of the Cinquecento. The painter died in 1517 or 1518 in his native town, to which he had returned just a short time before.

Landscape as a primary subject of painting was discovered simultaneously on both sides of the Alps: by Dürer on his wanderings through the Tyrol, by Cranach and Altdorfer south of the Danube, by Joachim Patinir for the Netherlands, by the painters of Venice and Lombardy for Italy. The Alps played a major role in this development: the sculptural character of the mountains, the spaces of the valleys, the rocks and trees, the castles and high-perched mountain villages presented an irresistible challenge.

At first, landscape served as the background of religious paintings, replacing a flat golden ground that had come to be too confining to the Quattrocentists striving for a sense of space and depth in their pictures. But it was only very gradually that the landscape could be permitted to be an end in itself; almost always figures were added to give the picture a human content. In Venice, Giorgione was the first to create paintings in which the character of the landscape *was* the content.

COAST WITH TWO MEN FIGHTING

Poplarwood. 32 × 53 cm.

PROVENANCE: *Cima painted this picture about 1510. The mountains in the background greatly resemble those in his St. Jerome, in the Kress collection of the National Gallery in Washington, a fact of essential importance in the attribution to Cima of this painting, which has occasionally been claimed for Giorgione. (See Bernard Berenson,* Italian Pictures of the Renaissance: The Venetian School, *London, 1957. Originally published in 1894.)*

85   To do justice to the achievement of a landscape painting of the early sixteenth century, one must keep two things clearly in mind. First, the painter did not set up his easel out of doors, for a direct view of his subject, but created the picture in his workshop. Secondly, perhaps the power of imagination that stored up details and impressions culled from nature, to be re-created from memory, was greater then than it is in our time. One may assume that a painter like Cima da Conegliano occasionally also made sketches from nature. His backgrounds give the impression that certain scenes have been faithfully rendered. But his rocky mountains, piled high with fantastic castles, were invented for the sake of his composition. The painting in the Berlin gallery also shows the ordering hand of a conscious master of composition.

The landscape is the coastal stretch of a large body of water; the dueling scene, considering the presence of the gay flute player, must be considered as nothing more serious than a fencing lesson, the kind of thing that might have been part of the education of a hero like the young Roland.

Lorenzo Lotto

THE ARTIST: Lorenzo Lotto was born in 1480 in Venice. Whether he was a pupil of Giovanni Bellini or of Alvise Vivarini is still a subject of controversy. The many commissions he was asked to execute in Venice and Bergamo, in Treviso and The Marches, as well as in Rome (1508–1512), he owed to his excellent reputation as a painter of religious themes, especially of great altarpieces. He died in 1556 in Loreto.

Apart from his early altarpieces, done in the spirit of Giorgione, posterity has tended to value his portraits the most. Of the twenty-five or so portraits that are known to be by his hand, Berlin owns three especially good ones, which rival those of Holbein for clarity and naturalness.

Among the great artists whose birth dates so conspicuously cluster around the year 1480, Lorenzo Lotto cannot be ranked with stars of the first magnitude such as Giorgione, Titian, Raphael, and the German painters of this era from Dürer to Grünewald. But among those who succeeded in following the high aims of the Renais-

sance and fulfilling its striving for beauty and harmony, he has earned a place of distinction.

The Berlin gallery offers the opportunity to judge for oneself with what freedom and independence Lotto was able to profit by what he had learned from Bellini or Vivarini. It is important to remember that Vivarini was influenced by Antonello da Messina, who had done much, as a portrait painter and an admirer of Flemish and Dutch art, to shape the course of Italian painting, especially in Venice.

Lorenzo Lotto goes far beyond the Quattrocento. His altarpieces, in the spirit of the High Renaissance, show his striving for a great style. But his portraits most of all reveal his highly trained sense of form, especially what he had learned from the chiaroscuro of Leonardo and Correggio. Highly gifted, temperamental, and sensitive to impressions and influences that he could adapt to his own needs, Lotto excelled in one thing above all: the handling of light, and the mysterious way it plays upon bodies, as a basic stylistic device. Like Giorgione before him, he used gradations of light to give sculptural body and spatial variety to his portraits, without resorting to distracting details of perspective.

PORTRAIT OF A YOUNG MAN

Canvas. 47 × 37.5 cm.

PROVENANCE: *Signed on the balustrade at the right "L. Lotus pict." Painted about 1530. Acquired in 1815 from the Giustiniani collection in Paris. (See Bernard Berenson,* Lorenzo Lotto, *New York, 1955. Originally published in 1895.)*

With the genuinely painterly approach of a Venetian,   **86, 88** Lotto combines, in this portrait especially, a psychological tact not unexpected in someone of his sensitivity. It enables him to develop the form and content of his painting from the character of his subject. The intensity with which the subject's eyes regard the beholder is peculiar to Lotto, as are the formal interplay between eyes and temple, the vibration of the nostrils, the contrasting reds of lips and skin. The painter does not draw lines, but with a soft brush renders tonal values and transitions, intermediate shadings between dark and light, surrounding everything with that mysterious harmony of color such as only the Venetians seem to have been capable of.

Lorenzo Lotto likes to use a draped curtain as a colorful background for his heads. In this case, the luminous red curtain descending to a dark stone balustrade is slightly retracted to add depth and the suggestion of a statement about the subject. The slanted folds of the curtain allow a glimpse of the sea with some ships on it.

The ownership of merchant ships in Venice was a prerogative of the aristocracy; it follows that the sitter—sometimes supposed to be the painter himself, sometimes a man of Bergamo—was a Venetian nobleman. Since Lotto did not return to his native city until late in the

1520's, after many years of activity in Bergamo, this painting must have been made about 1530. It may be considered a result of the painter's contact with Titian, who considered Lotto worthy of his friendship.

A Master of Northern Italy

PORTRAIT OF A YOUNG MAN

Detail

Poplarwood. 32 × 26 cm.

PROVENANCE: *Painted at the end of the fifteenth century. From the collection of James Simon, who acquired this panel from a private owner in Vienna. Now in the museum storerooms.*

89   To gauge the achievement of the Italian Renaissance in the art of portraiture, the work of Lotto, which stands at its apex, is here juxtaposed to a portrait that follows the conventions of the Quattrocento as well as the type established for Venice by Antonello da Messina and Giovanni Bellini and represented by Solario in Milan. Though its size is exactly that of the two portraits by Antonello da Messina now in Berlin, it appears harder than these and yet sharper in its characterization, simpler and yet with more contrast in its coloring. The healthy brown skin tone is sharply set off by the blue background, with which the cinnabar-red coat forms a strong contrast. The painter here competes with the sculptor; but he lacks a spatial concept, so that the head seems to emerge without transition in relation to the body. The occasional supposition that this may be a portrait by one of the three masters named above is therefore unconvincing.

Giorgio Barbarelli (Giorgione)

THE ARTIST: Giorgione was born in 1478 in Castelfranco Veneto. Of the frescoes he created with Titian, we have only a vague idea; the number of paintings that indisputably bear his name is small. He died of the plague in Venice in 1510.

Giorgione is one of many masters who were born about 1480, a generation of decisive importance for the High Renaissance. He developed his art in Venice as a pupil of Giovanni Bellini and in close friendship with Titian. Considering how few are the works that can be attributed to him with any certainty, his far-reaching influence is all the more astonishing. He frequently heightens the emotional impact of his pictures by using landscape as a conscious accompaniment, and indeed it is sometimes the sole determinant of the rest. It is not by chance that Vasari praises his "musical" genius.

PORTRAIT OF A YOUNG MAN

Canvas. 58 × 46 cm.

PROVENANCE: *An inscription on the balustrade, "VV," has so far defied interpretation. The painting was in the Giustiniani collection in Padua and later went to Paris. It was acquired in Florence for Berlin in 1891.*

The fact that the sitter's eyes are looking straight at   **87** the beholder has led some to consider the painting a self-portrait, even though this is not the active, searching look into the mirror of the painter studying his appearence but is rather the quiet glance of the model at rest. We know how Giorgione looked from the *David* of the Brunswick Gallery, recognized by C. Müller-Hofstede as a self-portrait, and also from the woodcut accompanying Vasari's affectionate description of him: far more temperamental, with a passionate, tense expression and curly hair.

If one were to choose from among the many portraits in the Berlin museum a single painting in which the beginning of the High Renaissance is most impressively manifested, one would pick Giorgione's *Portrait of a Young Man.* Fiocco calls it, in his monograph dedicated to the master of Castelfranco Veneto, "the first modern portrait."

It is the inner freedom of this study of a young man that so directly appeals to the beholder. The great simplicity of the form is in perfect harmony with the emotional content. In contrast to the approach of the Quattrocento, this picture represents something complete in itself. There are no details: the painter's eye is on the whole, whereas Dürer, two decades later, still modeled the head of Hieronymus Holzschuher out of a combination of details (Pl. 59).

The artificially constructed balustrade (not shown in our reproduction) has a justifiable function: it serves as a resting place for the hand and so creates a break that enhances both the spatial and the sculptural effect. Both Titian and Sebastiano del Piombo adopted this device, which had been familiar to Antonello da Messina.

The noble spatial effect is emphasized by the coloring: the contrast between the dark-gray wall, somewhat lightened just behind the head in three-quarter profile, and the fine gradations of the lilac tones of the quilted coat is tender and lyrical. The abundant hair with its metallic sheen frames the healthy flesh tones of the handsome head with those large eyes and the still-youthful lips.

Titiana Vecellio (Titian)

THE ARTIST: That Titian was nearly a hundred when he died in 1576, is a legend that tries to express the miracle of his vitality. Today he is thought to have been born around 1490, which would make him about eighty-six at his death.

He was born in Pieve di Cadore, an Alpine mountain town. He came to Venice, where he was the pupil of Giovanni Bellini, and developed as an artist with his somewhat older friend Giorgione. He worked chiefly in Venice, but also occasionally elsewhere—for example, in 1511 in Padua, in 1545–1546 in Rome, in 1548 and 1550 in Augsburg—where he met Lucas Cranach—at the behest of Emperor Charles V, who considered him the greatest master of his time. From 1522 until his death, Titian regularly sent paintings to the Spanish court. According to Borghini, he died of old age while the plague was raging in Venice.

That visionary quality that raises Venice, of all the cities of the world, to a dream image above reality gained its perfect embodiment in the art of Titian. Although he did not paint the scenery of Venice, everything he created is Venetian in attitude and conception, intensity and transfigurative power: saints and Madonnas, before whom the Doge kneels in adoration; the ecstatic rise to the heavens of the Assumption *(Assunta)*; the reclining Venus with her thoughtful gaze; the tremor of Danäe; the glorification of manly dignity and womanly beauty in his portraits. The image of man serves Titian as the basis for his image of the divine, but his art also raises what is human to perfection and gives it a higher validity.

A DAUGHTER OF ROBERTO STROZZI

Canvas. 115 × 98 cm.

PROVENANCE: *Signed on the upper slab of the pedestal " Titianus f." and on a tablet on the wall, upper left, " Annor II. MDXLII."*
The daughter of Strozzi shown is probably Clarice, who married Christofano Savelli in 1557 and died in 1581.

90   Children were rarely painted by themselves in the sixteenth century; if a child appeared in a painting, he was usually with an adult. When, therefore, the noble and rich Florentine Roberto Strozzi, then living in Venice, commissioned a life-size portrait of his little daughter from Titian that was to be executed on a canvas more than a meter high and nearly a meter in width, it was an event that attracted much notice. Pietro Aretino wrote his friend Titian an enthusiastic letter about the "marvelous painting."

Titian fulfilled his unusual task not without humor. He painted the child as a future young lady. The graceful little girl is posed before a dark architectural background beside a pedestal showing a sculptured relief of two dancing *putti*. Behind her appears a wide landscape, over treetops and on to a distant mountain range. More than half of the background is composed of a dark wall setting off the luminous white-silk dress. The gaze of Clarice's intelligent dark eyes is slightly to the side,

corresponding to the slight twist of her curly head in the direction opposite to that of her body. The dainty jeweled belt, with the long chain ending in a golden ball that reaches nearly to the hem of the long dress, also testifies to the mobility of the temperamental child by its suggestion of a slight swing, as do the strong little hands, one of which is grasping the remains of a twisted bun, the other keeping a firm hold on the pet spaniel somewhat uneasily perched on the pedestal. The group forms a perfect triangle in the exact center of the picture, in accordance with all the rules of High Renaissance painting.

The charm of the portrait consists in the combination of the infantile quality with that of a personality already formed, as befits a descendant of two of the richest and most aristocratic families in Florence, the Strozzi and the Medici. The rivalry of these families, to be sure, had just then led to the banishment of the child's father from Florence. But the picture gives no hint of such upheavals in outward circumstances; what Titian succeeded in expressing was rather the happiness of a sheltered childhood.

VENUS WITH THE ORGAN PLAYER

Canvas. 115 × 210 cm.

PROVENANCE: *Signed at lower right " Titianus f." Purchased in 1918 from an art dealer in Vienna, with the help of private donations. Until 1914 the painting is said to have been in Italy, in the possession of a prince of the Spanish branch of the Orléans family. Related compositions: two at the Prado in Madrid, one at the Uffizi in Florence, and one in the United States.*

Reds and pinks, a nearby green and a distant blue, above three tones of white, with a sheen of gold and golden blond—such is the color harmony that seems to be rising out of the organ like a melody. This musical quality that pervades the visual imagery is the true Venetian element in this Venus, which was probably executed in Rome, if not in Augsburg.   91

When Titian painted it, he had found a style that permitted the fusion of the individual colors into a chromatic harmony of an essentially musical character. He strengthened this impression by including a portable organ, a so-called portative, such as came into use in the later Middle Ages. The diagonal placement of the row of pipes also aids in establishing perspective, which enhances the sculptural effect of the figures created by the illusion of space surrounding them.

The organist, an aristocratic gentleman with a short sword in his belt, has just finished playing, and while the last chords are still vibrating on the air, he has turned around to gaze at the naked beauty behind him. She is identified as Venus by the presence of the infant Cupid —she is wearing rich jewels as she reposes on red velvet, spread over the bed on the open loggia and draped behind the white pillow so as to form a rich background for the heads of mother and son.

The spaniel in the lower-right corner and the obvious resemblance of the boy—Cupid by virtue of his wings and a child of no more than three years—to the organist testify that this is a sufficiently realistic representation of a beautiful woman with her noble lover and their child in front of a familiar landscape, perhaps the Campagna—with a mythical-allegorical topdressing as a pretext.

The organist is generally thought to be Philip II of Spain, the son of Charles V. But he would have been about twenty when this painting was made, which conflicts with the apparent ages of father and child. It would seem more plausible to seek the model among the princely family of the Farnese. Pope Paul III, a scion of that family, had legitimized his natural son and made him, successively, Duke of Castro, of Parma, and of Piacenza; this son, Pier Luigi, was about twenty-seven at the time of this painting, which makes him a far more likely subject than Philip of Spain.

But of course the identity of the sitters matters little. This work of Titian owes its great significance to the perfection with which it captures the Renaissance ideal of beauty.

SELF-PORTRAIT

Canvas. 96 × 75 cm.

PROVENANCE: *Painted about 1560. Acquired with the Solly collection in 1821.*

93 Titian brought to perfection the concept of the artist as prototype of man the creator. This can be seen in the attitude and composition of this self-portrait, which shows the master at the height of his powers, although he had probably passed the seventy mark.

The painting is unfinished, but by this very fact it gains an impressionistic immediacy that captivates the beholder. The agile fingers of the right hand in their playful yet vigorous gesture, those fingers with which he created so many immortal works, are only sketched in. The left hand (not shown) expresses the dignity and pride of the man whom the Emperor, the ordinarily icy, lonely Charles V, deemed worthy of his friendship and made a count. Wound fourfold around his neck, the chain of knighthood glitters against the silky carmine red of his doublet.

The eye of the beholder is drawn to the face, seen in three-quarter profile, by lines of perspective, beginning with the position of the hands, and by the lines of the light-green drapery from the target of the model's glance to the far right. The chromatic composition also leads the eye through the reddish and dark tones to the face, set off by the white of the collar. The healthy skin tones are luminous above a full gray beard; the glance of the dark eyes moves diagonally in the direction of the composition, which determines the spatially and plastically suggestive effect of the painting. While the figure is pushed backward by the table in the foreground, the spatial effect of the background is achieved entirely through dark shading. This raises the picture into a visionary realm—it lets us surmise what titanic power animated the eyes of that greatest among the many luminaries of Venetian painting.

Jacopo Robusti (Tintoretto)

THE ARTIST: One generation younger than Titian, Tintoretto is considered to be, in the series of great Venetian painters, the last of the great masters of the Renaissance. Born in 1518, he was nicknamed Tintoretto (the Little Dyer) because he was the son of a dyer (*tintore*). He studied briefly, in 1539, with Titian, and an inscription above the door of his workshop bore witness to his allegiance to him as well as to Michelangelo: "*Il disegno di Michelangelo, il colorito di Tiziano*" ("The drawing of Michelangelo, the color of Titian"). Tintoretto formed his style independently, without leaving his native city, combining his personal stamp with a sense of the times that opened the gates to the art of the baroque. He died in 1594.

When he was asked which were his favorite colors, Tintoretto replied: "Only black and white." This is an amazing statement from so great a master of color as the painter of the brilliant murals in the Church of Madonna dell'Orto in Venice, the magnificent allegorical and mythological works in the Doges' Palace, the powerful cycle of the Sacred History in the Scuola di San Rocco. It becomes understandable, however, when one looks at the portrait of a patrician of Venice, masterly because of its extreme formal restraint, and strikingly small in format.

PORTRAIT OF AN OLD MAN (GIOVANNI MOROSINI)

Canvas. 58 × 44 cm.

PROVENANCE: *A late work, done about 1579. Purchased from an art dealer in England in 1908, having previously been in the Kilényi collection in Budapest.*

Apart from the gleaming golden yellow of the border **92** and the buttons, significant though they are in the composition, the effect of this painting is determined by black and white in combination with only one color: the red in the doublet and in the flesh tones. The intermediate flesh-color and gray tones subdue the colors; their somberness underlines the effect of solemnity so characteristic of Tintoretto's late works.

Contour and detail are not a matter of drawing, as in the case of Dürer's *Hieronymus Holzschuher,* which was painted a half century earlier. The head is not separated from the surrounding atmosphere, as in Dürer's portrait, which was built up line by line; instead, it is the air space between the painter and his subject, that is, as if it were included in the portrait. By this means, as well as by the sidelong fall of light in exact correspondence with the three-quarter turn of the head, but most especially by the softening of contours, Tintoretto achieved, with purely painterly devices that are nowhere linear, a kind of modeling that surpasses even the achievement of the greatest portraitist of Italian art, Titian. What is characteristic of Tintoretto is the sureness of his brushstroke, which aims, however, not at the pinning down of detail, but at the formation of the whole. The unusual composition gives the portrait an element of movement, reinforced by the diagonal leading from the edge of the coat to the brightest point in the picture, the bit of white collar. In contrast to the frontal composition of the Dürer portrait, this work thus shows a formal drive beyond the Renaissance to the baroque.

The sitter's gaze, from deep-set, dark-rimmed eyes, is fixed with great intensity upon the beholder. One might see in these eyes a burning anxiety over Venice, the Queen of the Adriatic, whose splendor was inevitably waning.

Yet it must be remembered that the painting was done in the decade that began with a glorious victory for Venice, then a great power whose fleet helped to defeat the Turks at Lepanto, staving off the threat to her domination over the eastern Mediterranean. Something of the strength of her resistance lives in the features of the sitter, who is thought to be Giovanni Morosini, a member of that old aristocratic Venetian family well known to historians. A phrase of Hugo von Hofmannsthal seems to have been coined for this Venetian: "The strength of patrician breeding lies in resistance."

Antonio Allegri (Correggio)

THE ARTIST: The master, who called himself Correggio after his birthplace, became the greatest painter of Parma. He was born in 1494, in Correggio, but he lived and worked in Parma from 1518, although he occasionally revisited his native town, where he died in 1534.

Because of Correggio, Parma may claim equal rank with the neighboring cities of Ferrara and Bologna as a seedbed of art. Correggio might be called the founder of illusionism because of his ceilings alone, on which the modeling with light and light-and-dark—Leonardo da Vinci's *sfumato*—opened new possibilities to art and prepared the way for the baroque.

LEDA AND THE SWAN

Canvas. 152 × 191 cm.

PROVENANCE: *The picture was painted about 1530, having been commissioned by Duke Federigo II of Mantua, who presented it to Emperor Charles V. In 1603, Count Khevenhüller bought it for Emperor Rudolf II, so that it went from Spain to the latter's favorite residence, Prague. There the Swedes picked it up as part of their loot at the end of the Thirty Years' War (1618–1648) and took it to Stockholm. Queen Christina brought it to Rome after her abdication and her conversion to Catholicism, It then went from hand to hand and so to the Prince Regent Philip of Orléans, whose bigoted son Louis cut it up in a fit of religious frenzy, destroying the head of Leda and of the servant next to her. Judging as best one can by the etching made before the painting was mutilated, this head of the Queen of Sparta, with its expression of surrender, may have been the most perfect example of Correggio's sensitive art. Charles Coypel, court painter and Inspector of the Prince Regent's Collections saved the picture from total destruction by hiding it in a chimney. He repaired the damage and repainted the two heads. From Coypel's estate the picture went into the Pasquier collection. In 1755 the Prussian ambassador bought it for King Frederick II of Prussia, who planned to exhibit it prominently in his Sans Souci gallery, which was completed in 1763.*

In 1830 it was transferred, with many other pictures, to the newly founded Berlin museum. There Schlesinger, a good restorer but an adherent of the Biedermeier style, again restored the head of Leda. It unfortunately turned out too large and with features not delicate and young enough. It seems that Schlesinger did not realize that there are two more representations of Leda in the painting, else he might have made his version more like the lovely head looking upward after the departing swan. The viewer must use his imagination to see the painting as it was originally. On the painting of Leda from the circle of Leonardo, of which only an old copy exists in the Galleria Borghese in Rome, there can be seen, besides Castor and Pollux, Helen and Clytemnestra, also a pair of twins, one of whom was sired by a god, the other by a man (Leda's husband, Tyndareus, King of Sparta).

The oneness of man and nature transfigured by beauty in the sense of Renaissance Neoplatonism, the ideal underlying the pantheistic mood of Correggio's depiction of the Leda myth, was translated into words by Goethe, who owned two copperplate engravings of the famous painting. His version, in the second part of *Faust,* is one of the most beautiful descriptions of a picture ever written: 94, 95

> Fair scenery!—Waters, moving
> In forest shadows: women there, undressing,
> The loveliest forms!—the picture is improving.
> One, marked by beauty, splendidly expressing
> Descent from Gods or high heroic races,
> Now dips her foot in the translucent shimmer:
> The living flame of her sweet form displaces
> The yielding crystal, cool around the swimmer.

But what a sound of wings! What rapid dashing
Across the glassy pool, what fluttering, splashing!
The maidens fly, alarmed; but only she
The queen, looks on, composed and terror-free
And sees with proud and womanly delight
The swan-prince press her knee with plumage white,
Importunately tame: he grows acquainted.—
But all at once floats up a vapor pale,
And covers with its closely-woven veil
The loveliest picture ever dreamed or painted.

Goethe grasped the essence of the nature myth in these words, spoken by his homunculus; nothing more beautiful can be said about Correggio's painting. Nevertheless, Goethe's description is wrong. The poet did not realize that Correggio painted not just one Leda and several of her servants, but presented her in three separate scenes, meant to depict a sequence of events: one showing the arrival of the god, shyly fended off by the courted young woman; another, her surrender; and last —perhaps the most beautiful of all—the moment in which she follows the departing swan with her eyes as she is about to slip into the garment held by the servant behind her—having tasted his love, fulfilled, yet with a hint of sorrow in her smile.

There are, in fact, four scenes, for at the left we see Leda's twin sons, the Dioscuri. One of them, probably Pollux, accompanies Amor's playing on the lyre with his flute; he is the immortal son of the god. His brother, Castor, is the mortal child of Leda's earthly husband, King Tyndareus of Sparta.

Correggio achieves his pictorial illusion by means of the light pouring over the bodies. But his canvases are not free of a certain slickness; he smoothed away every trace of his brushwork. Nevertheless, he fulfills in his painting what the subtle humanist Pietro Cardinal Bembo, Titian's friend, said about love: "When it encounters a well-formed face," it creates the highest perfection by means of light and shade and "pure line."

"Correggio arouses, knows, and paints the most delicate stirrings of the nerves." With these words did Jacob Burckhardt characterize the art of Correggio in his *Cicerone*. But there is one aspect of it that has not been fully appreciated until quite recently: in his treatment of a landscape, of trees for example, the mysterious play of light in the shifting darks and lights of the foliage—the gradations of his distances, and the transparency of his skies—he exhibited a perception of nature that was centuries ahead of his time.

Francesco di Cristofano Bigi (Franciabigio)

THE ARTIST: Franciabigio is yet another of the distinguished generation of 1480, the shapers of the High Renaissance. But he is less an original creator than a gifted synthesizer. At first he was a pupil of Mariotto Albertinelli and perhaps, briefly, of Piero di Cosimo. His crucial relationship was with Andrea del Sarto, whose assistant and friend he became. His Madonnas are reminiscent of those of Raphael. While he shows little independence in his religious paintings, his portraits gain a certain originality from his adaptation to them of the High Renaissance style. He lived and worked in Florence, where he died in 1525.

The ripe achievement of the art of Florence, as it was absorbed by Francesco di Cristofano Bigi, called Franciabigio, who was born in that flowering city in 1482, is contained in the conception and the composition of the portrait of a young humanist that he completed on October 24, 1522. Only a year older than Raphael, Franciabigio profited by all the influences that Raphael, too, put to his own uses when he came to Florence in 1504.

PORTRAIT OF A YOUNG MAN

Poplarwood. 78 × 61 cm.

PROVENANCE: *Signed "FRA CR" (for Francesco di Cristofano). Dated October 24, 1522. In 1829, one year before the Berlin museum was opened, this painting was purchased through the mediation of Herr von Rumohr.*

It is unimportant that the arrangement of the details in the picture is quite arbitrary. To indicate the sitter's literary activity, the painter has included a table with a lectern, an open book, an inkwell, and a little note showing his signature and the date of completion. But he moved the desk to the side at a right angle; it is merely a prop and does not represent, as in Holbein's Gisze portrait, any spatial reality. The landscape in the back, a bit of Tuscany with a house toward which two tiny figures are moving, is also only a stage set.

This defiance of realism is justified by the exigencies of spatial composition. It also makes possible an effective arrangement of the hands, the one in the act of writing with a goose quill, the other with a signet ring on the index finger. The right hand is active, the left at rest, just as the grave visage, facing almost fully forward, is divided into an illuminated and a dark half. The black mantle over the tightly pleated white shirt adds to the solemn mood of the painting, which is composed in planes rather than in three-dimensional space—a mood in which contrasts are turned into harmonies, as in the attitude and expression of the model. The subject is thought to have been Matteo Solferoni, the young humanist who was a friend of Franciabigio.

A comparison of this portrait with Bronzino's portrait of the young humanist Ugolino Martelli, also in the Berlin gallery (Pl. 97) but painted almost two decades later, is tempting: in the case of Andrea del Sarto's pupil, the Renaissance is reaching a point of perfection; in that of Pontormo's disciple, while there is a greater clarity in spatial composition, the work evinces the chilliness with which mannerism began in Florence.

Agnolo di Cosimo di Mariano (Bronzino)

THE ARTIST: Agnolo Allori, called Bronzino, was born in 1503 in Florence. With the exception of a brief period of work on behalf of the Carthusian monastery of Val d'Ema and another with his friend and teacher Pontormo in Urbino in 1530, he worked in Florence, where the Medici Grand Duke Cosimo I had appointed him court painter. His task, which accorded well with his own inclination toward courtly distinction in subject and style, was to paint representative portraits of the Grand Duke and his spouse, the coldly beautiful Eleonor of Toledo.

As a leading member of the academy that was founded in Florence in 1561, Bronzino stands for the formal, aristocratic style of the Florentine late Renaissance, when it had already frozen into mannerism. He died in Florence in 1572.

"The times keep changing, and we change with them." These words of Ovid are illustrated by the further development of the Renaissance soon after the death of Raphael and Leonardo—superficially, a further elaboration of its ideals; in reality, an accelerating decline from the heights of its achievement. The now dominant mood has been termed "mannerism" by the art historians of our day.

A master like Bronzino appears to be fulfilling in his work the ideas that Count Baldassare Castiglione outlined in *The Courtier,* based upon the aesthetics of Plato. The portraits of the first half of Bronzino's career—until approximately 1540—therefore depict personages who might have exemplified Castiglione's definition of the perfect nobleman: the Duke of Urbino and all the noble lords and ladies as they look down upon the visitor from the walls of the Uffizi and the Pitti galleries. In accordance with Castiglione's prescription for the representational portrait, a book generally appears in one hand, to indicate the sitter's intellectual leanings.

PORTRAIT OF UGOLINO MARTELLI

Poplarwood. 102 × 85 cm.

PROVENANCE: *Painted about 1540. The painting went from the Palazzo Martelli to the Palazzo Strozzi in Florence, then to the Berlin museums in 1878.*

97   One of these early portraits by Bronzino is that of Ugolino Martelli, with its significant detail. The sitter was a member of an aristocratic Florentine family who lived next door to the town palace of the Medici, where a street still bears the name Martelli. The architectural background of the picture is part of a palace in the noble style of the Florentine Renaissance, thought to be the work of Domenico d'Agnolo. On a handsome pedestal in the background stands the *David* of Donatello, a preliminary study for which is in Berlin, while the original is in the Widener collection of the National Gallery in Washington. Donatello's statue shows the shepherd boy in a short, sleeveless tunic; his left foot is set on the head of Goliath—a symbolic gesture of liberation highly popular in Florentine art. When Bronzino's picture was painted, this symbol had of course quite lost its relevance to current reality: the Medici were ruling Tuscany with tyrannical cruelty.

It would seem that the young Ugolino Martelli had given exact instructions on how and with what props he should be represented. That he knew Greek is demonstrated by his right hand resting on the open pages of Homer's *Iliad,* Book IX, where the subject is the wrath of Achilles. While the Homer indicates his classical learning, the book serving as a support to Ugolino's left hand, the author of which was the humanist and churchman Pietro Bembo, shows his awareness of the current literature of distinction. Every inch a scholar and a gentleman, he sits bolt upright at the table, his intelligent eyes, in the unusually tight casing of their lids, gazing thoughtfully into the distance as though musing upon his reading.

We know of Ugolino Martelli (1519–1592) that he lived entirely for his learned pursuits and once wrote a treatise on an ode by Horace (IV, 3). He eventually took Holy Orders and received, probably more as a benefice than as a sphere of activity, the bishopric of Grandèves in southern France.

The young scholar's age at the time of this portrait has frequently been estimated as sixteen or so. But there is, in the great Kress collection in Washington, another, much simpler portrait of him done by Bronzino's teacher and friend Pontormo. This shows Ugolino a few years earlier, portrayed as a young cavalier with a plumed beret. The pure, almost boyish lineaments and dreamy expression of this face appear quite changed in the Bronzino portrait into those of a mature consciousness. There must have been several years between the two portraits, which would make the age of the sitter in the Berlin picture about twenty. Its date is therefore probably about 1540, when, following the murder of a reigning though illegitimate Medici, Cosimo I made himself Duke of Florence—the man who subsequently appointed Bronzino as his court painter.

Michelangelo da Caravaggio

THE ARTIST: His surname was actually Merisi, but he adopted the name of the place where he was born, in

1573, a town located between Milan and Bergamo. He began his apprenticeship at the age of twelve in Milan and in 1590 went to Rome, where his gifts were soon recognized. But he had great difficulties even there, for his uncompromising sense of reality brought him into conflicts with the representatives of mannerism. His passionate temperament repeatedly got him into trouble; he once killed an opponent in a duel and had to flee to Naples. From Naples he went to Malta, where in 1608 he was made a knight of the Maltese Order. But he soon found himself in hot water again and fled to Sicily. There he painted altarpieces for Messina, Palermo, and Syracuse. On his return journey to Rome, he was mortally wounded in an assault by bandits near Naples and died of a fever in 1610.

Despite the storminess of his life, Caravaggio brought decisive new impulses to the development of art in the seventeenth century through the boldness and directness of his realism and the form-giving power of his chiaroscuro. As leader of the chiaroscuro painters, the so-called Tenebrosi, Caravaggio decisively influenced both Italian and Dutch artists. Of those who followed his example, only one may be considered his peer—Rubens.

Out of the conventions of the High Renaissance, mannerism had developed. The painters who admired this style approached their subjects with predetermined formal objectives instead of seeking an intensification of reality in the work of art. A master of Caravaggio's stature felt this to be a diminution of his possibilities, a bloodless abstractionism that ran counter to his powerful, almost violent realism. The saints and gods he created were seen as realities; the expressiveness of their glance and gesture, the light that irrupted into the dark heightened the sculptural effect and intensified the reality that it simultaneously transfigured.

THE HOLY FAMILY

Canvas. 105 × 82 cm.

PROVENANCE: *From the early period, about 1590. An old copy is in a museum at Tours. Acquired in the art market, 1923.*

98, 99 Of the three works by Caravaggio in Berlin, *The Holy Family* shows both his realism and its intensification by means of light as a transfiguring element. Opinions differ as to whether this is an original or a copy, yet it must be taken into account as an essential link in his life's work. Besides, there is nothing in this canvas with its boldly contrasting elements, that suggests a hand other than the artist's own. One of the principal characteristics of Caravaggio's art, his way of making the figures seem to be moving forward out of their frame because of the intensity of his lighting and modeling, is here brought to perfection.

The spatial composition shows three planes: in the foreground there is the infant John in front of the balustrade, behind which, in the middle plane, towers the group of mother and child, behind whom, third and last, Joseph bends forward, his hands reaching out to suggest a wide, sheltering embrace of the others.

The child is unusually large; the glowing color in which he is painted determines the dominant effect of the picture. Mother and son are clinging to each other; the sense of their tender intimacy is enhanced by the fact that the infant Jesus has his arms around her neck. This is no Madonna of unruffled beauty, as mannerism demanded; there is a premonition of tragedy in that face, and the child's embrace seems protective. This gesture—both formally as a horizontal element of balance and emotionally—is an innovation in paintings of the Madonna with the child and must have mattered a great deal to the artist, for he reinforces its impact by paralleling the movement in the right arm of John along the balustrade which is grasped, as though in need of support, by the left hand of Mary. The expressiveness of the hands, revealing the inner tensions, is a characteristic trait of Caravaggio's art. The head of the young Italian woman who appears here as the Madonna is familiar from other paintings of his: she appears as the lamenting Magdalen in the *Burial of Christ* in the Vatican, as St. Catharine in the Caravaggio in the Thyssen collection in Lugano, as Judith in his Casa Coppi painting in Rome. The Berlin canvas is considered an early work of the master, who lived to be only thirty-seven.

LOVE TRIUMPHANT

Canvas. 154 × 110 cm.

PROVENANCE: *Painted as commissioned by the collector Giustiniani. Acquired with the Giustiniani collection in 1815.*

100, 101 In *Love Triumphant*, the art of Caravaggio appears at first as pure realism, designed to reproduce faithfully the body, the instruments, the textures. One finds it hard to credit this knowing boy, who has such a strong young body and those almost too real belly folds, with the wings of a god. But the plumage is so marvelously painted that it carries its own conviction of reality, a reality no painter had ever before succeeded in bringing to any angel or Cupid.

Caravaggio painted this picture during the transition from the sixteenth to the seventeenth century, from Renaissance to baroque, for his patron, the art lover and collector Giustiniani in Rome.

At about the same time, a *Conquest of Divine Love over Earthly Love* was painted by a rival of Caravaggio, Giovanni Baglioni. Both pictures can be seen in the same room of the Dahlem museum in Berlin. Baglioni's "opposition" painting bore the name of Caravaggio as late as 1904, when it was installed in the Kaiser Friedrich Museum. As artist, the conqueror is Caravaggio. He succeeded through his realism, which he had developed to the peak of perfection, and above all through his ability, exceeded by none, to achieve sculptural tangibility and spatial depth by means of strongly contrasting darks and lights. This realism, which conquered the euphuistic pose of mannerism, led to a new departure in painting: *verismo* with chiaroscuro. Unlike many a more superficial observer, Goethe recognized in the realism of this painting a certain demonism. He visited the Giustiniani collection several times during his stay in Rome, and had access to the city's other collections. A principal work in the collection, Caravaggio's painting hung at the end of a long exhibition hall in such a way that it could be seen through a series of rooms. The impression may have worked on Goethe, consciously or not, and led him to write the following poem:

Cupid, you loose-living, headstrong fellow!
You begged me for only a few hours' shelter.
How many days and nights you have stayed on now!
You give the orders, master in my own house!

You have driven me from my own wide bed,
I sit upon the ground all night, tormented;
Your wantoness stirs flame after flame on the hearth,
Eats up my winter's hoard, sears my poor skin.

My instruments you've tumbled helter-skelter,
I search for them as though grown blind, half crazy.
You make such a disturbance; I fear that my darling
Will run away frightened, and leave me alone in this
shack.

Although the poem takes a graceful turn at the end, with a plea for the continued presence of the beloved, the poet has expressed his intuition regarding the deeper meaning of this outwardly playful painting—a meaning, moreover, very much in tune with Caravaggio's character: that love is wantonly destructive.

Georges de La Tour

THE ARTIST: Like Poussin and Louis Le Nain, Georges de La Tour was born in 1593, in Vic-sur-Seille, near Nancy. He settled down in Lunéville in 1620. King Louis XIII, who owned his painting of St. Sebastian, conferred on him the title Peintre Ordinair du Roi. Little else is known about his life; he died in 1652, the victim of an epidemic. In age he stands between Rubens and Rembrandt. The chiaroscuro of his painting shows an affinity to masters such as Caravaggio.

The artist lived in Lorraine at a time when plague, war, and conquest by France ravaged his native country. For a long time, his name was quite forgotten. When one of his few extant pictures occasionally attracted attention as a work of art, it was baptised "Caravaggio" or "Le Nain" or even "Gerard van Honthorst." He was rediscovered, but not until 1915, by Hermann Voss. Since then he has been esteemed as a great painter of the Velázquez-Rubens-Rembrandt era.

ST. SEBASTIAN MOURNED BY ST. IRENE AND HER LADIES

Canvas. 160 × 129 cm.

PROVENANCE: *In about 1631, in a time of war and pestilence, La Tour created two paintings of St. Sebastian, who is considered the guardian saint against pestilence. The painting simultaneously served to celebrate St. Irene, whose name signifies "peace." One of these pictures—we do not know which one—was painted for Duke Charles IV of Lorraine, who lost his domain to the French in 1632. The second was purchased by King Louis XIII of France, who was spending a few weeks in Nancy, having just won it by conquest. The King so valued this work that he banished all other paintings from his chamber in order to leave himself entirely under its spell. The painting in Berlin came as a gift of the Matthiesen Gallery in 1928. Art historians generally consider this the original, the one in Broglie the replica. Moreover, this painting is the higher by a few centimeters, showing even more clearly that Sebastian has been found tied to a tree, the place of his martyrdom. A final decision as to which of the two pictures is the original cannot be made until all La Tour's works can be brought together in a single exhibition, to make comparison possible.*

In the light shed by the torch's white flame, we see four women approaching the scene of martyrdom (archers had executed Sebastian at the order of the Emperor Diocletian). The light separates the bright and dark colors in mysteriously intensified and yet restrained harmonies. The sharp shadow of the arrow falls across the youthfully handsome body of the saint beneath the tree of his martyrdom, so that the beholder shudders to think of the tortures suffered by the young captain of the Praetorian Guard who would not abjure his Christian faith. **102, 103 104, 105**

Pain and grief are most movingly expressed by the figures of the women. The torchbearer, whose red dress gives the picture its dominant note of color, looks sorrowfully down on Sebastian as she lifts his arm with a delicate gesture. The principal figure is St. Irene, who has sunk to her knees and, recognizing that life has not entirely left his body, holds out both hands with an expression of grief mingled with hope. Behind her are two more women: one in dark garments, so that only her prayerfully folded hands and bent head can be seen; the other, in the light of the torch, hiding her weeping face in a white kerchief.

The painter apparently followed the familiar legend that Sebastian was not killed by the arrows but was saved by St. Irene. It is said that he later appeared once more before the Emperor and avowed his faith again, whereupon he was beaten to death and his body cast into a deep pit which, according to one interpretation, is visible in this picture.

In keeping with his strong sense of form La Tour did not merely retell the story; he gave it embodiment. He captured, in plastic terms, grief and tender concern in a way done before him only in paintings of the burial of Christ. He knew how to vary the expressive gestures of the rescuing women above the uplifted hand of the apparently dead man to deeply moving effect.

The artist struggled with this subject twice. In the picture in the museum in Rouen, he showed Sebastian being cared for in the house of Irene; the light from a lantern falling on her, she is seen drawing the arrow from the martyr's body. This picture is almost too dependent on its single central source of light.

In the second treatment, seen in the Berlin painting and in a smaller version in the little church at Broglie, the artist gave expression to more than a single motif. The work brings together a number of elements, expressing his subject by "transition" from one to the other, as the baroque preferred it. It is interesting to note that the diagonal structure of the composition bears a resemblance to Caravaggio's *Burial of Christ* in the Vatican gallery in Rome.

Joachim de Patinir

THE ARTIST: Patinir war born about 1485 in Dinant near Lüttich. Some think he was born in Bovines, on the other side of the Maas River. But his family at least must be from Dinant, since he called himself Dionatensis. The principal scene of his activity was Antwerp, where he was made a member of the painters' guild in 1515. Widowed early, he married again in 1521—a wedding attended by Albrecht Dürer as guest of honor. Patinir's fame rests on the fact that he made landscape an independent subject in the art of the Netherlands. He died in 1524 in Antwerp.

When Dürer was in Antwerp in 1521, much honored and feted, he wrote in his diary for May 5: "The Sunday before Holy Week Master Joachim, the good landscape painter, invited me to his wedding and did me honor in every way."

In this diary entry, the phrase "landscape painter" is used for the first time as the designation of a special genre; with it, the importance of Joachim de Patinir is defined. It is true that landscape had meant a great deal before this, in the paintings of Gerard David and Hieronymus Bosch—both of whom had decisively influenced Patinir—but still only as a background or setting for religious subjects. Dürer and the masters of the Danube school had also painted landscapes in aquarelle or on small panels, but only Patinir had made himself a specialist in this field. He did "justify" his landscapes by including some elements of religious legend in them, but his chief concern was nature itself.

If Patinir's pictures nevertheless seem far more old-fashioned than, for example, the landscape aquarelles of Dürer and the paintings of forest scenes by Altdorfer, there is a reason: Patinir does not paint an impression of a specific landscape, but builds his landscapes up with painstakingly exact details, ending up with a composition seen from two perspectives—his distance and horizontal strata are seen from above, his rocks, buildings, and trees from below. The viewer's eye sees the entire landscape from above, but sees the details as if in direct confrontation with them on the ground. Patinir successfully combines the great mass and variety of details into a harmonious whole.

REST ON THE FLIGHT TO EGYPT

Oak panel. 62 × 78 cm.

PROVENANCE: *Purchased in 1821 with the Solly collection.*

The painter's naive approach, which gives him a vast expanse of space well filled with detail, and his delight in storytelling, blending scene and events together, combine to make this *Rest on the Flight to Egypt* a richly colorful gem. The center of the landscape is dominated by a hollowed out mountain of rock, with a fantastic circular structure, among others, nestling in its rent core. The towering jagged rocks, crowned here and there with castle-like buildings, are a recurrent motif, for such formations were familiar to the painter from his homeland, the upper Maas River region. Water, too, figures importantly in the scene, especially in the right half of the picture, where a wide river leads to a distant city, possibly Jerusalem, which was only two hours by road from Bethlehem. Bethlehem, in the middle distance, is clearly identified by the mill above it, a reminder that *béthlekhem* in Hebrew means "house of bread," and by the tiny figures enacting the Slaughter of the Innocents (a picture-within-a-picture done by the painter as miniaturist).

On the left, surrounded by more modest houses, stands a castle—David, the future King, was born in Bethlehem, which is significant in view of the prophecy of the Savior's birth. On the gently curving road, we see Joseph, followed by his donkey.

The landscape with its abundant detail, done partly in the style of a Gobelin, partly in that of miniature painting, serves as background for the group of mother and child, the apparent subject of the painting. In contrast to the deep greens of the foreground and the dark grays of the rocks, the jewel-like colors of enamel painting are gleaming here. The carmine of the cloak, the blue of the dress, the iridescent lining, the gleaming white of the coif, and the delicate flesh tones combine into an effect of such sumptuousness that it draws the viewer's attention to this little group as the main focus of the painting. A mass of narrative details "caption" the scene here as well: the covered basket, a familiar prop in the pictures of Patinir; the kettle on the fire; the little bird on the bare branch whose song the infant joyfully attends while Mary's hand seems most gracefully to follow its beat—it is as if she had just told the child to listen. The little bird on the basket, as well as the spring

106, 107
108

220

that, according to legend, gushed forth at the place of rest, shows that the figures are more than just props. Though it is known that Patinir occasionally let other painters, such as his friend Quentin Massys, paint figures into his landscapes, the ones shown here appear to be so well integrated into the entire composition that one would be most reluctant to accept the view of some critics that another painter added this pleasing little group as an afterthought.

Adam Elsheimer

THE ARTIST: Elsheimer was born in 1578 in Frankfurt am Main. He was trained in Italy, at first in Venice, then in Rome, where he died in 1610, at thirty-two. In small paintings done mostly on copper, he satisfied the seventeenth-century liking for landscapes as idyllic images of nature.

Adam Elsheimer was a landscape painter by nature. As such he stands at the beginning of the great development of seventeenth-century landscape painting. In the Rome of the early Settecento, his landscapes, so modest in size, can be said to have been revolutionary in effect, not least upon the Netherlanders, who were seeking new ways in art in Italy. Rubens, who was his friend, wrote under the impact of Elsheimer's early death: "In my opinion there was no one to equal him in the painting of smaller figures and landscapes."

LANDSCAPE WITH PENITENT MAGDALEN

Copper. 18.5 × 24.3 cm.

PROVENANCE: *Gift to the gallery from Frieda Hinze, Berlin, in 1926.*

109   As the painting in Berlin shows, the religious or mythological motif was to this German-Roman painter only a pretext for yielding to the new and unprecedented demand for landscape paintings. This had been true even of Patinir (Pls. 106–108), who followed similar paths in Antwerp almost a century earlier.

Painted on copper, like most of Elsheimer's pictures— he was also an etcher—his landscape with the penitent Magdalen shows the master's style in his handling of perspective, the way he achieves a sense of depth by the gradual progression of increasingly more delicate tones. The foreground with its towering tree trunks arrests the eye at the left, whence it travels over the tops of the trees in the center and far beyond into the distance.

The Magdalen, however, kneeling before the skull and crucifix, seems alien to the picture, and this is the reason that occasional doubts are expressed regarding the attribution of the singularly beautiful landscape to the Ro-

man painter from Frankfurt, Germany. However, the picture, small as it is, shows a scale of conception of which anyone other than Adam Elsheimer was hardly capable at the start of the seventeenth century.

Pieter Brueghel The Elder

THE ARTIST: Born about 1525 in Brueghel, near Breda, Holland, Pieter Brueghel the Elder seems to have begun his apprenticeship in 's Hertogenbosch, the native town of Hieronymus Bosch, whose art decisively influenced his own. His subsequent training was received in the Antwerp studio of Pieter Coeck van Aelst, whose daughter he married. After his master's death, he went on to work with Hieronymus Cock, and himself became a master of the painters' guild in Antwerp in 1551. Soon thereafter, in 1553, he journeyed to Italy but returned to Antwerp after a time; he died in 1569 in Brussels, where he had been working since 1563. He is the founding father of the well-known family of painters and was nicknamed the Peasant Brueghel because of the subjects of his pictures, a designation that also suggests the folk themes and the new social element in his art. He differs from Bosch in being a humorist rather than an obsessed accuser. The weaknesses of humanity offer the artist such a splendid variety of subjects, far less oppressive and more charming than the virtues. And so the Peasant Brueghel became a forerunner of the seventeenth century and an originator of modern genre painting.

"The last of the primitives, the first of the moderns," is the way Pieter Brueghel the Elder and his position in the evolution of Western art have been characterized. His relationship to Hieronymus Bosch and his paintings of the months and seasons, adapted from the tiny illuminations of the Book of Hours to works of monumental size and splendor, link him to the art of the Middle Ages. He inaugurated the realism of the seventeenth century, and his work is of great significance, especially for the development of landscape painting.

Brueghel, not only stands at the crossroads of time but also opposes the fashionable manner of his own period, in which the Netherlanders had yielded to Italian influence to the point of surrendering their own individuality. He resisted the "Romanism" that sapped the art of his country of its originality, though it justified itself to some degree in becoming one of the sources of inspiration for the work of Rubens.

THE DUTCH PROVERBS

Oakwood. 117 × 163 cm.

PROVENANCE: *Signed at lower right "Brvegel · 1560." Acquired from a private owner in England in 1914. A replica is in the museum at Haarlem.*

Brueghel used his talent for characterization to capture the typical rather than the individual, and his choice of themes in *The Dutch Proverbs* is an excellent example of this aspect of his art. More than a hundred folk sayings capable of being stated pictorially—not all proverbs, more often figures of speech—are here crowded into a single canvas. With great sophistication in its formal structure, the work presents an appearance of folk naiveté, liking it to those artless cartoons used by street balladeers at county fairs to illustrate the moral tales they sang in doggerel as they pointed with a long stick to the picture accompanying each stanza.

In the attic window at the upper left, for example, a man is "looking through his fingers"—that is, he meets provocation (symbolized by the knife hanging by a cord) by pretending not to see it. The pair of wooden shoes on the same windowsill illustrates another popular expression: "He stands on wooden shoes," meaning that he is waiting in vain.

Brueghel's ability to combine a profusion of detail into a unified whole evidently owes a great deal to Bosch. Formal devices, such as the diagonal moving the beholder's eye from bottom left to the sailboat in the upper-right-hand corner, account for much of his success. Beginning with the maid trussing up the Devil, the eye moves to the man banging his head against a wall, the sheep shearing, the gossiping women, the wife "putting a blue cloak on" (cuckolding) her husband, the pig with a knife in its belly, the foxy fellow who catches fish with his bare hands, the man aggrieved because the sun shines on the water, the monk who hangs his habit on the fence (*i.e.*, abandons his vocation), the hungry man watching the dancing bears, until we finally reach, in the sailboat, an illustration of a genuine proverb: "it is easy to sail with the wind."

Above the diagonal there is a staggered arrangement of buildings and fields. At the left one sees the typical Flemish house with sloping roof on which the "pancakes" grow; in front of it is the little temple where someone "lights a candle to the Devil and confesses to him"; beyond this a pillory illustrates the expression "to toy with the pillory"; then there is the city gate with the man who falls "from the ox to the donkey"; and on the tower sits the "climber" who "hangs his coat into the wind" (the turncoat). Finally there is another tiny group showing "the blind leading the blind."

Underneath the diagonal, many kinds of human folly are illustrated. At bottom center there is a man who "covers the well after the calf has drowned in it" (the same fellow who locks the barn door after the horse is stolen.—Tr.); behind him a man is casting roses (pearls) before swine; in front of the low hut sits Christ, and a man kneeling to him "hangs a flaxen beard on him." Behind the man who "catches an eel by the tail," another proverb is illustrated in the hut with a roof of wooden slats: "The pitcher that goes to the well once too often." To the right of this is a man "cutting wide straps from other people's leather."

One can wander thus from scene to scene—sometimes confused by the overlapping of figures and groupings, sometimes lured on from one to the other—in this garden of folk wisdom and folly presented by the Peasant Brueghel in his characteristic folk manner.

Johann Liss

THE ARTIST: Johann Liss, called Pan, was born around 1590 in Oldenburg, north of Lübeck, Schleswig-Holstein, Germany. His early work was decisively influenced by his stay in the Netherlands. He lived in Amsterdam from 1615 to 1618, but he undoubtedly had seen the work of Jacob Jordaens of Antwerp, who was of the same age as himself. He went from Holland to Paris and Italy. In Rome he came under the influence of Caravaggio, and about 1620 he settled in Venice, where he died in 1629.

Like Elsheimer, Liss is one of the most gifted German painters of the early seventeenth century, and in his art he is even closer to the Italian masters. As one of the leading masters of the baroque, he influenced Tiepolo by the bold monumentality of his Venetian compositions.

SATYR WITH A PEASANT FAMILY

Canvas. 120 × 184 cm.

PROVENANCE: *Acquired in 1963 from the Kaiser Friedrich Museum Association with the aid of a donation from the Berlin Lottery.*
Liss often did more than one version of a painting; of this one, too, there is a replica in Washington. K. Steinbart authenticated both as originals in his last publication, which was devoted to Johann Liss.

The story behind this painting concerns a satyr who **114,115** was invited into a peasant's hut after the peasant had seen the creature marveling at the way the man was warming his hands by blowing into them. Now the satyr sees the man cooling his soup by blowing on it. He can't understand this; it looks like black magic to him. He leaps up to escape from the domicile of such a sorcerer. This is the moment captured by the painter. At the low table sits the peasant, blowing on the hot liquid in the spoon. The peasant's wife, her youngest child in her arms, regards the frightened satyr with amusement; behind him an older son peers out.

The painter is clearly interested in the forceful movement and countermovement of the figures so characteristic of the baroque style. Peasant and satyr are contrasted in two bold diagonals. The peasant's smock, with its dark gathers, is as much an exhibition of painterly virtuosity as is the nude study of the satyr. Here, incidentally, the painter gives himself away: he must have used as a model for the satyr a Roman fisherman or the like whose head, neck, and hands were sunburned but whose body was pale. A "genuine" satyr would have been tanned all over. The picture also reveals a great deal about Liss's progress as a northern German who received his early training in the Netherlands but then, modeling himself upon Caravaggio, developed an international style showing Italian influences.

He might have picked up the subject from Jordaens, who had repeatedly painted the scene of the satyr in the peasant's house. Even though Liss's conception is far more dramatic and his composition more disciplined, an echo of the Netherlands, especially in the characterization of the peasant family, is unmistakable. But the style in which it is painted is the chiaroscuro of Caravaggio, whose light effects and overemphasized shadows give a sculptural quality to the figures that far exceeds in brilliance the rather flat, Gobelin type of painting. The spatial composition, with the emphasis on the source of light— the narrow window slit, reminiscent of the type found in Holland—shows that Liss was capable of assimilating independently and vigorously the stimuli he found abroad. He is no eclectic, however. This painting, particularly significant as an early work, shows that this German painter of the early seventeenth century deserved to stand beside Jordaens, Caravaggio, and Rivera.

Peter Paul Rubens

THE ARTIST: Rubens was born in 1577 in Siegen, Westphalia, where his father, an alderman of Antwerp, had been forced to flee after his expulsion as a Calvinist. From 1600–1608 he lived mostly in Italy—Venice, Mantua, Rome, and Genoa—with a year in Spain. In 1608 he returned to Antwerp, where, the following year, he married Isabella Brant. In 1609 he became court painter to the Archduke Albrecht, Regent of the Netherlands. In 1610 he painted the great altarpieces for the Antwerp Cathedral.

Rubens was inundated with commissions and honors, entrusted with diplomatic missions, and finally ennobled. From 1603–1604 he was in Madrid, then again from 1628–1629; he went to Paris several times between 1621 and 1627, to London between 1629 and 1630. In 1622 he began to paint the works ordered for the glorification of Marie de' Medici. After the death of Isabella Brant, he married, in 1630, the sixteen-year-old Hélène Fourment, whose beauty he celebrated in portraits and in mythological and religious paintings. In his last years he also painted landscapes. He died in Antwerp in 1640.

To understand Rubens and his art properly, one must not let the passion that glows in his work blind one to the sensibility that is the secret of his nature. His glorification of elemental nature was an expression of longing for something he lacked, rather than of something he possessed in his makeup.

Jacob Burckhardt called Rubens the greatest storyteller on earth next to Homer. By this he meant that the heroic figures that appear in the works of both men "live in the moment of action, and that moment lives in them."

In their capacity for seizing the moment and for letting their heroes and saints fulfill themselves in their surrender to it, both the poet and the painter are strikingly effective. But Burckhardt's bold comparison also draws attention to the contrast between the ecstatic sentiment, the exaggeration in the baroque and the epic calm and naturalness of the Greeks.

Rubens had to find a way to combine his native Flemish idiom with the foreign idiom of "Romanism" and to overcome mannerism by means of the earthy, Flemish sense of reality. His art displaced the spiritual conception dominant before his time; his emphasis was on dynamic forces of elemental being.

When Rubens went to Italy in 1600 for a long stay, he made himself the northern heir of the great Venetians, whose followers in Italy had gone into decline. Titian had died in 1576, Veronese twelve years later, Tintoretto in 1594. In the next century, Velázquez, Rubens, and Rembrandt were to be the great masters. After the early death of Caravaggio in 1610, Italy had no painter to match this trinity, though it had Bernini, the magnificent sculptor and architect. The great age of Italian painting was over.

It was providential that Rubens came first to Venice, where he was emboldened to use color and free, daring brushwork. But it was owing to his wealth of inner resources that he adopted not only the splendors of Venetian color but also the plastic force of Caravaggio.

Mantua, where he had come to be Duke Vincenzo Gonzaga's court painter, does not seem to have inspired Rubens; the Italian art of Mantegna's century remained alien to him. But the Duke sent him to Spain on a diplomatic mission, and there Velázquez became his friend. It was not *what* the great Spaniard painted but *how* he painted that influenced Rubens; the bold, wide brushstroke became his own as well.

Upon returning to his homeland, Rubens entered the service of the Regent of the Netherlands, the Archduke Albrecht and his wife, the Duchess Isabella. He flourished —not as an artisan of the guild but as a great gentleman who employed a large number of apprentices in his workshop and took on diplomatic missions between times. Rubens went once again to Madrid, and when he came to England at the Regent's behest, King Charles I, the patron of Van Dyck, knighted him, as the Emperor Charles V had once knighted Titian.

Few men have ever risen to the heights of achievement in art as well as to the summit of intellectual and social life as Rubens did, though he always put the unfolding of his creative powers before anything else.

THE LAMENTATION OVER CHRIST

Oak panel. 34 × 27 cm.

PROVENANCE: *Painted about 1612. Acquired in 1880 in Florence from the Demidoff collection.*

116 This small early work, hardly noticed by gallery goers, sketchy, painted in free, quick strokes without any break in the ecstasy of creation, is a work of genius that fully reflects the artist's creative excitement.

One senses that this picture was made without any previous drawing, which might have led to a calculated schematic treatment. The formal structure is determined by the almost harsh rectangular composition, quite unusual in the baroque. In the lower half of the painting, which is only a little more than a foot high, the horizontal figure of the Savior on his bier stretches across the entire width of the panel. On the right, the torches rise vertically, their flames illuminating the corpse bedded on linens. In the center, the two lamenting women stand out against the darkness of the grotto. The contrast between the violent grief of the weeping women and the rigidity of the corpse makes for a dramatic tension typical of Rubens.

The master was still young at the time of this painting, when his impressions of art in Italy, especially the lighting effects of Caravaggio, were still fresh in his memory.

Even the arm hanging down accords with the emotional and moving conception of the early Italian baroque. But the brushstrokes—which do not draw but sharply separate light and dark, thus giving plastic form to the body —and the visionary quality of the lighting are true Rubens. Only Rubens could have conceived and executed such deeply stirring effects as the sudden impact of the flaming torch lighting up Mary's gesture of self-abandonment in lamentation while the Magdalen leans forward in her grief.

LANDSCAPE WITH THE SHIPWRECK OF AENEAS

Canvas. 60 × 98 cm.

PROVENANCE: *About 1620, when this picture was painted, Rubens was portraying nature for its own sake. He did not contemplate landscape—he boldly dramatized it. And while landscape was not one of his major interests, he did paint forty such pictures, unique in their vitality. The engraving done by Schelte van Bolswert is captioned by a stanza from Vergil's* Aeneid *in the original, given in translation below. The engraver added two figures in the costume of his period at bottom left. This painting was a gift from Alfred Beit in London to the Kaiser Friedrich Museum Association in 1899. The painting was formerly in the collection of Lord Francis Pelham in Clinton Hope.*

117 Although tradition has it that the scenery in Rubens' painting of the shipwreck of Aeneas is modeled on an actual scene at Portovenere, near La Spezia, the precipitous headland shown seems nevertheless to have been formed and composed entirely in the artist's imagination. He has given more than a view; he has rendered the conflict of the elements. The raging sea has smashed the ship on which the hero escaped the destruction of Troy; the despair of the shipwrecked men is shown, but also their survival of disaster. Aeneas and the others are approaching; the earth has saved the stranded men, the fire is warming them, the threatening storm clouds in the sky are breaking up, the rainbow promises peace. We experience these dramatic events as only the impassioned art of the baroque can portray them.

Baroque, too, are the plunging curves of the composition: the line of the coast, the pathway leading past the shattered tree into the abyss, above which towers the steep rock upon which the ship burst asunder. Dark and bright, storm and calm, thunderheads and rainbow are sharply contrasted. Nature is caught in movement and struggle; the onlooker feels the wind that shakes the treetops and threatens the bird's flight. Through the heavy gray of the sky, the red undercoating shimmers mysteriously.

Motion is primary, not only in the flooding waves, the threatening clouds pouring gusts of rain on the sea in their retreat, but throughout the entire composition, as well as in its effect on the viewer. Rubens painted the tempest itself, and so he did justice to the verses in which Vergil lets the hero of his epic describe the power of the elements:

Tum mihi caeruleus supra caput astitit imber,
noctem hiemque ferens, et inhorruit unda tenebris.
Continuo venti volvunt mare, magnaque surgunt
aequora; dispersi iactamur gurgite vasto.

When o'er our heads descends a burst of rain,
And night with sable clouds involves the main;
The ruffling winds the foamy billows raise;
The scattered fleet is forced to several ways . . .

ST. SEBASTIAN

Canvas. 200 × 128 cm.

PROVENANCE: *Painted no later than 1614. Rubens mentions it on April 28, 1618, in a letter written, as was his custom, in Italian, to an English art lover, Sir Dudley Carleton. It is also thought by some that this Sebastian, dated 1614 by general agreement, may have been painted in Italy—that is, by 1608. The picture had been part of the collection of H. H. J. Munro, sold at auction in London in 1878. It was purchased for Berlin a year later in Paris.*

118 In a letter to an English art lover, Rubens expressly called a nude Sebastian by his hand "the flower of my things." Since many of his paintings were completed with the participation of his apprentices this statement of authenticity is of great value. As a representation of the human body, the work is of the same importance as the later *Andromeda*, which he also kept in his house. It is instructive to compare these two paintings, which are among the great treasures of the Berlin gallery, for they represent the ideal male and female figures as conceived by a leading master of the baroque period. That a Christian and a pagan subject may be so closely associated is also significant—as they were, in fact, in the *Venus* and *Sebastian* of Botticelli, both of which are also in the Berlin museum. Botticelli's paintings represent the early Renaissance; those of Rubens, showing his conception of physical beauty about one and a half centuries later, come at the close of that great era, when the Renaissance found its last vital expression in the style of the baroque.

Botticelli's Sebastian looks more like a model; the arrows seem to be an afterthought, and there is no inevitable relationship between the figure and the landscape. Rubens' Sebastian is seen purely as a martyr. The lines of the body are determined by the pain of the wounds; the quiver with the arrows at his feet appears as an essential element in the picture. There is a sense of disturbance in the landscape, where the tree trunk and foliage in the center strongly contrast with the glaring yellows of the sunset that emphasize the tragic scene. The body contorted by spasms conveys its pain to the beholder; the face of the fettered martyr is transfigured.

The colors are luminous: against the dark tree with its green foliage, the flesh tones of the strongly sculptured body appear almost golden. If it were not for the arrows and the bleeding wounds, the viewer would think he was looking at a pagan god or a ruler of late classic times such as Rubens had seen depicted in Roman works of art during his years in Italy.

ANDROMEDA

Oak panel. 189 × 94 cm.

PPOVENANCE: *A late work. The* Andromeda *at the Prado in Madrid is similar in pose. There are gold copies of the painting, probably from Rubens' workshop, in the Prado and in private collections in Paris. This picture was No. 85 in the auction catalogue of Rubens' estate. From the estate of his son Albert, where it was known to be in 1657, it went to the Duke of Richelieu. It was purchased for Berlin in 1885 from the collection of the Duke of Marlborough at Blenheim.*

119   This is a much later work than the *St. Sebastian*. In contrast to other representations of the story of Andromeda's liberation by Perseus from the monster guarding her, Rubens concentrates on the beauty of the body; the face shows the features of his second wife, Hélène Four-

ment. Here, too, the painter must have felt that he had achieved a kind of perfection—he kept the painting in his house, as we know from the catalogue of his estate.

But it is also possible that Rubens could not bring himself to finish the work, which was actually intended for Philip IV of Spain, in order not to have to part from it. His disciple Jordaens is thought to have worked over several uncompleted details after his master's death. Jordaens probably made the head of the monster emerge more distinctly from the whitecaps surrounding it; he may also have made more distinct the figure of Perseus galloping to the rescue through the sky—his arrival is announced to the captive by the god of love—not to the advantage of the otherwise so unified composition.

However, Rubens' own hand is clearly evident in the treatment of the body, raised to an intense luminosity with fine, delicate brushstrokes that allow the white undercoating of the panel to shine through. Other parts of the painting show a brown undercoating—for example, the dark background on the right; it seems that Rubens began the distribution of his lights and darks with the grounding of the canvas. The reflections of the red cloak that has slipped to the ground and the cool shadows of the veiling make an incomparable framework for the warm-blooded, richly gleaming body.

Anthony Van Dyck

THE ARTIST: Among the students and apprentices of Rubens, Anthony Van Dyck holds the first rank. Born in 1599 in Antwerp, he became a master of the painters' guild there as early as 1618. With his restless temperament, he moved several times before finally settling down in London. In 1620 he went from London to Italy, then returned to Antwerp, then from 1623–1627 worked mostly in Genoa but also in Rome and in Venice, where he came under Titian's influence. He was in Antwerp again between 1627 and 1632, and many of his religious paintings are from this period. In 1632 he returned to London, where King Charles I appointed him his court painter and knighted him. From 1634 to 1635 he was once more in Antwerp. He married in 1639, one Mary Ruthven, a lady of the Queen of England's court. In 1641, Van Dyck died in a London suburb.

When Petrus Christus portrayed the young lady who is commonly called Lady Talbot (Pl. 47), a panel of 26 × 21 cm. sufficed for the modest requirements of the low-ceilinged paneled rooms of the late Gothic period. The proud palaces of Genoa's noble families and the showy style of the baroque, which gave even to the interiors the pillared look of the facades, demanded very different dimensions. The painting of the Marchesa Geronima Spinola, painted almost two centuries later by Van Dyck, with its height of 2.21 meters, testifies to the baroque striving for monumental impressiveness.

PORTRAIT OF THE MARCHESA GERONIMA SPINOLA

Canvas. 221 × 147 cm.

PROVENANCE: *Formerly in the Palazzo de Fornari, Genoa. Acquired in 1904 from the A. Thiem collection in San Remo and presented as a gift to the Berlin museum.*

120, 121 This picture must be imagined within the framework of the Genoese palaces, where some of the principal works of Van Dyck are still hanging in the place they were designed for, as in the Palazzo Rosso. This explains why the portraitist had to use architectural elements, such as a column, a step, or both of these connected by a portal, in the background of a portrait intended for a specific interior. In this way, the picture of the beautiful, proud lady, a Doria by birth, fitted into the palazzo of which she became the mistress through her marriage to Filippo Spinola.

Formally, the painter's task was to combine figure and interior into a unified whole. The use of the step introduces an element of motion: the lady, dressed in elegant black, with her delicate left hand lifts the hem of her dress, revealing a gleaming violet petticoat. Her head with its golden blond hair, the black cap richly jeweled, the light ruff, the fine-boned hands set off by entrancingly painted red cuffs, the flower in the right hand, the sapphires set in the gold of her necklace— all are effectively contrasted with the blacks and dark grays of the background. The viewer seems to have caught a momentary movement in which the grace, the superior poise, and the searching glance—not without a youthful curiosity—of this beautiful, noble creature are all fully expressed.

Frans Hals

THE ARTIST: Frans Hals was the scion of an old, established Haarlem family, but he was born in Antwerp, presumably about 1580. His parents had temporarily left Holland as a result of the unrest during the struggle of the Netherlands for freedom. But he grew up in Haarlem, where the museum still shows his famous works. In freely executed group paintings, Frans Hals celebrated the community life of the Dutch, who took pride in their struggle for independence. During the 1630's, Hals was at the height of his productivity and was overwhelmed with commissions. He died in 1666, impoverished and forgotten, and is buried in the choir of St. Bavo Kerk. The Frans Hals Museum of Haarlem is on the Heiligland Straat, where the painter had his workshop.

The art of portraiture enforces a certain restraint upon the artist's temperament. Frans Hals, aiming for spontaneity, expressive movement, and tension, broke through the conventional restrictions and conquered new dimensions for the art of the Netherlands by way of the genre portraits he created. He painted jolly lute players and laughing children, barmaids and singing, drinking, smoking young men, tipplers old and young, boys and girls fishing, and, repeatedly, one old woman— the mad Babette, an innkeeper.

The Singing Flute Player is an outstanding work of this type. Frans Hals liked to capture facial expression in movement, the play of the muscles in laughter, in speech, and in song, which intensifies the modeling of the face. He had worked out a new technique: instead of blending his colors, he boldly set his brushstrokes side by side or overlapping; indeed, he even did his modeling with relatively narrow strokes set at angles to one another. According to Arnold Houbraken, Van Dyck said that he had never seen a painter who could outline a portrait as Frans Hals could, in one movement, without connecting strokes or corrections, by means of light and shade. It was precisely through his many genre portraits, the models for which were probably his own children, that he acquired the freedom and daring that made him so skillful in the execution of his public commissions, especially the group paintings.

MALLE BABBE OF HAARLEM

Canvas. 75 × 64 cm.

PROVENANCE: *Formerly wrongly called Hille Bobbe. Acquired in 1877 from the Suermondt collection in Aachen.*

122 Frans Hals painted Babette, the old innkeeper, frequently. He was amused by her laugh, the raucousness of which seems to be audible from the portrait. He was interested in seizing, by means of highlights and strong shadows, the grimace of drunken screeching that makes the facial lines angular. He wanted to catch the depression in the low brow above the nose, the glazed eyes of the drinking woman, the twist of the mouth. He was probably charmed by the way the reddish-yellow face emerges from between the no-longer-clean white of the cap and collar, which in turn pushes the woman's dress into the background.

The body is twisted around in a manner typical of the baroque, suggesting the crazy tippler's habit of lolling on the bench at the tavern table, tossing off her coarse jokes to the unseen audience. The stocky body makes a diagonal with two pronouncedly vertical elements: at the lower left, the pewter tankard, the soft, gray-shimmering metal of which is marvelously painted; and at the upper right, on the old woman's shoulder—and not unlike her—the brown owl. Between the rigid tankard and the owl the woman's spontaneous movement is all the more dramatic; she has just turned around to give one of her mad answers to the innkeeper or one of her companions.

This is no faithfully copied reality. It is a fantasy made out of brushstrokes that are angular and yet suggest the roundness of the object, leaving it to the eye to complete the illusion. This is not the least of the devices by which the picture gives the effect of immediacy, of capturing the accidental and momentary.

THE SINGING FLUTE PLAYER

Canvas. 62 × 54.5 cm.

PROVENANCE: *Signed "FH." Painted about 1625. Purchased with the Suermondt collection, Aachen.*

123   The *Flute Player* is remarkable for the way in which color and form blend into one, with the individual colors subordinated to the whole—the effect Hals strove for at all costs. The subject is a young fellow sitting at his music stand, studying the melody he intends to play on the flute. His left hand—one of the best-painted hands in European art—tentatively accompanies the melody that the lively, radiantly life-loving boy is singing to himself.

The player's head is placed relatively low in the picture, as Hals liked to have it, especially in his early paintings. Form and color are strongly concentrated below, loosening as the movement goes upward from the rising line of the left hand toward the blue-tinted ostrich plume on the boy's beret.

The diagonal movement emphasized by the flute determines the composition of this portrait, which comes to life so effectively against the emptiness of the background. The painting links tone to tone, rising from dark to light, itself a melody harmonizing with the glowing ease with which the boy surrenders to his delight in music.

Rembrandt Harmensz van Rijn

THE ARTIST: Rembrandt was born in 1606 in Leiden, Holland, where he pursued his studies until he came under the influence of Pieter Lastman in Amsterdam. He returned to Leiden, a university town, where Hercules Seghers later awakened his interest in landscape painting. In 1631, Rembrandt settled permanently in Amsterdam, marrying in 1634 Saskia van Uijlenburgh, whom he was destined to lose in 1642, following the birth of his son Titus. In 1649, Hendrickje Stoffels entered his household and faithfully took care of him and his small son. After her death, in 1661, life became very lonely, for Titus also died before him, in 1668. The style of his last phase, which has come to be considered one of the greatest of an extraordinarily fulfilled art,

tragically failed to be understood by his contemporaries. He was sixty-three when he died on October 4, 1669, in Amsterdam.

The art of the Netherlands reached its apogee in the work of Rembrandt. His chiaroscuro style, mysteriously bound up with his inner life, was brilliantly original. He was at first highly successful as a portrait painter, an art that had come to be greatly appreciated in his time. His good fortune continued during the life of his wife, Saskia, whom he painted often. His famous group picture called *Night Watch* was painted in 1642, the year of Saskia's death, when his days of triumph ended with the public rejection of his work.

THE RAPE OF PROSERPINE

Oak panel. 83 × 78 cm.

PROVENANCE: *Painted about 1632, the picture was ascribed for a time to Rembrandt's pupil Jan Joris van Vliet. Waagen was the first to recognize it as a Rembrandt. It is first mentioned in the inventory of Castle Honsholredyk, where in 1707 it was listed as No. 144. It may also be identical with a picture listed as No. 43, "Lievens," in the 1632 inventory of the gallery in the Stadhouderlijk Kwartier of the House of Orange in The Hague. It came to Berlin in 1720 with a number of other pictures from the House of Orange collection, and in 1763 it was in Frederick II's gallery at Sans Souci.*

124,125   About 1632, when he painted the famous *Anatomy Lesson of Dr. Tulp*, Rembrandt, aged twenty-six, had reached the first great summit of his art. It was about this time that saw the creation of what might be considered the most perfect painting of the era, *The Rape of Proserpine*, full of the mystery of that ancient myth.

The art of Rembrandt, who had just moved from Leiden to Amsterdam, already embraced a wide choice of theme: the New and the Old Testaments, portraits, and those naive representations of goddesses for which he dressed his model as Minerva or undressed her for a Diana bathing. In no other painting of that period does the visionary element that characterizes the art of Rembrandt, that mysterious quality created by the painter's chiaroscuro, assert itself more powerfully than it does here. In the way it contrasts heightened with deepened tone values, warm and cool colors, the painting is truly peerless. Golden brown is intensified by hints of red; light glitters in the form of blond hair, startles as the gleam of the metallic lion's head on the prow of the chariot as it is about to plunge back into the depths. Pluto has dragged Proserpine from her innocent play in a flowering meadow. Her bright figure is threatened by the dark god of the underworld; the folds of her pale-blue gown, to which her companions are clinging in an effort to pull her back, emphasize the steep diagonal of the composition. But the movement of the chariot, drawn by black horses toward the abyss, cannot be stopped. The delicate blue-gray shadings of the flower-strewn meadow and the foliage near the rock are overshadowed by clouds rising like dark vapors from the underworld. In a way that might be called Shakespearian, Rembrandt grasped all the possibilities of the scene and brought them to their highest intensity. By comparison, the mythological pictures of most of the masters of the period appear cold and academic; even the art of Poussin, who was more than ten years older than the miller's son from Rijn, pales before the energy and the passion of the master who drew on the deepest instincts of his rich humanity. Rembrandt heightened the drama of the scene partly by making reality fantastic; even the golden lion's mask on the chariot wears the grimace of the Hound of Hell. What he depicts is not merely myth—it is the struggle of the powers of darkness against light, the despair of a young life that must go down into the kingdom of the dead. Poussin presents us with a tableau; Rembrandt makes the myth timeless and universal.

THE VISION OF DANIEL

Detail

Canvas. 96 × 116 cm.

PROVENANCE: *Painted about 1650. This painting, like the one of Susanna, comes from the London collection of Sir Joshua Reynolds, who owned a number of Rembrandts. It was purchased in Paris in 1883 for Berlin.*

126   Rembrandt is probably the only artist who dared to paint the scene of Daniel's vision, based on the eighth chapter of the Book of Daniel. There the prophet describes his vision of the mighty Medes and Persians and of a cruel king. Daniel had his strange dream near the palace of Shushan, beside the river Ulai: at the river stood a ram with high horns, which he thrust toward three points of the compass; no beast could resist him or be saved from him. But then a he-goat appeared from the west, with a powerful single horn growing between his eyes; with this he knocked down the ram and trampled him. "And an host was given him against the daily sacrifice by reason of transgression, and it cast down the truth to the ground; and it practised, and prospered." The power given him was to be limited in time, however.

Then God commanded the angel Gabriel to go to Daniel, who fainted before that figure of light. The angel touched him and explained the terrifying vision: the ram with the two horns signified the King of Media and the King of Persia, the he-goat was the King of Greece; he would devastate the land and destroy many of the people, but he in turn would be broken. This sounds like something far away and unreal, but it is the vision of evil that keeps bringing devastation upon the earth.

The two beasts hidden in the darkness, depicted by Rembrandt in the natural proportions of ram and goat, are not a major element in the picture; its focal point is the grouping of the angel and Daniel: the emergence from the sheltering darkness of the vision in white, the fine blond hair, the hand that the heavenly messenger lays upon the shoulder of the young prophet, who is getting up after having fallen in a faint, the hand stretched out in the act of interpretation, the awakening of the youthful Daniel (for whom Titus probably served as his father's model). Here Rembrandt's mystic chiaroscuro reaches the height of perfection.

In the background appears the palace of Shushan with its great tower, as we know it from the painting of Susanna, whose story is connected with that of the prophet Daniel, the just judge and visionary who saved her from death and punished her persecutors. Rembrandt, a zealous reader of the Bible, gave his own pictorial form to what he read.

JOSEPH'S DREAM

Mahogany panel. 20 × 27 cm.

PROVENANCE: *Painted in 1645. A sketch for this is in the Albertina Museum in Vienna. This is one of the paintings that came to Berlin as part of the Prussian King's inheritance from the House of Orange in 1720, and it was eventually transferred to the Berlin museum from the royal-palace collection. Another treatment of the same subject, with a different grouping of the figures on a vertical panel more than a meter in height, painted about 1650, may be seen in the National Gallery in Budapest.*

Rembrandt's chiaroscuro rendering of figures and   127 space as creations of the surrounding light is seen most clearly in his smaller paintings. For this version of Joseph's dream he chose a panel of imported mahogany not quite ten inches high and not much more than ten inches wide. The light of the angel's pathway enters the broken-down manger from above, enhancing the visionary appearance of the dream figure shown. Joseph is shown sunk in sleep on the floor, while Mary sleeps leaning protectively over the bundle of straw on which the carefully wrapped infant is bedded. Behind Joseph, touching his shoulder, stands the radiant figure of the angel with wings outspread, warning him to flee in order to save the life of the newborn child.

In the representation of mysterious events, chiaroscuro serves to express a heightened intensity of feeling. Hovering above the objects, it transfigures reality and makes the spiritual world visible.

In his book *The Old Masters,* written when French impressionism was in flower, Eugène Fromentin defined Rembrandt's approach with a painter's instinct: "His chiaroscuro is undoubtedly the native and necessary form for his impressions and ideas. It is the form of mystery par excellence... light, airy, veiled, restrained;

it suggests the power of things unseen, invites curiosity...
it can express a sentiment, an emotion, an uncertainty,
the indefinite and the infinite, a dream and an ideal.
And this is why it had to become the poetic and yet so
natural element in which the genuis of Rembrandt never
ceased to dwell."

SUSANNA AND THE ELDERS

Oak panel. 76 × 91 cm.

PROVENANCE: *Signed at lower right "Rembrandt f. 1647."
This may be the painting Adriaen Banck bought from Rembrandt
in 1647 for 500 guilders. Fully executed studies for the figure of
Susanna without the elders are at the Louvre (Collection La Caze)
and at the Mauritshaus, The Hague. Other drawings and
sketches are in the Berlin collection of etching and engravings.
The picture remained until 1795 in the collection of Sir Joshua
Reynolds (etching by R. Carlom, 1769). It was purchased for
Berlin in Paris in 1883. Susanna alone—showing a resemblance
to Saskia, according to Wilhelm von Bode—appears on the painting in The Hague (dated 1637).*

128,131   "For Rembrandt reality exists only to the degree that
he is able to heighten and spiritualize it into an expressive truth, by a strong concentration of his human
sympathies." In these words from his book on Rembrandt, Émile Verhaeren, the Flemish poet, summed
up the essence of the master's art. Rembrandt's ability
to intensify and spiritualize also gives its deep humanity
to his painting of Susanna in the act of repulsing the
two lecherous judges threatening her purity.

Rembrandt tackled the problems of composition and
the Biblical details of the painting several times. His
point of departure was a painting by his teacher Lastman,
now in the Berlin gallery, and there is a special study of
Susanna alone. It was not only the beauty of the body
gleaming against the mysterious dark background of
the garden that attracted him but also the expression of
a double shock: Susanna is still shivering from the first
dip into the cold water, when she is frightened by the
lustful judges pouncing on her. They had been hiding,
unbeknownst to each other, by the pool, watching the
bathing woman and awaiting their chance to seize her.

Despite the strong red of the discarded robe, the
painting's color scheme is dominated by the luminosity
of the nude body shimmering against the semidarkness.
The towering architecture of the palace of Shushan
(Susa), rather like a fortress, in the background; the
foliage of the trees still glowing in the heat of the waning
day; the colorful Oriental dress of the persecutors; the
mirror-like surface of the pool and the marble steps
leading into it—all these tones, veiled by the twilight
atmosphere, serve only as a foil for the splendor of the
shining body. Next to those of Danaë and Bathsheba, it
is the most magnificent body Rembrandt ever painted—
not in accordance with any canonical definition of
beauty, but as a vigorous expression of life.

POTIPHAR'S WIFE ACCUSING JOSEPH

Canvas. 110 × 87 cm.

PROVENANCE: *Inscribed above Joseph's coat "Rembrandt f.
1655." Acquired in 1883 in Paris. Formerly in the collection
of Sir John Neeld in Grittleton House.*

The false accusation of the rejected woman, the   129,130
awakening wrath of Potiphar, and Joseph's expression
of alarm are all captured in a scene whose dramatic
tension reminds one that Rembrandt's life began in the
time of Shakespeare.

Characteristic of Rembrandt is the part played by
the surroundings: the white linen on the bed, the play
of chiaroscuro under the canopy, the bronze-green coat
of Joseph under the foot of the enraged lady. The
painter's problem is the rendering of the figures catching
the light against a dark background, related to one
another by means of their eloquent hands and the distribution of the light. Chromatically, the seductress is
in the center, dressed in a gold-tinged pink. An extremely
artful touch is the way her bright shoe stands out against
the dark coat of Joseph. The olive hue of Joseph's garment, despite the red belt, gives a subdued effect, while
the mixed green and brown of Potiphar's clothing harmonize with the darker green of the curtains guarding
the crepuscular atmosphere. The light effects gleam gold
and white, singly and disturbingly, yet they coalesce
into a full but disquieting accord.

There is a tangible relationship between this painting
of 1655, set in a interior, and the mood of the *Susanna*
painted eight years earlier. Both pictures have a twilight shimmer as a painterly device for enveloping the
theme of slandered virtue in a mysterious union of the
spirit and the senses. He who understands this interior
vision has an "open sesame" to the art of Rembrandt.

PORTRAIT OF HENDRICKJE STOFFELS

Canvas. 86 × 65 cm.

PROVENANCE: *Painted about 1659. Acquired at auction in Paris
in 1879. Formerly in the collections of Graham White and John
Wardell of London.*

The subject is Hendrickje Stoffels, Rembrandt's faith-   132,133
ful housekeeper after the death of Saskia, who stayed
with the increasingly lonely man and cared for him and
his son. After a creditor has brought about the artist's
bankruptcy through rascally machinations, she found
a way to save him from total ruin. This portrait, painted
about 1659, when she had been with him for ten years,
was an expression of his gratitude—a personal motive
that should be taken into account.

Characteristically, Hendrickje is here seen both in
action and in thought. She is standing at the window

she has just opened, her right hand still on the knob. Rembrandt may have observed her at such a moment, which he then recaptured in this portrait. She looks out of the frame at the beholder; but the beholder is Rembrandt, who stands before her with his easel.

Hendrickje is richly and colorfully dressed: the master, whose virtuosity with color this painting teaches one to appreciate, painted with evident delight the red fur-trimmed cloak and the matching cap of golden ribbons held together with a broad red band. He lovingly bedecked her with pearl earrings, a pearl bracelet, and a ring, probably wanting to make partial atonement for being unable to marry her, the mother of his daughter Cornelia, for fear of losing Saskia's inheritance. The consistory cruelly forbade her to take communion, and so she had to suffer much bitterness until her death in 1661. After Rembrandt lost his devoted companion, there followed the bitter years of solitude.

Jan van Goyen

THE ARTIST: Jan van Goyen was ten years older than Rembrandt. He was born in 1596 in Leiden and was a pupil of Isaack van Swanenburgh, but he was chiefly influenced by Esaias van de Velde at The Hague. After his return from travels in France and Belgium, he worked in Leiden until 1632, then at The Hague, where he died in 1656. After overcoming the unevenness of his earlier phase, he reached his greatest achievement in the mature works of the 1640's.

The pictures of Jan van Goyen, which decorate the galleries in large numbers, can be recognized from afar by their warm, golden, slightly veiled tone, dominating the color detail but capturing all the more effectively the interplay of light and shade, the momentary nature of light, the significance and reflective function of water. The new style of landscape painting, in the creation of which Van Goyen was an important participant, did not set isolated details side by side; it sought, rather, to render their appearance within the atmosphere, so that the sections of landscape shown were now of an unprecedented vastness, in the spirit of the baroque.

Working indefatigably, he developed his style with growing consistency, so that the works he created in The Hague in the 1640's are considered particularly characteristic of him. The picture in Berlin of Arnhem am Rijn, the capital of Gelderland, shows Goyen's work at its height.

VIEW OF ARNHEM

Canvas. 90 × 105 cm.

PROVENANCE: *Signed at bottom right "vGoyen 1646." Acquired in 1874 with the Suermondt collection, Aachen.*

As with so many Dutch masters, the land takes up only about a third of the picture's height; but the impression of distance matches the height of the sky, so that the effect of depth, sustained by the vaulting sky, determines the feeling of space in the painting. Line, shading of color, the direction in which the eye is made to move—all are conducive to the creation of perspective. The eye glides over the foreground, which is held together by the shadows cast by clouds, to the middle distance, where the sharply outlined city is set and where the broad tower of the Church of St. Eusebius, rising above the horizon, is clearly visible. Sharply outlined against the river behind it, the city with its ornamentation of towers and turrets and the wings of a windmill is most vividly pictured. Built upon a rising riverbank, it dominates the wide plain, the horizontal lines of which guide the eye into the far distance.

This is not merely a sober, objective view of a city; the artist has caught the moment at the approach of evening when a fine mist begins to sink over the landscape under moving clouds, when the changing light makes for a dream-like transfiguration of the scenes. It is as though on this late afternoon, with twilight approaching, time were standing still. It is that hour between light and dark that makes the onlooker feel most deeply the vastness of the world and the consonance of earth, water, and sky.

Jacob van Ruisdael

THE ARTIST: Jacob van Ruisdael was born in 1628 or 1629 in Haarlem, where he died in 1682. From 1657 to 1681 he worked in Amsterdam, painting landscapes exclusively. His portrayals of nature in her melancholy moods exerted a great influence on the landscape painters of the German romantic school. In the following passage, Goethe spells his name "Ruysdael," although the artist himself signed all but a few early paintings "Ruisdael."

Jacob Ruysdael, born in Haarlem, 1635, working industriously till 1681, is recognized as one of the most excellent landscape painters. To begin with, his works satisfy all the demands the outward senses can make of a work of art. With the greatest freedom, his hand and brush achieve perfection. Light, shadow, the character and the effect of the whole leave nothing to be desired. Every amateur and connoisseur is convinced of this at a glance. But at the moment we would like to consider him as a thinker, indeed as a poet, and as such, too, we must confess that he is deserving of high distinction.

When Goethe called Jacob van Ruisdael a thinking artist, indeed a poet, he meant that this master of landscape painting was the first to perceive and to express the inner life of nature, its echoing of human sensibility.

We know little about the painter's life, only that he was unmarried, lived in Haarlem and Amsterdam, suffered from a lingering disease, and finally was taken from Amsterdam to Haarlem, to die in the poorhouse of his native city. His paintings tell us a great deal more than that about the man: they sound a melody that knows all the scales of sensibility; it is acquainted with the tragic forces of nature but also with that tender feeling for nature that is expressed in the phrase "sweet melancholy." But above all, whatever he paints—the vastness of the landscape around Haarlem, the woods of Westphalia across the border from Holland, the sea, the coast, the dunes, rushing water, a windmill by a river— everything lives and breathes in the atmosphere. It is as though one could measure the temperature and the moisture in the air and tell the time when the clouds that are casting their shadow on the ground will discharge their burden. Ruisdael sees things—house and tree, earth and water—not for themselves alone but fatefully involved with the wind and the rain.

As Eugène Fromentin puts it, "Ruisdael sees no object without linking it with the point corresponding to it in the atmosphere." In this fashion, he expanded the prevailing conception of man's relationship to nature and brought a new, more profound vision of nature and its vicissitudes.

LANDSCAPE WITH OAK WOODS

Canvas. 114 × 141 cm.

PROVENANCE: *Signed "J v Ruisdael." The picture is from the artist's best period, about the middle of the 1660's, when after his years of preparation in Haarlem, he moved to Amsterdam. Acquired in Paris in 1891.*

135   It is said of Jacob van Ruisdael that in the summer he liked to go from Haarlem, and later from Amsterdam, to Bentheim (in Westphalia, Germany), where the oak woods, the hills and ponds, or the old feudal castle provided the themes for his paintings. In contrast to the plains of Holland with their low horizon, which he depicted in so masterly a fashion, especially from Haarlem, nearby Westphalia offered the gigantic trees and bizarre outlines that appealed to lovers of the baroque. One of the most magnificent examples of his dramatic manner is the *Landscape with Oak Woods*, a prize possession in the series of paintings by this master who is so well represented in the Berlin gallery, thanks to Wilhelm von Bode's collecting zeal. All the elements of Ruisdael's art and the baroque conception of landscape are here combined in a unique synthesis: the diagonal division of the surface; the richly varied outline of the treetops; the counterpoise of the barren, dying tree; the reflections in the water; the stratification of space by the hill, with its rising line in a direction opposed to that of the line of the treetops. The picture is boldly, thoughtfully composed, rich in details of growing things that surround the lake and cover part of the water—a piece of

nature and at the same time a destiny, Shakespeare's *Lear* transposed into pure landscape.

Composition and color scheme are in perfect harmony: a saturated brownish green in the foliage of the trees, with some branches already tinted by autumnal decay, serves as background for the blasted beech tree familiar from other paintings by Ruisdael, with reddish wounds where it has lost its branches, its tall upward curve like a shrill outcry. This counterpoint is framed by the yellow of marsh flowers and the bright green of the plants floating on the water; what matters is the contrast between the darkness of the depths and the bright growth on the lake's surface. From this foreground the eye moves to the distance, where the sand-yellow shore yields to the blue-gray of the sky. A gold-rimmed cloud is threatened by dark rain clouds—the same dramatic counterpoint again.

Adriaen van de Velde

THE ARTIST: This painter belongs to a famous family of artists that produced five masters, active mostly in Amsterdam. The son of Willem van de Velde the Elder, a court painter who died in London, and the younger brother of Willem the Younger, Adriaen was born in 1636 in Amsterdam, where he died in 1672. He served an apprenticeship with his father and was most strongly influenced by Jan Wijnants and Philips Wouwerman of Haarlem, as well as by Paulus Potter of Amsterdam. In 1653 he was working in Italy, and subsequently he was active in Amsterdam and Delft. He painted landscapes, in which the figures were so carefully worked out that occasionally masters like Ruisdael let him paint figures into their own landscapes. He also distinguished himself as an etcher.

Though we are accustomed to low horizons in landscapes by the Dutch masters of the seventeenth century—who were painting the low-lying coastlands of Holland —the special charm of the river landscapes by Adriaen van de Velde stems from the fact that the land occupies less than one-fourth of the total height of the canvas, and even this is curtailed by the water in the foreground.

FLAT RIVER SCENE WITH GRAZING HORSES AND SHEEP

Canvas. 41 × 66 cm.

PROVENANCE: *Acquired in 1874 from the Suermondt collection, Aachen. Formerly in the Schönborn collection, Vienna, until 1866.*

What we see in this picture is in perfect accord with   **136** some verses by Joost van den Vondel, the great Dutch poet of the period, whose poems celebrate the pensive beauty of his native landscape:

Terwyl de wint in't loof,
de beeck langs d'oevers speelt....

The while the wind caresses
The leaves, the brook its banks....

The strips of land, with houses, a little castle, some scattered trees, stand out in their varied contours, an effect magnified by their being reflected in the water. The spit of land with grazing sheep and the white horse with its luminous reflection in the water add depth; and the sky, with the contrasting movement of its brownish-gray, light-rimmed clouds, is made to appear so wide and so high that it seems to encompass a piece of infinity. The colors are muted: the bluish mist drifting over the water, which mirrors the treetops and the brick manor house, is done in a scale of tones that proves Van de Velde to be one of the leading Amsterdam masters of landscape painting. One becomes aware of his originality as well as of the solidity of his tradition: along with his father and his brother, the marine painter, he has a delicate touch in the rendering of water. The white horse recalls Wouwerman, whose pupil he had been in Haarlem.

Aert van der Neer

THE ARTIST: He was born in 1603 in Amsterdam, where he died in 1677. For a time he studied in Gorinchem, where he was influenced by Raphael and Joachim Camphuysen. But he soon returned to his native city, and he is accounted one of the best of its landscape painters. Despite his great productivity, he had little success late in life, when the fashion changed; he ended up running a hostelry and died in poverty. His paintings, which are to be found in many museums, are recognizable by their dramatic uses of light. His landscapes gained a supernatural intensity from their lighting effects, and if the sun and moon did not suffice, he was not above adding a fire to provide a further source of illumination. This predilection provided him with his favorite subject matters: landscapes with canals in the moonlight, winter skating scenes, fires raging in the night.

LANDSCAPE BY MOONLIGHT WITH SAILBOATS ON A RIVER

Oak panel. 32 × 46 cm.

PROVENANCE: *Monogrammed at bottom right "AV DN." Purchased in 1843.*

137 Aert van der Neer achieves the transcendence of reality and the sense of transcendence in nature by the use of moonlight. Sky, earth, water, light, the four elements themselves, are fused in his pictures.

He accordingly does not make so sharp a distinction between earth and sky as does, for example, Jan van Goyen: the dark clouds rising above the treetops of the ascending riverbank belong, in this composition, more with the land than with the white, light-rimmed cloud formations approaching in an opposing movement from the background. The bright shimmer on the horizon is mirrored in the wide surface of the water, which, as it gains in depth, constitutes the beauty of this painting. The dark sails outlined against the sky add mystery and suggest the height of the vaulting canopy above them. The little picture—painted on an oak panel only eighteen inches wide—manages, by means of contrasting darks and lights, horizontal and vertical elements, to capture a mood without sentimentality, uniting in a grand baroque synthesis all its carefully observed details, from the fisherman mending nets in the foreground to the last small sail in the far distance.

Jan Vermeer van Delft

THE ARTIST: Jan Vermeer was born in Delft in 1632, the son of an innkeeper who was also an art dealer. He is one generation younger than Rembrandt, whose handling of light crucially influenced him. He is thought to have been a pupil of Carel Fabritius, himself a pupil of Rembrandt. When Fabritius lost his life in an explosion in the arsenal, a poem of the period commented:

The Phoenix Fabritius, swallowed by fire,
Was reborn as the painter Vermeer.

As a master of perspective, Vermeer excels even Pieter de Hooch, who worked in Delft for a time. The father of eleven children, eight of whom were alive at the time of his death, Vermeer had gone through hard times as a result of the war between Holland and Louis XIV of France, which put an end to his best work as an artist. He died in 1675.

We associate the name of Vermeer with the perfect rendering of interior light. Nor was there anyone to equal him in modeling by tender palpations of light, so that figure and room were fused into a whole.

In his special field of genre and interior painting, he brought to masterly fulfillment the great task that Jan van Eyck was the first to recognize. Unlike Pieter de Hooch, who loved complicated interiors with ingenious arrangements of perspective, Vermeer generally formed his interiors by means of only two walls, one to indicate depth and foreshortening, the other to provide a background and to close up the space. He surpassed all other painters in his ability to suggest a physical presence, the depth of a room, by means of lighting—even if it is no more than a gleam on the lid of a pewter tankard or the shading of a wall from a warm yellow-white to a cool blue-gray. Above all, his colors are of a rare beauty: he alone has this particular blue and yellow, brought forth by magic with flat brushstrokes from a gray undercoating; he alone has this nobility of cool tones, against which a rose-like luminosity of red—never a shrill red—warmly glows or the gold of a picture frame highlights a dark-green landscape on the wall. His colors gleam softly between light and dark, blending into a rare harmony in which discretion equals dignity.

The question that engages Vermeer is the same for every real painter: "How does a picture, abstracted from reality, come into being in the painter's eye?" He is not really concerned with the "story," and in this sense it is wrong to call him a genre painter. What his painter's eye notes as worthy of being made into a picture is the moment in which a definite situation, of no particular significance in itself, achieves a certain unity as an optical impression by the right combination of structure, color, and light. This is what makes a picture in the painter's eye and becomes worthy of being set down as such in permanence. Vermeer's art is basically that of the still life, painted in accordance with his own compositional and chromatic intention—even though Vermeer uses actual still life only as a picture-within-a-picture, like the chair with the lute in the picture here. Life, incessantly changing, stands "still" for him; it becomes a picture, but is harmonized within it.

Life in Holland, a country of long twilight evenings and mysterious half-lights along the coast of the North Sea, is conducive to a deep pensiveness of temperament. It is this that enabled Vermeer to grasp the mystery of transition, to make time stand still in a picture. It is no mere coincidence that Vermeer belonged to the same generation as Spinoza, Holland's great philosopher. Starting out from the insights of Descartes, whose philosophy had been translated into visual terms a generation earlier by Poussin (Pl. 156), Spinoza declared the unity of thinking and being; he spoke of the ideal form that made possible the recognition of substance and of its expansion into reality in the form of matter. And Vermeer? As a painter, he substituted vision for thought. As thought was to the philosopher, so vision was to him the ideal expression of being.

MAN AND WOMAN DRINKING WINE

Canvas. 65 × 77 cm.

PROVENANCE: *Acquired in 1901 from the collection of Lord Pelham in London.*

138, 139   What happens in this picture? A still-youthful gentleman has come for a visit, as his hat and cloak indicate. There is only one wineglass, and he lets the girl, sitting at her own table, drink from it. Has she been singing to the lute, or is she about to do so under his direction? We do not know. The interpretation that this is a complaisant young woman, such as Vermeer has painted elsewhere, is not convincing. It is contradicted by her rich,

upper-middle-class style of dress, the valuable painting on the wall, the Persian rug on the table, the coat of arms in the stained-glass window, all of which suggest a wealthy home in which a music lesson is about to begin. But interpretation of the "content" is beside the point. What matters is the harmony of the composition, the way the eye is guided into the room, by means of the diagonal position of window and chair on the one side, the grouping of the two figures on the other, the fore-shortening of the table, and the emphasis on the center, which has been slightly moved to the left by the positioning of the painting on the back wall. What matters is the "how" and not the "what" of the picture. It is a question of color, space, illumination, not of a situation in a story.

THE PEARL NECKLACE

Canvas. 55 × 45 cm.

PROVENANCE: *Inscribed on the tabletop "J v Meer." Acquired from the Suermondt collection, Aachen, in 1874.*

In the portrait of the young lady putting on a pearl **140** necklace in front of her mirror, there is more than a study of the subject; the viewer's interest is heightened by the fact that the eye of the beauty adorning herself is looking across the room at the mirror on the wall opposite, which has been foreshortened to create a third dimension. The painter's daring in giving over the greater part of his canvas to a white wall depicted in light and shade succeeds particularly because the composition gains in tension by the girl's glance having to bridge so much of that wall space to reach the mirror.

Chromatically, too, the painter achieves a balance between the two sides of the picture: at the left there is the cool lemon yellow of the curtain, complemented on the right by the same color for the blond girl's jacket; the yellow dust brush on the table points toward her, linking the two chromatically as well as deepening perspective. The yellow gives a bluish shimmer to the gray tones in the picture, but the blue of the upholstered chair back serves as a contrasting color and gleams in the vigorous ultramarine decoration of the great faïence vase at the left. No painter has ever excelled Vermeer's skill in catching—indeed, in transfiguring—the special color tone of Delft ceramics. The vase has a spatial function as well: defining the foreground as it does, its gray-blue darkness moves the female figure further back in the room.

Jan Vermeer, of whose work only some thirty-five examples are known, frequently shows only a single person in a room, as in *The Pearl Necklace, The Letter, The Lute Player, The Milkmaid.* Basically it is these canvases that reveal most clearly what he strove for: the transfiguration of what Spinoza called "Substance" by means of a vision that defines being as allied to light itself.

Pieter de Hooch

THE ARTIST: Pieter de Hooch can be claimed by several cities of his native country. Born in 1629 in Rotterdam, he was accepted as a master by the painters' guild of Delft in 1655, of which the slightly younger Vermeer was also a member. In 1667 we find him in Amsterdam, where he died, presumably sometime after 1677. Compared with Vermeer, whose cool tonality is unmistakable, his colors are warmer, stronger. Both painters have an inner serenity of vision.

Pieter de Hooch and Jan Vermeer belong to the same generation: the similarity between the two masters of the interior and its lighting is clearly evident; a certain mutual influence, even perhaps a mutually stimulating rivalry, may be suspected.

Pieter de Hooch is more realistic and does justice to the details he represents in a way different from that of Vermeer, whose treatment of light raises reality, with the aid of chiaroscuro, to a higher dimension. Although the tonal effect of a Vermeer is unattainable by anyone else, several works of Pieter de Hooch, such as his *The Mother* or *Woman Weighing Gold*, can decidedly hold their own beside those of the master of Delft. While De Hooch's colors are more realistic, they are also more intense. He does not dare, as Vermeer does, to depict a simple white wall in such a way that the shading of light alone make a pictorial phenomenon of it (Pl. 140); instead, he chooses a curtain or a leather wall covering in which color or touches of gold fill the entire picture with warmth.

WOMAN WEIGHING GOLD

Canvas. 61 × 53 cm.

PROVENANCE: *Painted about 1664. This canvas is clearly influenced by Jan Vermeer's* Woman Weighing Pearls *(now in the Widener collection, Philadelphia). Property of the Kaiser Friedrich Museum Association, it was acquired in 1910 in the Paris art market, into which it came when the Brun collection was sold at auction in 1841.*

141 The subject of the painting is obvious: a young woman is weighing some gold pieces on a scale; in those days the value of a gold piece was determined by its weight—paper money had not yet come into use. Therefore the gold scale was an inevitable part of the furnishings of any respectable burgher's establishment, as shown by the painters of interiors in Delft. But since the weighing of gold was usually done by men, particularly the jewelers, who were also the bankers of the period, it may be assumed that the picture has a symbolic significance. There is a proverb that goes back to the prophet Jesus ben Sirach about weighing each word on the gold scale, and it is tempting to speculate that this is how the young woman is weighing her lover's protestations. Many a picture of the time can be understood as a reference to some popular saying.

But, of course, it is not a question of meaning. The painting must be regarded not as a subject for thought but as an object for the eyes. Despite the suggestion of movement in the diagonals of the half-open window, in the folds of the rug table cover, which has been pushed back, and in the books, the unhurried balancing of the scale, the wait-and-see attitude of the young beauty help to establish an atmosphere of tranquillity. De Hooch has also made the wall a subject in its own right, but this wall is covered with costly figured leather, on which the evening sun brings out mysterious gleams of gold. The same muted shimmer recurs in the adjoining room, where a mirror reflects an unseen window; this, too, is a motif of pensive calm, in character with De Hooch's style, which is here clearly under the influence of Vermeer.

THE MOTHER

Canvas. 92 × 100 cm.

PROVENANCE: *Painted about 1659 to 1660. Acquired in 1876 in Paris at the auction of the Schneider collection.*

142, 143 Here is the realm of the mother, the interior of the 144 house breathing order and peace. Everything has its place, where it is kept clean and polished: the gleaming bedpan hanging slightly left of center beside the curtain of the sleeping alcove, the floor tiles so highly polished that the puppy's legs are reflected in them.

The rather risky division of the painting into two parts is annulled in the foreground; but in the upper part, the brilliant red cloak hanging on the side wall, with its long vertical folds, emphasizes the separation in the center. For it really is two pictures we have here: at left, the mother with the basket cradle; at right, the vestibule with the older child, a little girl of about three. The mother is preparing to give the breast to her newborn infant, bringing an unobtrusive element of motion and a scenic form into the picture, as Pieter de Hooch liked to do. The open door to the vestibule, through which sunlight pours into the room, is a motif in itself. The dog connects the two halves of the picture not only optically but also subjectively, through his evident indecision over whether to follow the girl outside or stay with his mistress.

We are familiar with these figures from other paintings by De Hooch; he has probably depicted his own home and wife and captured something of the domestic happiness that fills his work with its inner harmony.

Gerard Terborch

THE ARTIST: Terborch was born in 1617, a year before the beginning of the Thirty Years' War, in Zwolle; he worked in Holland's cosmopolis, Amsterdam, and in its aristocratic residential town, The Hague. As a highly esteemed portrait painter, he was in Münster and Osnabrück in 1648, at the end of the Thirty Years' War, and there he painted the diplomats negotiating the Peace of Westphalia. Having gained an international reputation, he traveled in Europe and, when in Spain, was much impressed with the art of Velázquez. He died in 1681, an honored Town Councillor in Deventer, where he had settled in 1675.

As a portrayer of the social scene, Terborch perfected what had been begun by lesser painters such as Buytenweg: a picture of daily living, done almost like a still life, with "still" the appropriate word for the calm reserve of his pictures.

His portraits, in contrast to those of Frans Hals, for example, are not impressionistic; they have something of the objectivity of a Holbein without the latter's sculptural and monumental quality.

THE KNIFE GRINDER'S FAMILY

Canvas. 72 × 59 cm.

PROVENANCE: *Monogrammed on the wall at lower right "GTB." Etching by Weissbrodt. A free replica is in the Metropolitan Museum in New York. Purchased in Berlin in 1837; formerly in the collections of the Duc de Choiseul and the Duc de Berry in Paris.*

145 In this painting the setting dominates, with the figures serving to characterize the picturesque milieu and to lead the eye from the right foreground to the background. Its uniqueness among the artist's works makes it all the more significant.

Terborch, who has been called "the most aristocratic painter of the Dutch school" and who painted the portraits of the delegates and statesmen at the peace congresses of Münster and Osnabrück, here went to work purely as a painter. This is a genre painting—an impression, one might say. The subject, a most unexpected one for Terborch, is a poor workman's yard and home, executed with a delicate feeling for color and nuance and contrasted with the proud mansion boasting a turreted gable behind it. The gray-blue slate roof above the barn, the browns in the crumbling wall of the building constructed on a ruin, the yellowish tones of the plastering, the red bricks and tiles of the hut's roof—all compose a background for the figures: the woman dressed in blue at the right forefront, delousing her little daughter; in the center, standing in front of the barn, dressed in yellow and blue with a red cap, a peasant waiting for his scythe to be sharpened; and at his left, barely visible in the gloom of the barn, the knife grinder, whetting the scythe on a stone wheel. The overturned chair in the foreground leads the eye into the central scene.

This painting, faithfully capturing a scene from life, is eloquent testimony to Terborch's gifts as a painter. It serves to demonstrate the meaning of Wilhelm von Bode's praise for this Dutch artist's "perfected painterly conception and execution of his pictures."

A GALLANT SCENE (FATHERLY EXHORTATION)

Canvas. 70 × 60 cm.

PROVENANCE: *Another treatment by Terborch of the same scene, with the inclusion of a dog, can be seen at the Rijksmuseum in Amsterdam. There is also an old copy (dated 1655) by Caspar Netscher in the museum at Gotha, Germany. The lady in the satin dress, alone, may be seen in the Dresden gallery. The misleading title* Fatherly Exhortation *appeared for the first time on George Wille's engraving in Goethe's private collection. Acquired in 1815 in Paris from the Giustiniani collection.*

Three Figures in a Room would probably be the best **146, 147** title for Terborch's well-known masterpiece. It shows him to be the equal of Vermeer and De Hooch.

Seen from the back is a youthfully slender female figure, magnificently painted in the delicate hues of the silvery, shimmering satin dress with the black collar, the blond hair above the peach-like graceful neck. At her right sits a cavalier in profile, his blue-and-yellow-plumed hat on his knee, his sword at his side. In his uplifted right hand he is holding a coin (this gesture was interpreted by Goethe as one of moral exhortation), probably the fee for the procuress in black sitting behind him, sipping at her glass.

The chamber is dimly lit, in a way only the Dutch of Rembrandt's century had of rendering the atmosphere. The curtains of the tester bed are brownish dark, the tablecloth bright red. The painter was concerned with color and light, not really with the anecdote, which possibly illustrates a popular saying about the power of gold.

However, the less one worries about the "meaning" and the more one takes pleasure in the harmony of the colors and the dim halftones, particularly the incomparably painted satin dress, the closer one is to the real import of the work as a painting and to an appreciation of the painter's delicate mastery of his craft.

Jan Steen

THE ARTIST: Jan Steen was born in Leiden in 1626, enrolled at Leiden University in 1646, and then became a pupil of the painter Nicolas Knüpfer in Utrecht; but he is rumored to have worked with Adriaen van Ostade in Haarlem and with Jan van Goyen, whose daughter he married, in The Hague. He continued his training under the influence of Frans Hals and was accepted by the painters' guild of Leiden in 1648. From 1649 to 1654 he lived in The Hague, from 1661 to 1669 in Haarlem. He died in Leiden in 1679.

"His laughing eye was turned to the light, and the light was mirrored in his laughing eye." With these words of Heinrich Heine, W. Martin, formerly the esteemed director of the Rijksmuseum of Amsterdam, begins his book about Jan Steen. Of all the pictures that the life-loving master of Dutch genre painting left to posterity, it can be said that light reflected itself in them. He has both the marvelous freshness and gradation of color and the twilit chiaroscuro that lends depth and form, so that G. F. Waagen, the enormously knowledgeable first director of the Berlin gallery, was of the opinion that Jan Steen was "unconditionally the most brilliant painter, next to Rembrandt, of the entire Dutch school."

Although stricter criteria for the art of the Dutch masters have come to be used, the virtuosity of Jan Steen has continued to delight the world. But while the earlier evaluations tended to emphasize the subjects of his paintings and take pleasure in his narrative gifts, to cite his humor and the hearty vigor with which his art mirrored the folk life of the Netherlands, more recent critics have begun to appreciate the unique gift for composition that makes these paintings so effective. His ability to stage a scene with figures in space has also been praised, as has his skill in placing props such as baskets, pitchers, and overturned chairs so that they will lead into the picture and help to shape the room.

THE TAVERN GARDEN

Canvas. 68 × 58 cm.

PROVENANCE: *Signed on the table "J. Steen." Transferred from the royal-palace collections.*

148,151 This famous painting from the royal-palace collections, which were so rich in paintings from the Netherlands, shows all the master's fine points. The beer garden of the tavern is painted with complete naturalness—rich summery green for the shade trees, red-brown shading into grays for the earthen floor, luminous red for the woman's blouse. Strong contrast is typical: the white of the tablecloth juxtaposed to the darkest tone in the picture, the black coat tossed across the other end of the table. From this point the eye is led, with the preference of the baroque for oblique lines, by the diagonal of bench and table to such an effect that the prawn seller appears to be in the center, although he is actually standing quite left of center. And this despite the fact that he is only a background form to the principal figures in the scene: the painter Jan Steen with his wife, child, and dog, enjoying the coolness of the beer garden in the late afternoon. He is busily peeling a herring with his skilled hands, and the dog is waiting for the skin to be tossed down to him. His wife, Margret, sits opposite her husband, her motherly concern concentrated on her blond son, whom she is feeding.

The linear composition makes her the figure around whom everything revolves. The painter, sitting at the side, looks forward, out of the scene and at the beholder, as he does in many of his paintings. Jan Steen painted himself almost separately, as a picture-within-a-picture; probably he did it at home in front of a mirror.

We are familiar with his smiling face, his wife, his boy—and, not least, his parti-colored dog—from many of his paintings, as actors in many different situations (the family picture at The Hague, for example). A radiant love of life and reverence for the woman as mother give the work its human warmth. Houbracken, the Vasari of Dutch art, made the following memorable statement about Steen: "His pictures are like his style of life, and his style of life was like his pictures."

THE BRAWL

PROVENANCE: *Signed at bottom left on the stone "J.S." In Oldenburg until 1827. In 1828 owned by Philips; in 1842 part of the Gunthorpe collection in London; in 1855 auctioned with the J. L. Nieuwenhuys collection in Brussels. Acquired for the Berlin museum with the Suermondt collection, Aachen, in 1874.*

149,150 Just as Shakespeare expressed his delight in characterization by including scuffling peasants even in a work of transcendent poetry such as his *A Midsummer Night's Dream,* so Dutch painting of the seventeenth century, with its serene interiors as depicted by Vermeer van Delft and Pieter de Hooch, includes the tavern scenes of Jan Steen. When a Hollander wants to suggest the acme of disorder and confusion, his favorite expression for it is: "Just like a painting by Jan Steen." Next to the idyll of the beer garden in the Berlin gallery hangs a picture by Jan Steen unusually large for him, also set in a beer garden, but showing a fight that has developed from an argument over a game. A cavalier has been playing backgammon with a peasant; a violent argument has arisen; the peasant threatens the gentleman with his knife; the gentleman has half-drawn his sword but is being restrained by a woman who is apparently also shielding him from the peasant's companions.

At the rough outdoor table sits an older man who bears the features of Jan Steen. He does not seem to be taking the situation too seriously, nor do the other onlookers, notably those enjoying the ruckus behind the cavalier's back.

What is intended as a scene of wild disorder is actually based on a carefully planned and executed composition: the overturned pewter tankard, the game board fallen to the ground, the tabletop in the center are all elements of conscious spatial arrangement by the painter; the child trying to restrain the furious cavalier with its little hands, its colorful dress contrasting with the twilit background, is a dazzling sample of painterly virtuosity. Even the dog—Jan Steen's familiar dog—does honor to his master's skill, to say nothing of the bravura effect of the piece of chalk on the slate scoreboard on the table that marks the exact center of the picture.

Pieter Claesz van Haarlem

THE ARTIST: The name means Pieter, son of Claesz of Haarlem. He was born in Burgsteinfurt, Westphalia, about 1590, and accordingly belongs with the earlier generation of Dutch still-life painters. His presence in Haarlem is first documented in 1617, but it may be assumed that he was active there before that date. Pieter was the father of Nicolaes Pietersz Berchem, who became known through his landscapes and etchings with Italian landscape motifs. Pieter Claesz died in Haarlem in 1660.

To make a picture of an article of domestic furnishing became an objective of Dutch painters after Jan van Eyck made the re-creation of a lamp, a mirror, or a little carved lion on the Madonna's throne an essential task of his art. In the seventeenth century, this aim became an end in itself. The still life—theretofore a subsidiary element on altar panels and occasionally, as with Holbein, an aid to characterization in a portrait—became important in its own right. The usual subject was flowers and fruits vibrant with color, and a favorite color note was often supplied by the blue of the faïences made in Delft. Each of the Dutch schools developed its own specialty in this regard: the painters of Leiden, a university town, always included books; Amsterdam gloried in magnificent arrangements of flower pieces and vessels, preferring the tall format; there and in Haarlem, the pleasure taken in materials brought forth paintings in which the sheen of silver, the strong reflections of a wineglass, and the mother-of-pearl gleam of a nautilus goblet were given their due.

STILL LIFE WITH GOBLET AND OVERTURNED SILVER BOWL

Oak panel. 42 × 59 cm.

PROVENANCE: *Monogrammed on the knife blade "PC." Acquired in 1845.*

152,154 A still life in the Würzburg University collection and another in the Darmstadt museum attributed to the same master are brought to mind by the picture in Berlin. Pieter Claesz, competing with the famous Heda, his contemporary, worked in truly painterly fashion. He or the more inventive Heda may have been the first to think of overturning a silver goblet or a stemmed bowl for the sake of contrasting the unpolished silver inside the base, less mirror-like and lighter in sheen, with the polished surface. The diagonal progression from the hollow base to the stem and the rim of the bowl satisfied the baroque love of movement.

On a green cloth set off from the sober gray of the wall, such objects as an overturned footed silver serving bowl on a pewter dish and a pewter plate with oyster shells behind it are grouped around an ornate tumbler half-filled with Rhine wine—the principal object, but placed slightly off center, in the manner of the baroque. Unlike most Dutch still lifes of the period, this one has been restricted to comparatively few objects; in addition to those already mentioned, there are four nuts and, as a painterly accent of high sophistication, a single olive on a metal platter, in which the showy silver bowl is reflected. The color value of the olive is highly effective there, despite the extensive green of the tablecloth and the brilliance of the wineglass. The knife, with the artist's monogram on its blade, leaning against the platter is another fine bit.

Despite the sparseness of the ensemble, the artist's superb rendering of the materials and the harmony of his golden, green, gray, and silvery tones combine to make a most convincing demonstration of his virtuosity.

Willem Kalf

THE ARTIST: Born in 1622 in Amsterdam, where he was a popular painter of still lifes, Willem Kalf died in his native town in 1693. Like Pieter Claesz, he loved to put silver vessels into his still lifes, contrasting them with round or tall wineglasses or sometimes with Chinese porcelain. He painted any object that could demonstrate his skill in the depiction of materials, which excelled even that of Claesz, who presumably influenced him in Haarlem. In Amsterdam he was impressed with Rembrandt's chiaroscuro, especially with his luminous style of the 1640's and 1650's.

In contrast to the smoother manner of, for example, Jan Davidsz de Heem, Kalf's pictures, influenced by Rembrandt, are distinguished by a chiaroscuro executed with great sensitivity to tonal values and transitions. His art achieves the highest refinement of painterly effectiveness in its ability to represent materials—fruits, a lemon with the spiral of its peeled skin, glass, metals, porcelain.

STILL LIFE WITH CHINESE TUREEN

Canvas. 64 × 53 cm.

PROVENANCE: *Acquired in 1899 in the Paris art market, at first for the Strasbourg municipal gallery, by which it was exchanged for another still life by the same master.*

Kalf's masterful composition is particularly evident   153,155
in this still life. Against the rich brown background, the vivid colors in the center appear in a soft, shimmering light: the yellow of the lemon beside the deep ultramarine patterning of the Chinese tureen, the blue band of the gleaming gold pocket watch, the dark-red wine in the tall glass, the metallic tones of the silver platter, and the bright reflections in the agate handle of the knife all harmonize with the muted shades of the rug and the

reddish-violet of the tabletop. Enameled colors, contrasting with pastose textures, add effectiveness to the whole.

Nicolas Poussin

THE ARTIST: Poussin was born in Villers, near Le Grand Andely, Normandy, in 1594. He received his early training in Paris but went to Rome in 1624. There he remained, visiting France only once, from 1640 to 1642.

Rich in poetic inventiveness, Poussin turned to classical antiquity and the poets of the Augustan age for inspiration, which he found most of all in Ovid, the poet of the *Metamorphoses*. His feeling for nature and a conception of art in harmony with the rationalism of his period increasingly determined his special development. A certain unevenness in his use of color in his early work was overcome in the rarefied beauty of his mature works, in which the influence of classical sculpture and the seventeenth century's sense of landscape are fused into masterly compositions. In his later phase, the artist increasingly showed an inclination toward heroic landscape. He died in Rome, his adopted city, in 1665.

Academic art began with Poussin. It was didactic and philosophical, abandoning Christian motifs for classical subjects and substituting for indigenous traditions of craftsmanship an "international" style trained in the imitation of antiquity and the masters of the Renaissance. Education was also being determined by the growing interest in classical antiquity and literature. The center of the new aesthetics was Rome, where Poussin became the grand master of French painting upon an alien soil.

He found his inspiration in classical mythology, particularly its conception of nature. Poussin was no imitator but, rather, a late-born Roman of the Augustan age, choosing Ovid as his guide. In the era of Richelieu, who initiated the *grand siècle*, Poussin stands as an equal beside Corneille, the poet, and Descartes, the philosopher-mathematician and founder of French rationalism, as one who fulfilled the French national spirit of his time.

To understand Poussin is to understand rationalism as the belief in logical principle and inner order and to grasp what became, through Poussin and the French sense of tradition, the pivotal principle of French art until the advent of Ingres and Cézanne.

JUPITER AS AN INFANT, NURSED BY THE GOAT AMALTHEA

Canvas. 97 × 133 cm.

PROVENANCE: *An early acquisition for the royal-palace collection of the King of Prussia.*
The same theme was treated in two paintings by Jordaens. An antique sculpture in the Giustiniani collection in Rome, which *includes even the tree, may have been the source of Poussin's inspiration for this painting.*

156, 157

Poussin's way led from religious themes to those of mythology, and through this, in an unconscious parallel with seventeenth-century Dutch painting, to landscape. The mythological painting presupposes a flair for narrative. This is shown in one of the master's principal works, a scene from the infancy of Jupiter, who is being nursed on milk and honey by the nymphs Adrasteia and Jo (unless the painter meant the latter to represent Melissa, the queen of the bees). The milk is supplied by the goat Amalthea, who was rewarded by being made immortal: as Capella, Jupiter set her among the stars, and Poussin painted her.

After the manner of his time, Poussin gives his scene much movement. Since the jar the nymph is holding to the child's lips is rapidly being emptied, the satyr prepares to milk the patient goat anew, while the second nymph leans backward to take a honeycomb out of the hive to sweeten the divine boy's drink. So much for the meaning of the scene, with its two elements: the feeding of the child and the preparation of the divine food.

Poussin painted this canvas when he was at the height of his powers. It combines the relief style of antiquity with a landscape done in the grand manner, and achieves a compositional fusion of both elements to an unprecedented degree if one considers, for example, Elsheimer, more than a decade older than Poussin, whose figures are inserted into rather than integrated with his landscapes. In Poussin's painting, the tree with its vine-covered branches swinging out ranks as a physical presence of equal importance with the five living beings of the group. The diagonal sweep of the trunk and the horizontal movement of the left branch are rhythmically integrated with the movements of the figures: the branch, the incomparably beautiful arm of the nymph holding the honeycomb, and the kneeling satyr's arm stretched along the goat's back form the three strong horizontals of the clear, conscious composition; the trunk of the tree makes a counter poise to the body of the reclining nymph who is letting the honey drip on the plate.

Poussin's composition is characterized by this emphasis on horizontal lines, further intensified by the folds of the garment beneath the main group and by the lines of the Campagna landscape in the background. The baroque love of movement is shown by the fact that the painting has no center, such as the Renaissance preferred. Instead there is displacement, a crisscrossing and overlapping of diagonals in folds directing the eye this way and that, charming it by the liveliness of the scene. At the same time, the anecdote is subordinated to the meticulously planned composition. Rest and movement make a contrapuntal harmony, just as the contrast of cool and warm color tones are unified by the same shimmering light. The cool blue and yellow in the garment of the kneeling nymph contrast with the red cloth and brownish-red skin of the satyr; the warm brown and green in the foreground set off the cool gray of the rocks and the distance. All in all, the painting may be considered a model of French classicism in the studied care with which it was created, but it is expressive nevertheless of a deep inner life. The onlooker comes away with a strong sense of movement and color. Poussin's striving to do justice to each detail, while nevertheless achieving a great style, is evident. The master used to say of his pictures: *"Je n'ai rien négligé."*

Antoine Watteau

THE ARTIST: Watteau was born in 1684 in Valenciennes. In 1702 he went to Paris for his training. The ornamental art of his teacher Claude Gillot freed him to create a new, original, light manner that emphasized gracefulness in opposition to the heavy emotionalism of the baroque. Watteau was elected to the Royal Academy of Painting and Sculpture in 1717. In 1721, after a brief stay in London, he came back to France an incurably sick man and finally succumbed to lung disease at Nogent-sur-Marne, near Vincennes, in the same year.

Watteau could be realistic—as, for example, in his pictures of the Italian and French theater or in the famous *Gersaint's Shop Sign*, painted for a friend, the art dealer Gersaint. But he also painted visions of gay festivities and of a carefree enjoyment of life that he himself never achieved.

Valenciennes, the home of fine lacemaking, was formerly Flemish and became French in 1678, during the reign of Louis XIV. When Watteau chose Paris as his home, he brought to French art a practitioner of the Flemish tradition, with something of the superior feeling for form of Peter Paul Rubens and also something of the easy gaiety of David Teniers.

Born in the year that saw the death of Corneille, whose plays typified the strict classicism of the French baroque, Watteau freed painting from the academic tyranny of the strict rules enforced by the great Poussin's petty followers, who were leaning on the authority of the classical dramatists. With a refreshing and revitalizing effect, Watteau championed instead a purely painterly approach. The tradition he created was to be the glory of France all the way to Degas and Renoir.

Watteau was always aware of the Flemish tradition behind him—a painting by Rubens was his most cherished possession—and his Parisian teachers had nothing to offer him but their craftsmanship. He modeled himself upon the masters of Antwerp and, secondarily, of Venice. He was a painter first of all, but he was also a poet who created a festive realm above the merely terrestrial world.

His paintings tend to present not nature unalloyed but the scenery of the stage and parks, where art and nature join hands. In this he expressed the early eighteenth century's love of both the theater and nature. Heir of the French baroque, this was the period that in all the arts and in all aspects of life turned from solemn dignity to charm, from pomp to grace. As the painter of sheer loveliness, Watteau is as unexcelled as Mozart is unsurpassed as the composer of loveliness—the painter founded, the composer fulfilled the art of the rococo.

Watteau's quality of loveliness has a tragic undertone; it is the dream born of longing in one condemned by chronic tuberculosis to feel excluded from life. He gave to his longing an immortal greatness of form.

THE ITALIAN COMEDY

Canvas. 37 × 48 cm.

PROVENANCE: *Engraving by C. N. Cochin (1734). From the holdings of King Frederick II, who owned nineteen paintings by Watteau. This painting remained in the Sans Souci gallery until 1830. It is listed as No. 69 in Goncourt's* Catalogue raisonné. *The painting of the Italian comedians in the National Gallery in Washington shows the group on the stage.*

Here they are, the figurines of the Italian comedy, **158, 159** lined up together in front of the dark bushes of the park, barely suggested by the pale moonlight but carved out of the darkness by the flame of the torch in Mezzetin's hand. They have come back to Paris, whence King Louis XIV's chauvinistic command had banished them; the life-loving Regent, Duke Philip of Orléans, has made them welcome.

Now Paris delighted once more in the familiar masques and pranks of the entertainers, whom Watteau painted several times. In the center stands Pierrot, in blazing white, plucking the strings of his guitar. Behind him dances Harlequin, puppet-like with bent knees, and Scapin and Brighella can be dimly seen. Pierrot is not frustrated, like the ever-doting, never-favored Mezzetin, for the graceful Colombine stands nearby, coquettishly holding up her black half mask. Near the lantern we discern other figures as well; that long nose must belong to the Dottore da Bologna. The modulated play of the colors against that mysterious dark background affects one like music. We seem to be hearing the song of the comedians. Watteau's colors are melodic in themselves, especially here, where moonlight, torch, and lantern add a touch of unreality.

These gay figures of the Italian *commedia dell'arte* were a favorite subject of artists and craftsmen up to the time of Bustelli's procelain figures made in Nymphenburg. Mezzetin, half clown, half Falstaff, had become a familiar type in Paris through Callot's drawings of the popular comedian Angelo Constantini.

Watteau's friend, the archaeologist Count Caylus, reported that the artist kept in his studio all sorts of costumes in which to dress his friends and his models before painting them. It is possible that Watteau has immortalized in the painting in Berlin not the Italian troupe itself but only the Italian costumes. An etching made of a similar painting has the following revealing caption:

> Les habits sont italiens,
> Les airs français, et je parie,
> Que dans ces vrais comédiens
> Gît une aimable tromperie.

> The costumes are Italian,
> The actors French, believe us;
> They may be good comedians,
> But they are gay deceivers.

GERSAINT'S SHOP SIGN

Canvas. 163 × 308 cm.

PROVENANCE: *Watteau's last work, which captured the essence of an entire era, was a shop sign. Originally topped with a shallow arch, the beginning of which is discernible at the left, near the fourth stone of the column, it was mounted above the entrance to the art dealer's shop on the bridge over the Seine.*

However, the rapidly finished canvas had been hanging there for only two weeks when an art lover of note, the parliamentarian De Gluq, was so enchanted with it that he purchased it. He soon passed it on to his nephew, Monier de Julienne, who published the great collection of engravings based on Watteau's paintings. Julienne did not keep it for long: King Frederick II of Prussia, the greatest collector of Watteaus, had his ambassador buy the painting for him. It was hung in the royal palace of Charlottenburg, where, divided into two companion pieces, it decorated the royal flautist's concert hall.

160, 161
162, 163 Watteau had the brilliant idea of giving the prospective visitor to the art dealer's gallery a look at what went on inside. As on the stage, there is no fourth wall, so that one has the impression of being a spectator at a play, perhaps something by Molière. Near the door, two shop assistants are packing pictures into a crate, one of them clearly a portrait of Louis XIV, a reminder that Watteau's friend Gersaint originally named his shop Au Grand Monarque. But the time of the Great Monarch had passed. He is being crated off.

A young lady, seen from the rear, elegantly dressed in a gown pleated "à la Watteau," is ascending the step, conducted by a gentleman whom tradition identifies as the painter himself. But the principal scene is enacted on the right side of the painting. The art dealer is showing a *tondo,* the beauty of which is being admired by the kneeling Chevalier de la Roque and an elderly lady with a lorgnette. Behind the counter sits Mme. Gersaint, showing a costly mirror to the Juliennes, man and wife. The husband and his uncle, De Gluq, are admiring the lacquered frame; the young lady with unconscious coquetry, seems to be more interested in her reflection in the mirror—a joke of the painter, who was a friend of hers.

Among the works of Watteau, the Gersaint painting is unique, but not within the development of French art as a whole. In the studied yet natural interrelationship of figures and space here, it brings to fulfillment what Largillière was striving for in his group pictures, though these, unlike the Watteau, were painted for the sake of the portraits.

Through its popularity as an engraving, this painting came to have a decided influence on the development of the group picture. Only one man ever came to equal the greatness of the original: Hogarth.

Giovanni Battista Tiepolo

THE ARTIST: Born in 1696 in Venice, Giovanni Battista Tiepolo was not a scion of the well-known patrician family, as is so often stated, but merely the son of one of their retainers who followed ancient custom in taking the name of their masters. The sheer size and festive splendor of his conception were best expressed in his frescoes, painted in the churches and palaces of Venice, the Archbishop's palace at Würzburg (1750), the Villa Valmarana (1757), and the royal residence in Madrid (after 1761). He was the last great master of the Venetian school. To suggest the expansion of space through illusions of perspective and the effectiveness of painted light was the high point of his art, which followed in the footsteps of Tintoretto and Veronese, expressing the baroque's thirst for infinity. His power to create space, his light color scale, juxtaposing warm and cool tones with brilliant effect, the bold freedom of movement and lighting, the dazzling magnificence of attire and draperies make even his altarpieces and easel paintings decorative and monumental in effect.

After his return from Würzburg, Tiepolo became the director of the academy of arts founded by Piazzetta. But the last ten years of his life were spent in Madrid, where he died in 1770. His influence on Goya, especially in his drawings, is clearly discernible.

Tiepolo knew how to combine history and legend and bring them to life with poetic vision. His themes came from Homer, Ariosto, and Tasso. His ability to fuse the earthly and the divine and to surround with glory even the agony of martyrdom gives its special stamp to his religious paintings, especially his tall, narrow altar panels.

THE MARTYRDOM OF ST. AGATHA

Canvas. 184 × 131 cm.

PROVENANCE: *Painted about 1756. Tiepolo had done a painting of this subject once before, in 1735, for an altarpiece in the Cappella Buzzacarini in St. Anthony of Padua, which was damaged by fire in 1752. A sketch for the picture in Berlin can be seen in the Museo Civico in Venice. Acquired in 1878 in Paris; formerly privately owned (Munro collection) in London.*

In about 1756, three years after Tiepolo had created the boldest ceiling frescoes in history for the palace in Würzburg designed by Balthasar Neumann, he was asked to accomplish the almost impossible: paint the martyrdom of St. Agatha. The breasts of Agatha, a wellborn daughter of Catania, were cut off by order of the pagan governor of Sicily because she would not become his mistress and refused to abjure her Christian faith.

Tiepolo paints the scene following the horrible mutilation. Agatha, supported by a friend who is covering the saint's bleeding chest with a robe, has collapsed. Behind her, the executioner, having shifted the bloody sword to his left hand, his eyes regarding the merciless judge looking on behind the pillar, is seeking instructions on whether to lead the victim away. The saint, glorified by her martyrdom, is gazing upward, as though uttering the words attributed to her by legend: "My courage is founded on a mighty rock and made firm by Christ."

An etching of this picture made by the son of Tiepolo shows that it originally was rounded on top and that in this semicircle above the broken column and the dark ruin could be seen the crown of thorns, with the heart of Jesus in the center, all surrounded by the winged heads of cherubs in a gloriole.

The beholder of the fragment needs no more than the heavenward glance and the self-surrendering gesture of the hands, as well as the pitying look of the page boy holding the amputated breasts on a salver, to grasp the painting's religious significance. The painterly beauty of the work is what gives the effect of a transcendent vision. The cool, light values in the pale flesh tones of the martyred woman, her bright-yellow gown, and her cloak of that brilliant blue that has come to be known as "Tiepolo blue" contrast with the executioner's red clothing, his red flesh tones, and the red blood dripping from the wound. The heads of the onlookers almost disappear in the blue-gray of the background. The conscious contrasting of cool and warm—one is tempted to say "hot"—tones is characteristic of Tiepolo's ability to generate excitement with color.

Francesco Guardi

THE ARTIST: Guardi represents the apex of a long tradition of Venetian architectural painting. Even the masters of the Quattrocento had begun to use Venetian motifs for their backgrounds. But the great period of architectural painting for its own sake came in the eighteenth century, beginning with Bernardo Canale and his son Antonio, called Canaletto. Canaletto's nephew Belotto, who adopted his uncle's famous name, continued the tradition in the third generation. Francesco Guardi was Antonio Canaletto's most important pupil and successor. He was born in Venice in 1712 and died in his native city, where all his work had been done, on the first day of the year 1793, four years before Venice ceased to be an independent state.

The art of Guardi, which anticipates impressionism, can no longer be called vista painting in the traditional sense. His paintings are not so much portraits of buildings as they are visions of light, and thus they capture the magic of the sea-born city of Venice.

VIEW OF THE GIUDECCA IN VENICE

Canvas. 53 × 84 cm.

PROVENANCE: *Signed on a fishing boat in the center foreground "Fran.co Guardi." Acquired in the art market of Paris in 1899. Property of the Kaiser Friedrich Museum Association.*

A third of the canvas is given over to the surface of the water, above which rises a wide luminously blue sky with gray, sun-rimmed clouds. Between the water and the sky, the churches, towers, and buildings of the fabled city of Venice appear on both sides of the picture as if they had blossomed out of the water. From the middle of the canal, one sees at the left the Giudecca, with the little church called Santa Eufemia; opposite this on the right is the Fondamenta delle Zattere, the old piers for the rafts or logs upon which the buildings of the city on the lagoon were erected. The Church of Spirito Santo and, further back, that of Gesuati are clearly discernible. The water, going far into the distance, is enlivened by fishing boats and gondolas gliding on their own mysterious reflections.

The whole is viewed by the painter's eye in such a way that the shimmering and glittering of the colors, the interplay of light and shade, and the colorfulness of the little figures painted with a fine brush all appear to be there for their own sake. In this way, Guardi succeeds in capturing the magic of Venice, the magic that causes the city to appear to be a dream vision even in the light of day to one gliding along in a gondola.

Even the bizarre contour of the roofs, gables, domes, and chimneys, above which the Campanile rises in the distance, appears like something in a dream.

No one is likely to have described the charm of this city more perceptively than Hippolyte Taine, for whom Venice was tangible proof of his doctrine that style is born of an enviroment. He wrote:

The eye here discovers a new world. In place of the strong, clear, dry colors of the mainland, there is an iridescence, a diffusion, an endless shimmer of colors melting into one another and making a second sky, as luminous, but more colorful, more changeable, richer, and more intense than the first, formed from a mixture of fragmented tones combining into a harmony. One could spend hours contemplating these gradations, these nuances, this splendor. Is the coloring of the Venetian painters derived from such a daily display, such a natural scene that has inadvertently become a guiding force, and from an imagination filled perforce by this billowing and delightful appearence of things?

Francisco de Goya

THE ARTIST: Francisco José de Goya y Lucientes was born in 1746 in Fuentetodos in Aragon, near Saragossa, where his father was a gilder and where young Francisco's apprenticeship as a painter began. But he soon went to Madrid, where Anton Raphael Mengs and Tiepolo were leading artists. In his sketches for Gobelins, which Goya painted in great numbers, his relationship to the eighteenth-century tradition is evident. To be sure, Goya himself, whose style was not influenced by a stay in Italy (1771), designated as his teachers nature, Velázquez, and Rembrandt. Like Velázquez, who was court painter to Philip IV of Spain, Goya was appointed court painter (Painter of the Chamber) to Charles IV in 1789, director of the art academy in 1795, and First Painter to the King in 1798.

Goya's first period, with its serenity and kinship to the work of Teniers, Watteau, and Lancret, was followed by a tragic phase, owing to the artist's increasing deafness and the tribulations of Spain in its struggle with Napoleon, and finally by the style of his old age, when he, the heir of Velázquez, was an exponent of realism, in contrast to the classicism of his era. In 1822 he went to France on leave and settled in Bordeaux, where he died in 1828.

KING FERDINAND VII PRESIDING AT A SESSION OF THE COMPANY FROM THE PHILIPPINES

Canvas. 54 × 70 cm.

PROVENANCE: *Painted about 1816. The picture came to light in 1879 at the Laperlier auction, then again in 1884 at the Beurnonville auction in Paris. It is a color sketch for an official painting now in the museum of Castres, in southern France. In 1909 it was presented to the Berlin museum by Rudolph P. Goldschmidt of Berlin.*

168 Upon a black ground, which sets the somber tone of the painting, appear bright areas, lights, and spots of color. What is shown here is a session of the council of the Philippines Company, presided over by King Ferdinand VII of Spain. The wide chamber is lighted by two windows in this sketch, though by only one in the finished painting. From the ceiling hangs a chandelier, the crystals of which reflect the play of light.

On a dais three steps from the floor (two steps in the finished painting), the King is seated on a throne,

flanked by the dignitaries of the junta. They are ranged behind a table covered with red velvet, which hangs down to the floor. The members of the council are seated along the side walls, two groups facing each other, each individual characterized with a few strokes of a brush that apportions light and shade with a coolly contrasting effect. The satirist Goya, whose unmerciful eye does not merely see but sees *through* people, is here in evidence. He is the first realist of the nineteenth century, preparing the way for Daumier as well as Manet.

The modern character of the work appears all the more astonishing when one considers what precedent the artist, and perhaps also the King who commissioned the painting, might have followed. One possibility is revealed in a painting at the Prado, showing in a strikingly similar composition the Doge with his senators at a session in the conference chamber of the Doges' Palace. It was painted by the Venetian Pietro Malombra (1556–1618), who did the room in schematic perspective but depicted the figures as a sum of single portraits, not subordinating the many details to a single vision as Goya did by means of light and shade.

Disregarding the ostensible subject, one might consider Goya's theme here to be the struggle of light against darkness, a darkness repeatedly overcome by the shimmer of colors. Yellow and red tones gleam on the stone floor; the taut bands of light and dark dividing the walls boldly contrast with the horizontal of the table and the perspective of the floor; gold glitters on the King's raised throne and on the chairs of the councillors; white brushstrokes indicate the shirts; the red of a uniform lights up; heads and hands have strong flesh tones. And yet the colors are set down in this sketch—which surpasses the finished painting as a work of art—only as notes, as it were, for the planned painting. But how firmly those figures "sit" there in the light, against the blacks and grays of the background, and what a forceful impression of unity they give in their glittering variety!

It is as though the curtain had just gone up on a tragicomedy, or comical tragedy, called *King Ferdinand VII of Spain*—the story of that ruler whose hollowness Goya perceived and despised. Our painting would not represent the first act of the piece, which would have shown how Ferdinand had torn the crown from the head of his father, Charles IV, Goya's Maecenas. The second act would have depicted Ferdinand of Spain courting Napoleon, who was letting the Spaniard feel his superior power. The third act, the session of the council of the Philippines, shows the King apparently at the height of his power. But in fact he was only preparing the political confusion that was to cost Spain her lovely islands in the Indian Ocean toward the end of the nineteenth century. The portraits Goya painted of Ferdinand VII expose his unregal character. The First Painter to the King here turns revolutionary, and a new historical era proclaims itself.

DATE DUE	

GAYLORD   PRINTED IN U.S.A.